What They're Saying About Tik Maynard and
In the Middle Are the Horsemen

"In 1989 when I was 54 years old I started a Thoroughbred filly for the Queen of England. Upon Her Majesty's insistence that I write a book, I set out to write my autobiography, *The Man Who Listens to Horses*. Tik Maynard's book, like mine, is the tale of a young man committed to understanding horses and life. It is a fantastically written adventure story for horse fanatics and adventure lovers alike.

"My generation began a revolution in horsemanship, and it is Tik's that will continue it. For that I am grateful. A must read."

Monty Roberts
Horseman and *New York Times* Bestselling Author

"It's a shame you have to use the word 'natural' in front of 'horsemanship.' It should all be natural, the way you interact with a horse, the way you converse, teach, and perform together in this incredible partnership. In my day, they called it, 'It' and it was a kind of secret society because people were ridiculed for taking the time to understand the way horses think and learn, rather than just showing the horse who's boss. Today, it is becoming more the way, to train horses using love, language, and leadership; using psychology rather than mechanics no matter what your discipline, from recreational to performance.

"This is not horsemanship versus eventing; it is about laying a proper foundation before specialization. To see Tik Maynard bridging these two worlds in his quest to become a real horseman will inspire generations to come and contribute to making a better world for horses and the people who love them."

Pat Parelli
Bestselling Author, Founder of
Parelli Natural Horsemanship®

"Both a fascinating record of a young man's quest to find his place, and a vivid portrait of an industry and a culture built upon on one of our most ancient and transformative relationships, that between the human and the horse. Acutely observed, vividly told, and not to be missed."

Kathy Page
Author of *Alphabet* and
Paradise & Elsewhere

"People have a hard time being aware. Awareness of their environment, of other people, of what effects their actions have on others, animal or human. Self-awareness is even more rare. This is a book about self-awareness. How does one learn? How does one process the world? Observation is a necessity to be successful in an animal world. How one processes one's own observations is a key to being successful as a human being. Tik Maynard has opened up and shown his ability to be self-aware and observational. This is an insightful book about the journey to acquire knowledge and then use that knowledge to help others, human and horse. It's a joy to read."

David O'Connor
Fédération Équestre Internationale (FEI) Eventing Chair,
Former Chef d'Equipe US Eventing Team, Former President United
States Equestrian Federation (USEF), Olympic Gold Medalist

"Tik Maynard is not only a fantastic writer but a special horseman. His ability to work naturally through a horse's problems and to communicate what he does in a way people can understand is a gift. He has a never-ending want for knowledge about horses, and I hope he continues to share his experiences."

Lauren Bliss Kieffer
US Olympian

"Tik Maynard's writing is engaging and insightful. With each turn of the page I felt like I was right there, rooting with him through the triumphs and challenges of his horsemanship adventure. Loved the gems that came from his experiences and the honesty he shares. Anyone who loves horses and is passionate about becoming better with them will love this book!"

Jonathan Field
Horseman, Author of *The Art of*
Liberty Training for Horses

"About five years ago, I met Tik Maynard for the first time when he attended a clinic I was giving in Maryland. I immediately observed: Tik is a special person who has an equally good understanding for both people and horses. Tik can put himself in his partner's place and listens closely to the horse that has offered Tik his trust.

"Tik possesses the knowledge of both classical riding and natural horsemanship that is necessary to bring them together. Bringing together these two complementary approaches has helped him become a true horseman. He has traveled a rough road. But he never gave up. Over time, he was able to convert every discouragement, every rejection, into something positive. He's tried to learn as much as he can from each of his trainers. That still applies to Tik today and is the basis for this exciting book.

"What can the reader gain from this book? You should never give up and always keep your specific goal in sight—and you must do that in the face of all the adversities that a rider must overcome in the course of his education. In this regard, Tik is a role model for all of his readers."

Christoph Hess
FEI Dressage and Eventing Judge and
Ambassador for Training and Education of the
German National Equestrian Federation (FN)

"As with horses and life, actions speak much louder and mean more than words. I think this statement is true for horses and people: Horses don't care how much you know until they know how much you care. Tik Maynard should be proud to count himself as one of those people. I am happy and humbled to have played a small part in his horsemanship and life's journey."

Bruce Logan
Clinician and Horse Specialist

"Tik Maynard arrived at my barn like an energetic young dressage prospect—with plenty of cadence in his step and a joy that filled the arena. I knew this was going to be fun! With his unparalleled desire to learn everything he possibly could I was hooked. Here was a student who was going to push me, and together we could both become better—student and teacher—understanding our horses more deeply and sharing thoughts and experiences in our blessed lives with our horses. This is who Tik is: engaging, inquisitive, intelligent, and compassionate about his horses and the work he does with them. It takes a great student to become a great teacher, and Tik is both. It was a great joy and pleasure to share time with him."

Betsy Steiner
Dressage Trainer and Coach and Author of
A Gymnastic Riding System Using Mind, Body & Spirit

"Tik Maynard writes like a seasoned novelist but there is no mistaking the authenticity of his story. Whether you're crazy about horses or not, you'll enjoy this ride."

Rick Lamb
Co-Author of *A Revolution in Horsemanship*
and Author of *Human to Horseman*

IN THE MIDDLE
ARE THE HORSEMEN

Tik Maynard

TRAFALGAR SQUARE
North Pomfret, Vermont

First published in 2018 by
Trafalgar Square Books
North Pomfret, Vermont 05053

Parts of this book have been previously published in some form: chapters 1–15 in *Gaitpost* (www.gaitpost.com) and *The Chronicle of the Horse* (www.chronofhorse.com); chapters 16–30 and 43–46 in *The Chronicle of the Horse*; chapters 48 and 51 in *Off-Track Thoroughbred Magazine* (www.retiredracehorseproject.org/join-ottb-magazine); and chapter 47 in *Practical Horseman* (practicalhorsemanmag.com).

Some names and identifying details have been changed to protect the privacy of individuals.

The author is grateful for permission to reprint the lyrics from the song "You're Too Cool" © Zachary Gray.

Disclaimer of Liability
The author and publisher shall have neither liability nor responsibility to any person or entity with respect to any loss or damage caused or alleged to be caused directly or indirectly by the information contained in this book. While the book is as accurate as the author can make it, there may be errors, omissions, and inaccuracies.

Trafalgar Square Books encourages the use of approved safety helmets in all equestrian sports and activities.

Library of Congress Cataloging-in-Publication Data
Names: Maynard, Tik, 1982- author.
Title: In the middle are the horsemen / Tik Maynard.
Description: North Pomfret, Vermont : Trafalgar Square Books, 2018.
Identifiers: LCCN 2017039334| ISBN 9781570768323 (paperback) | ISBN
 9781570768859 (ebook)
Subjects: LCSH: Maynard, Tik, 1982- | Horsemen and horsewomen--Biography.
Classification: LCC SF284.52.M34 A3 2018 | DDC 636.1--dc23
LC record available at https://lccn.loc.gov/2017039334

Cover photographs by Kathy Russell (www.kathyrussellphotography.com)
Interior artwork by Erik Schmidt (OffshoreArtwork.com)
Book design by Lauryl Eddlemon
Cover design by RM Didier
Typeface: Minion Pro
Printed in the United States of America
10 9 8 7 6 5 4 3 2

Contents

PART TWO:
PROFESSIONAL

Calgary
Vancouver
French
Paso Robles
Loving
Ocal
Mexico City
Troncones

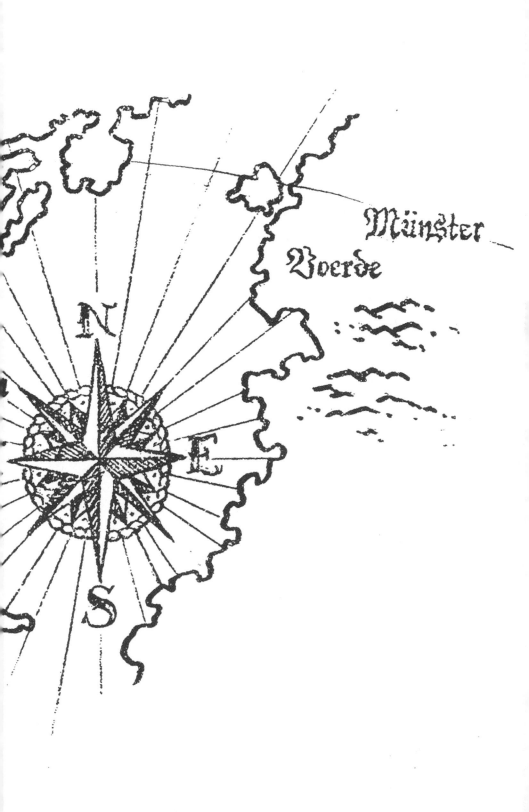

Münster

Voerde

N

E

S

＂ There is no such thing as a horse whisperer. There never has been and never will be. The idea is an affront to the horse. You can talk and listen to horses all you want, and what you will learn, if you pay close attention, is that they live on open ground way beyond language and that language, no matter how you characterize it, is a poor trope for what horses understand about themselves and about humans. You need to practice only three things, patience, observation and humility... ＂

From "Editorial Notebook; Death of a Legendary Horseman," *The New York Times,* July 24, 1999, by Verlyn Klinkenborg, Author of *The Rural Life; Timothy: Or, Notes of an Abject Reptile; Several Short Sentences About Writing; and More Scenes from a Rural Life*

PART I

WORKING STUDENT

CHAPTER 1

A Slap Across the Face

This is not *Eat, Pray, Love*. I will not wade through breaking up with my girlfriend, and the screaming, the crying confusion. Neither is this a story about Alexander Supertramp, nor Peekay, nor Tom Joad. I know and love those stories, but they are not *this* story. This story is about learning, writing, running, getting hired, getting fired (a few times). It is about other things too, even, maybe, *love*, if we get that far.

Most of all, however, this is a story about horses.

In 2008, the Beijing Olympics were just ending, and Obama was just getting started. I was twenty-six (a year older than my father when he married my mother—she was twenty-one). I was in Southlands, an area of Vancouver, Canada, where there were still a few farms, stranded like islands, in a swelling city. One by one these properties were bought, and barns were replaced with pools and tennis courts. My family, with our horses, dogs, cats, turtles, sheep, goats, ducks, chickens, garden, and orchard held out like the last burnt-orange leaves on a maple as winter sets in.

It was a funny time of life for me to be crawling out of hibernation, but waking up is a curious thing: We open our eyes, but we don't know what the day will bring. Only years later, when my mother would say, "Imagine if you had gone back to school," would

I realize the importance of that singular day.

I would look at her, as she knelt in her garden, weeds clumped around her legs, corn growing tall above her, and ask, "Do you wish I was a lawyer instead?"

And she would laugh—she is not shy about laughing—and declare: "Oh my God, Tik. I am *so glad* you are *not* a lawyer."

I would nod at her, and start to respond, and she would interrupt: "Now help me with these weeds. It will just take a minute."

I flung the door open and went straight to the old banana-yellow kitchen table. I opened drawers, moved books, spilled a vase, finally found a pen. Found paper. Still standing, I began to write.

If I could go and ride anywhere, and train with the most renowned trainer and most athletic horses in the world for one year, where would I go?

I was breathing hard from the run up to the house. My t-shirt and jeans were wet from the rain. I took a breath and continued.

I lost my job (as an athlete), my dream (the Olympics), my health (a broken collarbone), and my girlfriend (my fault, not hers—I'm an idiot). I need to get away.

Being a working student is the thing. An apprenticeship! I will see the world on a shoestring, train horses, labor for lessons, leave my troubles behind.

Step one. Where to apply?

Who is the most experienced, accomplished, renowned, horse trainer in the world? And how will I get a job with that person?

I stood there, thinking, tapping my pen on the pad where I'd scribbled. There was the scent of damp hay in the house. A duck watched me from the back door. She cocked her head. I stared at her. She tilted her head the other way, then stepped into the house. I recognized her. She was one of ours—a creamy white Indian Runner. Outside there were ponds and pools forming, but she was uninterested in acting like the other puddle ducks. She waddled in farther.

Precipitation in Vancouver is common, and our house was a long way from her friends, but I think I understood her: novelty is worth a gamble.

A portrait-size photo on the far wall showed my father standing, watching me ride his horse. Most of the photo was in shadow, but a ray of sun had filtered through the clouds, and in a lucky moment, caught the two of us, as if in a spotlight. It looked like one of those posters sold on the first day of college—the ones with a touching image above and an inspiring quote beneath.

That was how I felt—as if I had been moving in shadows, doing what was expected, and then suddenly, a spotlight caught me, and a voice roared: "Wake up!"

Not the most inspiring two words, but effective, like a slap across the face.

"WAKE UP!"

And I listened. I put pen to paper. It was a clear first step. Like the first step in a marathon.

I looked at my scribbled manifesto. I wiped my face with my arm and then used my shirt to sponge the drops off the paper. I held it up. I read it over.

It wasn't good, but it was honest.

I hoped that would be enough.

CHAPTER 2

"Not Many Decent Stables Are Interested in Taking Working Students"

The next two weeks I was on a computer more than I was on a horse. Not only would this "working student thing" take some research, but the editor of *Gaitpost* magazine—"Canada's Greatest Little Horse Mag!"—had replied to a query I'd sent out:

Sorry for my delay in responding. Your article is interesting, and I would like to run it if I have room. Do you have any photos of yourself you could send me?

I did have photos, and I sent them. I called the first piece "Chapter One." If there was going to be a "Chapter Two," I needed to figure out where I was going.

I wanted to achieve two things: the experience of living somewhere completely different and the chance to improve my riding. Becoming a working student—a notoriously difficult and unofficial apprenticeship of sorts, relied on by many in the horse world to both staff barns and provide mentorship—could offer me both.

As a child, riding to me was what church might have been to

other kids: something necessary and good, but not something I had chosen. My mother was a dressage rider and my father a show jumper; for both of them, horses were a career and a passion. At various times in their lives they had competed, taught, judged shows, owned tack shops, run a riding school, and even authored a book on equine photography. I spent many weekends with my dad competing horses and watching others compete them. I spent many car rides with my mother, debating riding theory.

In our family, when we talked about riders, character was as important as skill. And we used words to define that character: Were they *kind?* Or *cruel?* Were they *thoughtful?* Or *hasty?* Were they *professional?* There were always riders whom we looked up to as a matter of course: German dressage master Reiner Klimke was like an apostle in my mind. The American equitation king George Morris, as well. There was this almost unconscious notion that being a *good rider* was something important.

For years I had been putting off the decision about whether to commit to riding wholeheartedly. Now, if I was going to continue to ride, I wanted it to be *my* decision. I did not want to just *happen* to have horses in my life. I wanted to have to fight for them. To earn my way. To brawl with fate if needed!

And what discipline to choose? Show jumping was the sport in which I had the most experience, but I was curious about cross-country riding, part of the sport of eventing. It seemed more real and unfiltered, like swimming in an ocean instead of a pool.

At first, by not picking a particular riding discipline, I thought I might make the task of finding a working student position with some well-known trainer simpler. But as with any good dessert menu, I found that more choices only made the decision more time-consuming.

I began by talking to people who knew people. Although I had grown up around horses, I soon found that I was ignorant of the real Who's Who of the international equestrian scene, especially outside the world of show jumping. A friend was shocked that I had never heard of New Zealand's eventing hero Mark Todd (which was indeed embarrassing since a quick Google search revealed he was named "Rider of the 20th Century" by the Fédération Equestre Internationale, the governing body of international equestrian sport).

Once I started asking around, suggestions that were at first welcome came fast and often contradicted each other, and I was quickly overwhelmed and confused.

Let me give you an example:

Johann Hinnemann was a legend in the sport of dressage. Besides winning a bronze medal on Ideeal for Germany at the World Championships in 1986, he had trained many top horses and mentored some of the best riders in the world for almost half a century. At one point or another he was national team coach for Canada, the Netherlands, and Germany, and he co-wrote *The Simplicity of Dressage*, a book published in multiple languages that clearly explained the structure and program needed to bring along a dressage horse.

To some, Hinnemann could do no wrong. My parents in particular, both dressage enthusiasts, praised his training, so naturally he made my long list of possibilities. But when I asked another local dressage instructor about him I was shocked by her answer: "He rides okay, but I don't think you two will get along well at all. You should go to Kyra Kyrklund. I hear she's training in England now."

Everybody had an opinion about where I should go, where I shouldn't, who was hard to get along with, who was good, who was mean, who was overrated, and who was the "real deal."

Thankfully, another friend of mine suggested I check out Euro-dressage, a popular international website, where "want ads" for working students and grooms were posted. Immediately my search for a trainer seemed infinitely easier—within ten minutes I found that Germany's Ludwig Kathmann, Katrin Bettenworth, and Nadine Capellmann, and the American rider Leslie Morse, were all looking for riders. Even though I had never heard of them, I immediately sent off my equestrian résumé, along with a three-minute clip of me riding. I was uneasy about the video, but everyone who knew anything about the working-student selection process assured me it would be fine: "Trainers aren't looking for perfection. They are looking for potential."

My list of possible working student positions was long. I started eliminating names rapidly and ruthlessly. My criteria become clearer as I went.

One: The barn must be in a central riding location, someplace like Florida, Kentucky, England, or Germany.

Two: The trainer must have a deep understanding of the classical foundation of horse training. Riding has its classical adherents, always following the time-tested ways espoused by European masters, and it has its innovators. I wanted somebody who went "by the book." I believed the old way was the best way.

There were also people who talked about styles—French dressage versus German dressage versus Spanish dressage, for example. But I believed it was simpler than that: There is good dressage and bad dressage.

Three: The person must be a leading rider or trainer in whatever discipline he or she practiced.

Although I was tempted to include Western trainers, I decided to limit myself to the three Olympic disciplines—dressage, show jumping, and eventing. This was partly practical (it was in these areas that I had connections that might prove necessary in landing a position) and partly emotional (trying a Western discipline, like reining or cutting, would have been *way* out of my comfort zone).

The hodge-podge list of elite riders and trainers from around the world who ultimately made my short list included: show jumper Ian Millar (how could he *not* be top of the list for a Canadian-bred young rider?), dressage trainer Johann Hinnemann, eventers Mark Todd, Leslie Law, and Karen and David O'Connor, dressage riders Kyra Kyrklund, Leonie Bramall, Andreas Helgstrand, and show jumpers John and Michael Whitaker and Beezie Madden.

I would later look back and see this was an incomplete and unsatisfactory inventory. Obviously, there were many talented and illustrious individuals I did not ever consider. Omissions were almost entirely due to ignorance. My "greenness" was something I was aware of and not proud of, but I was hell-bent on adventure and gave myself no marks for research or comprehensiveness, only for originality and perseverance.

It was time to again send off applications (noting my hasty appeals via Eurodressage had not yet met with success). I underestimated how tricky completing this task would be. For many of the trainers, I could not even find an email address—I had to source them through friends and connections. I sent off about five emails, nervous about the kind of response I would receive. (In some cases, silence was to be my only response.)

But then, the next day:

Hello! Great to hear from you! Unfortunately, we don't have any spots at present for working students. However, I will definitely keep you in mind, and if I hear of anything I'll get right back to you! Take care!

That was from Leslie Law, winner of the individual gold medal and team silver in eventing for Great Britain in 2004.

I was undeterred. I had another response! It was from Leonie

Bramall. I had included Bramall on the short list because she was Canadian, she went to the Olympics, and she had become one of Europe's top trainers. She had trained with Hinnemann for fifteen years; that kind of loyalty, or staying power, is rare. Bramall was living in Germany, but she grew up only blocks from where I lived in Vancouver. I thought this personal connection might swing me an invitation.

However, her email was succinct and foreboding:

As things look with us we are full until the end of the year...not many decent stables are interested in taking working students.

But then, my third and fourth replies were much more promising. Johann Hinnemann and the O'Connors were both interested in seeing a video of my riding. I sent a movie clip by email to Hinnemann in Germany and a DVD of me jumping, performing basic dressage, and riding cross-country to the O'Connors in Virginia.

And the waiting game began.

I didn't hear anything for three long days. When I felt cooped up I went for a run. When I needed inspiration I read. First, *Life of Pi*, for fun. Second, *The Handmaid's Tale*, which was no laughing matter. I visited with our horses: Sapphire, a dark bay mare, nuzzled my hand. TJ, a big lanky gelding, threw his head and stomped his feet. When he was hungry he let us know! I ate little. I often lost weight when stressed or depressed.

When I finally got two invitations, they came within hours of each other. Johann Hinnemann was the first to respond (actually, it was his secretary, but seeing as he had thirty-five horses in his stable, I was sure he had more important things to do). I read and reread the letter. Although the wiser part of myself said, *Wait and see what other offers you might get,* my hands typed out an instant and enthusiastic reply, ending with: "When can I come?"

It was almost involuntary, my saying, "Yes!" Like a girl who plans to wait and see what kind of offers she gets to the prom…but then goes with the first boy who asks.

It would happen that right on the heels of my answer to Herr Hinnemann, Leslie Morse, one of America's top dressage riders (who I'd contacted in my initial flurry of online applications) offered me a job in California. I wondered if I had made the right choice. Despite her blatant warning that it was a sun-up to sundown job for the committed only, my mind conjured images of sunny, sandy coves and margaritas by the pool. Everybody gets a day off now and then, right?

With the Beach Boys' "California Girls" running though my head, I had an epiphany.

Going to only one place as a working student would not be enough.

If I was going to make this one year worthwhile, it should be a tour.

Sure, there was value in staying with one trainer for a year or longer; however, improving my riding was only *one* of my two criteria— the other being to experience living somewhere completely different.

Johann Hinnemann's stable in Germany would be my first stop, but why not do a little more research, and send out more applications? I could potentially train with three trainers in the year ahead, each one for four months. Why not learn at a dressage barn, a show jumping stable, *and* an eventing center? Well, *why not?* If I was really serious about improving my riding and seeing the world, to me, there could not be a better way.

CHAPTER 3

Lord of the Manor

I walked from the train station, schlepping two bags—one on wheels and one on my back. I took two wrong turns and stopped to look around. A sign on a building read *Dietrich Bonhoeffer Haus*. I continued to look at it as I took a swig from my water bottle. Hmmm. I took out the book I was reading and compared the house name to the author's name. They matched. The title of the book was *Letters and Papers from Prison*, and I had just happened to borrow it from my cousin Kenna, in Halifax, the day before. Strange coincidence, I thought.

I took off my jacket and my sweater, tucked them under one arm, and kept walking. As the brick houses gave way to orchards and paddocks, I broke a sweat for the first time in Voerde, a town near the river Rhine. I had my notebook in my back pocket and kept checking the addresses. Despite the cool weather I was down to my t-shirt by the time I stood in front of Krüsterhof 1. The rows of trees lining the long walk to the door were stern, straight, and evenly spaced—soldiers saluting me as I put on a brave face. I was nervously anticipating meeting the great riding master Johann Hinnemann for the first time. His brick house was covered in ivy, just starting to turn autumn red.

The entrance to Dressurstall Krüsterhof was a reflection of the whole property: nothing extravagant or decadent, everything purposeful and meticulous. Within days of being there, I realized it was a reflection of Hinnemann's philosophy, as well.

It was morning, and I arrived just as Herr Hinnemann came out of his house. He was dressed for the city, not for riding, in a dark suit. He had a ruddy complexion and short gray hair that bunched a little at the sides. I was walking toward him down the driveway, maybe sixty feet from him, when he noticed me through his wire-rimmed glasses. We made eye contact, but he said nothing. I waved, but he turned away and walked back toward the barn, which was next to the house.

Unusual, I thought, as I kept walking. Before I reached the barn he came out again with a young woman, and I put my bags down so I could introduce myself. I shook their hands—one large and firm, the other soft and cool. The young woman, I learned, was his secretary Julia—the one who had sent me the invitation to come. Herr Hinnemann left abruptly following the introduction, but Julia was happy to talk.

Julia had given up a career as an architect in order to manage Hinnemann's stable and, it seemed, his life. She led me through the barn, showed me the office, and finally to the living quarters. She wore a tidy blouse and on her face, a coy, smart smile. She could have passed for a lawyer or a young politician. She walked ahead of me, offering tidbits of information. "The original farmhouse was built in the 1800s." Her accent was elegant, her grammar perfect.

I was assigned a loft suite in the roof of the barn. It was one of nine apartments that were reserved for employees, students, and other hangers-on.

The interior renovations throughout the building were obvious: huge skylights and extra rooms for staff. My loft had a bed and a dresser. A single lamp rounded out the furnishings. I considered Julia. She was not much older than me. I wondered if her life was as organized as she looked.

"If you are not too tired, have a shower, get some food from the kitchen, and come out to the barn. I think there are horses on the board for you."

She tucked a stray hair behind her ear.

I was eager to do all three, and I told her so. After lunch, I got a short tour of the rest of the place before I found my way to the barn (and the first of five horses I was assigned to ride that day). In all, the property had two houses, the collection of standalone apartments and suites of various sizes, stalls for forty horses, indoor and outdoor arenas, several outbuildings, and five fields delineated by dark wood fencing, the largest of which had a sand track around the outside.

The peaceful picture was completed by fruit and nut trees spread out around the premises, as well as four masticating brown cows and one calf. These grain-fed, free-range cattle often had the run of the property. I do not presume to know what a cow likes, but it seemed an idyllic life for them. The herd unknowingly returned the favor to their owner by qualifying his equine operation as a legally functioning agricultural business. Of course, every year one of them paid the ultimate price.

In fact, our "Chef" (as in *Chef d'Equipe*—the name for equestrian team managers in international competition), as Hinneman was called around the barn, began his life as a farmer's son. But dressage would be his calling. As of 2008 he was one of only eight Riding Masters (*Reitmeister*) in Germany—Germany being a powerhouse of the discipline and sport of dressage, like ping-pong in China or curling in Canada. Hinnemann was the 1998 International Dressage Trainer of the Year.

But what impressed me was this: I met Coby van Baalen many times while I was working at Dressurstall Krüsterhof. Van Baalen was an Olympic silver medalist and a very successful dressage trainer in her own right, and when *she* wanted help, she came to Hinnemann! Perhaps, I thought, when looking for other trainers to work for, I should look at whom I admired, and then look at *their* trainers as potential mentors.

(While the others called Hinnemann "Chef," I tried it once that first day and gave it up. The informality of it made the word stick in my mouth like chalk. Later I heard riders his own age call him "Jo," but I was never at ease enough to call him anything but "Herr Hinnemann," or sometimes in my letters and writing, simply "Hinnemann.")

Everything about Hinnemann's place—the nine apartments, the caretaker, the cook, the self-sufficiency, and the wealth—reminded me of a medieval manor. And that's exactly how he ran it: like a lord. He could delegate and give orders like nobody's business. In brief military clips he organized the day: "Walk this horse thirty minutes," or "Warm up that horse for me," or "Longe the new horse for twenty minutes. And make sure the side-reins are correctly adjusted."

There was never a please or thank you, simply the complete and utter expectation that I knew exactly what he meant, and it would be done properly and efficiently. It was interesting that he expected this compliance from his horses as well. And in fact I often saw in other trainers a similarity in how they trained horses and how they trained staff.

In Canada I had never seen a man train an animal for such submissiveness, and he was talented at it. Watching Hinnemann ride those first few days, I was so impressed by him. I wanted to be able to sit like him. I wanted to learn how to teach a horse flying changes like him. But I was also uncomfortable around him.

Hinnemann saw everything. He was in and out of the ring constantly, riding and coaching, or—often—simply watching from his office that overlooked the indoor arena. During my first two weeks the only help he gave me was in the form of short, clipped directions, usually from horseback, with the understanding that I would then go and do my homework…and figure the rest out.

"Let the horse *stretch*!" he reprimanded me on my third day.

"Don't sit so heavily!" he growled at me my fourth day.

He did not speak to me for three days, and then: "You need to learn how to walk!" he said as he left the arena.

And so I brought my horse back to the walk. There were four other riders in the arena, and they continued trotting and cantering, not looking at me. I kept walking, but I was embarrassed.

Hinnemann's accent was thicker than Julia's, but his voice boomed easily across the arena. He almost always wore a dark sweater over a white, striped, button-down shirt. His boots were polished every day, and he made it clear mine should be, too.

He also had extra eyes in the form of his head rider. Steffi was twenty-four and had been a professional since she passed the German riding exam when she was eighteen, after only two years (it's usually three) of the state-run apprenticeship program. She was now licensed by Germany to teach dressage—what's called a *bereiter*.

At first it got my back up a little to have this young girl teaching me, but I realized quickly that she knew far more than I did. I decided I would take help where I could get it. In my first month she helped me a little almost every day. It was humbling and awkward. And eventually just what I needed.

Every day I rode between three and six horses. Sometimes I just walked them or warmed them up for Herr Hinnemann or Steffi; other times I worked them myself.

One morning Hinnemann breezed in and saw me riding his

ten-year-old black stallion, Timeless. I was having trouble with the canter-trot transitions. They were not smooth. The canter shortened and collected too much, and I ended up with a couple strides of a sort of half-trot, half-canter gait that was, as you might say in the business, "passagey."

"Your transitions aren't smooth," Hinnemann said. "Work on that!" he commanded as he left.

Well, thanks, I thought, but desperately wondered, How?

That's when Steffi, like a smooth west wind, stepped in. Her instructions seemingly solved all three: "Ride him shoulder-fore and a little rounder, use your voice, and keep doing transitions until he settles."

Bam! Just like that! Orders translated.

The place operated with military-like organization and competence.

I soon found I could not make the *brrrrr* sound that most of the riders used for downward transitions. They would vibrate their tongue behind their teeth, indicating to the horse to slow down or stop. Instead I *brrrr'ed* with my lips. I sounded like a kid blowing bubbles in a milkshake. The horses seemed to understand, but everyone else thought it was hilarious. The work—in the barn, in the yard, and in the care of the horses— like the training of the horses, was disciplined and structured, yet necessarily flexible. The days were long, but each evening I found the energy to write notes on what I was learning. The entries, looking back, were usually brief.

One day toward the end of my first month, Hinnemann—who had not spoken to me for a couple days—came out of his office, saw me trotting, and announced, "Work on your sitting trot." I *knew* I needed to work on my sitting trot, but I didn't know *how*. What exercises would help me?

Steffi was riding, too, and I waited until she was on a walk break, then asked her, "What can I do to get more help from Hinnemann?"

Her English, like most of the younger generation of Germans, was excellent.

"You need to practice what he tells you and not stop. You need to overdo it. For example, he just asked you to work on sitting trot, and you are already walking. Do sitting trot until he tells you to stop."

"Right now?"

"Right now." She did not smile. "Until he tells you to stop."

And so I did. I began a sitting trot and just kept going. Ten minutes. Twenty minutes. It was not going well. I bounced around like a small boat motoring over white caps. Through the door, behind the barn, I saw Hinnemann's car leaving the property. But I kept going.

I was pretty sore by the time Steffi called over to me, "I don't think he is coming back. You better stop."

I stopped. It was one thing for me to be a martyr, but I suspected the horse was enjoying the session even less than I was.

That evening I wrote: *I've been spoiled. Learning is such a privilege. I had no idea! When not learning, the mind craves it. I have taken learning for granted. Never again!*

I wanted to improve so badly. I put the notebook down and picked up Hinnemann's book. It was co-written with Coby van Baalen. I opened it, eyeballing the text.

Van Baalen has taken lessons from Hinnemann for more than ten years. His system is therefore hers, and Hinnemann's system is simply the German system.

I turned the page. My eyelids flickered shut, then opened again. I gritted my teeth.

"I'm certain," says van Baalen, "that any prominent German jumping or dressage trainer can immediately name the six concepts: rhythm, Losgelassenheit or suppleness, contact, impulsion, straightness, and collection."

I agreed, but I was losing focus. The walls felt so close around me. I loved books, but I could have read this one at home in Vancouver.

I should go for a run, I thought. I needed to move.

Relax, I told myself. Remain optimistic.

I lay back on the bed and looked at the ceiling, gathering my thoughts. I relaxed my muscles one by one, starting with my toes and working my way up to the top of my head, until I was calmer. Eventually I made a pledge, whispering to the empty room what I had already written: "I have taken learning for granted. Never again."

I put the book down and turned out the light. The dark rectangle of the skylight suddenly became the brightest part of the room. I looked out and repeated my promise: "Never again!"

CHAPTER 4

"Your Leg is Too Short!"

Each morning, actual riding started only after all the other chores were done. The days began at 7:00 A.M., and it took five of us two hours to do the morning chores—feeding, mucking, and sometimes ridding the corners of cobwebs or other odd jobs. The entire barn was swept three times a day, and we raked the edges of the rings by hand. We broke for breakfast and lunch, which we ate together, and worked until around 7:00 P.M. Then I would shower and prepare dinner, which I ate by myself.

After four weeks I was fed up. I was working twelve-hour days. I got one day off every two weeks. Many days I felt I had learned nothing. Hinnemann hardly even talked to me, much less helped me. I was not getting paid. And I didn't speak German.

I did, however, make an effort to learn.

I bought a small English-German dictionary for riders and studied it. Stallion was *der Hengst*. Mare, *die Stut*. Gelding, *der Wallach*. Thoroughbred was *das Vollblut*. A heavy horse, *das Kaltblut*. Saddle was *der Sattel*. Bridle, *der Zaum*.

And I learned interesting differences in how language might affect actions. In German a rising or posting trot was *leicht-trabben*, which translated literally as *light trot*. Not as definitive as the English term "posting," but more about how the action *seemed* to the horse and to the partnership. I liked that.

In German there was also the word *Losgelassenheit*, which had no direct translation. It meant, all at once, suppleness and relaxation on the part of the horse—both mental and physical. *Losgelassenheit* was like a child that had enjoyed recess and was now nodding his head at his teacher, ready to focus, ready to work.

Then there was *Durchlässigkeit*, which translated awkwardly. It meant the end result of years of horse training. A *Durchlässigkeit* horse was the partner every dancer dreams of: athletic, relaxed, focused. *Durchlässigkeit* is Baby, in her pink dress, dancing with Johnny to "(I've Had) The Time of My Life." It is her smile and her confidence, her enjoyment at being led.

I enjoyed learning German, but it was slow going. I still could not understand the others at the barn unless they spoke directly and slowly to me with simple words, or they spoke in English.

After five weeks, Hinnemann spoke to me again. It was while I was on a young gelding.

"You ride like a fucking rabbit."

I was not sure if the expletive was an adjective or a verb, but either way it was not a compliment. And it was not really that helpful either.

What are you doing? I asked myself that night.

You aren't good enough, I told myself. You're too old. This trip is silly. A waste of time.

Maybe my being there *was* ridiculous. There was certainly no denying I was under-qualified. One evening I wrote in my notebook:

I think my sitting trot is the joke of the month. They are laughing out loud at me. They were speaking in German so I don't know what exactly they were saying. But as I bounced along Steffi kept telling me I needed to relax my hips more.

After six weeks, I was still getting ordered out of the ring and sent back to the barn. If I had the wrong saddle pad, if I forgot to oil the horse's feet, if the horse wasn't clean enough, if *I* wasn't clean enough, if the wraps were crooked, I was directed to leave.

I wanted to talk to Hinnemann.

I thought I could catch him between one of his rides and a lesson, when he would be in the barn aisle. I planned my approach for three days.

Finally I saw him walking from the indoor to the barn, which was connected by a large room with cement floors, big enough to get on a horse and wait until the indoor arena was clear to enter. It also served the purpose of ensuring horse and rider never had to go outside in the winter.

"Herr Hinnemann?"

He paused but didn't quite look at me. I quickly asked him if there was anything more I should be doing to get the most out of my time in his employ. He wore a gray sweater over a collared blue shirt. His boots, as usual, gleamed. He didn't answer.

"What can I do to improve my leg?" I pressed.

He tilted his head, saying nothing.

"I want to be able to sit into the horse like Steffi," I tried again.

I waited.

"You don't have a nice long leg," Hinnemann finally replied. "Your back is too long and your leg is too short."

I didn't really know what to say to that. I started to tell him I would work on it, but he was already walking away.

Back in the barn I looked around. All the other riders were younger than me. For most, being a working student was something they did instead of college. It was equivalent to learning a trade. And there were some teenagers who maybe didn't considering riding a career, simply a hobby to be improved, who were doing this during their "gap year" between high school and university.

There *were* riders older than me who rode with Hinnemann, but they were professionals who shipped their horses in and paid for lessons, or they were amateurs who had their horses in training with Hinnemann. At twenty-six and in my position, I felt way behind.

I wanted to make the most of my time away from home, and I was getting impatient. I asked myself, How do I know when to wait and watch, and when to push for more help?

Many of the best riders in the world trained in Germany. Jessica Kürten, who was the top-ranked female jumper rider in the world, lived and trained just down the road. And what do you know, she came to Hinnemann for dressage lessons. She thought the flatwork would improve her jumping.

Another Germany-based rider I wanted to meet was Ingrid Klimke. The Klimkes were to German riding what the Kennedys were to American politics. Reiner Klimke, Ingrid Klimke's late father, won six gold and two bronze medals in dressage at the Olympics between 1964 and 1984. His daughter was carrying on the family tradition of winning Olympic gold medals, which she managed to do in Beijing, a few months before I arrived in Germany. Her facility was in Münster, about forty-five miles from Hinnemann's stable.

In my seventh week I wrote to Ingrid Klimke. I asked if I could visit her stable, and maybe one day become a working student for her. Three times I emailed. No response. I assumed she must be a very busy lady. So I bought a cell phone and called. She was just rushing out, but she said that in two days she was hosting an "Open House," and I was welcome to stop by.

Two days was not much time to make the necessary arrangements: I had to borrow a car, trade my day off with another working student, figure out directions, and set my mind to go—all while still getting my chores done and riding my assigned horses. But I did it.

There were a couple dozen men and women at Klimke's facility when I arrived. The first part of our "Open House" tour took us through her center-aisle barn. The horses on the right were eventing horses, the horses on the left were dressage horses, and the difference was immediately noticeable. The dressage horses had conformation and muscling similar to basketball players, while the eventing horses would have been long-distance runners.

We were led to the indoor arena to meet Klimke. She rode three horses that day: a young one to show the importance of the warm up, a dressage horse to demonstrate flying changes, and last, an event horse.

An assistant entered the arena with a simple, straight-backed, wooden chair—the kind you might use at a desk—and placed it underneath a jump. Klimke and her horse jumped the obstacle, which was over three feet high. The assistant removed one of the rails, and they jumped it again. The assistant methodically dismantled the jump, and Klimke and her horse cleared what remained every time.

Then, all that was left was the narrow, wooden chair.

Wow. I had never seen this before.

Klimke picked up the canter, and the pair approached the chair. The crowd held its breath. Woman and horse jumped it, smooth and true as an arrow fired out of a bow. Klimke came to a halt, smiling as we all clapped. In fifteen minutes she had taught her horse to jump a chair that was half his width! What this said about his connection to her and his attention to her aids was incredible.

Klimke gave the impression of having found the balance between humility and confidence, between joy and professionalism. It was a balance I had not seen before—part nun, part Ellen DeGeneres. I was impressed.

"Thank you for allowing me to visit, Frau Klimke," I said to her an hour later, back in the barn.

She offered her hand. "Call me Ingrid."

I took off my glove and took her hand. "Thank you, Ingrid."

I also made some new friends. What were the chances that Ingrid would have two Canadian working students at her barn? And both from British Columbia! Jamie, a serious boy, was from Vernon, and Eiren, a pretty brunette about my age, was from Vancouver…and we all got along famously. I promised to visit again.

I was jealous of the situation Jamie and Eiren had at Ingrid's. They seemed so…happy. They received instruction regularly, and they got along with Ingrid. They *talked* to Ingrid. But Eiren admitted it wasn't always like that for her. She explained she had worked for years in unrewarding, punishing conditions before she found this equestrian oasis. She and I became short-distance pen pals, of sorts, which in my situation felt like I had stumbled upon a glass of water while wandering lost in the desert. Eiren always wrote me back, and she offered advice freely, for which I was grateful.

Her hints were insightful:

As the weather gets worse and you spend more time walking in the indoor, really watch the other riders. When they do transitions—any transitions—watch the seat, the elbows, the lower-leg placement, everything. Try to develop a critical eye by comparing riders. Though Mr. H may not be the prettiest on a horse, I bet he has the best seat. Compare his position (and I mean you have to learn about details, like elbows) to the other riders and see what the better riders do differently.

They were practical:

When you're walking, drop your stirrups and really stretch your "jumper legs" down with your feet parallel to the ground (forget the heels down crap for now, just don't point your toes). Then LEAN BACK in the saddle, farther back than you think you need to. Feel when you're straight, then feel when your body is behind the vertical. If you can, check the mirror to see what's accurate, because I will bet that you will be almost straight when you feel you're too far back. Really explore this positioning by going too far and past your comfort zone (this is why we start at the walk). Then you can find balance.

And they were funny:

Always remember: Don't round your shoulders. A lot of men who ride dressage do this anyway, but jumpers are terrible for it. Don't think of pulling them back, that often will hollow your back, which ends up giving you the hunter-rider "duck butt" instead of a good seat. Instead push your shoulders down. Once your shoulders are down, imagine you're a girl with big boobs, and you're proud of them...like you want someone to notice. You'll have good posture in the saddle (and you don't have to tell anyone what you're thinking).

But isn't it true that every guy has wanted to know what it's like to have boobs?

Eiren made me laugh. I felt like she was on my team, which was valuable and rare. But I was still curious to know whether my working student experience was typical or not. I thought I would be getting more help from Hinnemann. I reached out again to my short-list candidate and fellow Canadian Leonie Bramall, who had this to say about working in Germany:

The problems you're having getting help with your riding are the same everywhere here. The German mentality is that you should feel privileged to even sit on one of their horses.... It will be much the same anywhere else you go. Don't expect too much.

Her advice? Summed up at the end of her email: "Learn by doing!"

Prior to my eighth week, Herr Hinnemann had not given me more than a few minutes of his time. Mostly he walked by me as if I was a saddle rack. As the end of my first two months neared, he spoke to me a few more times. Each was brief and to the point.

"*Tiefer*," he said, "lower," referring to the outline of the horse.

I guess if Hinnemann had a teaching style, it would be minimalist.

Despite feeling caught up in a place that wasn't right for me, I listened. I knew with my brain that everything he said was backed up by years of training countless horses and riders. But sometimes my heart wasn't in it.

Despite my frustration with Hinnemann's style of leadership, eight weeks after arriving, I finally felt like I was improving. I was assigned the young horses, and I was still not getting much help, but I *was* getting better. I was surrounded by excellence: expensive horses, educated riders, and a perfectly kept stable. So was I improving through osmosis? No. I was watching, and I was trying. I was sitting up taller, my legs felt longer, my hands were stiller, and my aids were subtler. This lesson—that by simply being around people and horses that were better than I was, I would improve—was one I have never forgotten. And I was learning by doing.

But I still continually wondered what the hell I was doing there. Each day that passed without a word from Hinnemann and very few from my fellow working students, I felt more trapped.

One day one of the regular clients said the horse I was on was good for me.

"Oh, why do you say that?" I asked.

In a rich accent she replied: "That is a good horse for beginners."

Internally, I went: Ohhh!

In that moment I fully realized the truth: At home I was a rider. Here, I was *not*. Here, I was just a beginner. I had to re-look at my situation. Right then, I wished I had a friend who wasn't miles away.

I had struggled to really connect with the others at Hinnemann's barn. They were mostly from Germany and had their own friends, their own culture, and their own language. Also, I suspected, it was becoming obvious to them that there was a distance growing between me and the management. In tough times people tend to pick a side.

The simmering tension I was beginning to feel was let out when I left the property for a walk or run. One Wednesday night, after work, I set out full of worry. The doubts creeping through my sub-conscious about the position were multiplying quickly. Running had always helped me work through problems more quickly. I craved it, especially when alone in a crowd. The group lunches at the farm were the most painful part of the day for me as I sat and ate in silence. The only words I spoke were "pass the salt" or "pass the bread," and if I could do without the salt, I did. I was utterly lonely…surrounded by people.

Perhaps running felt good because I needed my physical state to mirror my mental state, which was agitated and confused. Some say horses are like that—only after moving can they relax.

That night my body cast long gray shadows as I jogged under the few streetlamps. There were very few cars out that late, and soon there were none. The street lamps got farther and farther apart. It was an evening of cold and flurries—not so cold as to be painful, but cold enough I had to keep moving.

I soon found myself in an area I did not recognize. I turned a cor-ner and suddenly in front of me lay a cemetery. I stopped. I stared.

Before every headstone sat a flickering candle, melting a tiny circle of snow. There were hundreds of them! Maybe thousands! Around each candle, drifting snowflakes reflected the light and magnified it—it was beautiful.

I stood still and thought about that day…and about the coming days. Things were not going well, and I suspected something would have to change. A quote from Dietrich Bonhoeffer that I had copied down came to mind:

> *It is the characteristic excellence of the strong man that he can bring momentous issues to the fore and make a decision about them. The weak are always forced to decide between alternatives they have not chosen for themselves.*

Sometimes long walks, and his writings, gave me strength. Other nights, like this one, anxious or frustrated, I put on shorts, because despite the cold, I had to run. Had to race. Now, though, I jogged slowly home, the snow swirling around my face, and thought of many things, and had many questions.

Less than a week later I was fired.

CHAPTER 5

"We Can't Leave You Alone on a Horse for Five Minutes"

It was a day like every other, not notable in any way, except for two details.

The first was that it was a Sunday. On Sundays the stable was half-staffed, which was brilliant when it was my day off.

But that day I was working—and half the staff means twice the work. When my alarm went off that morning, my room was lit only by the eight stars I could see through my skylight. Dawn would break, unseen by me, usually around the time I finished my sixteenth stall of the morning. I would not have breakfast until I had mucked out ten more stalls, put in fresh straw, swept the barn aisles, and the driveway, as well.

The driveway was cobblestone...it took a long time to sweep.

The second detail, a very short meeting with Hinnemann, irritated and troubled me enough to note it down later in my journal.

Around the time I started my twentieth stall, Hinnemann wandered out, dressed in a dark suit with creases like knives. I watched his polished black leather shoes make their way through the courtyard to his Audi. I watched them step into the freshly vacuumed interior. I had been up already for almost two hours, but my arms and shoulders were used to the work by now, and I felt fresh. With every day and every week, I told myself: Stay positive. This will be the day when you finally start getting more help. I still craved the feeling that this was all *for* something. I wanted a lesson. I wanted to learn so badly my brain itched.

Sure, a part of me realized I was getting better, and though time has given me other perspectives, I felt like I was getting better *despite* Hinnemann, not *because* of him.

"Good morning," I called neutrally.

Hinnemann looked at me. We made eye contact. And then he turned his back to me and lowered himself into his new car. As he shut the door, I thought I heard a reluctant "*Morgen,*" but perhaps not. As his car wound along the tree-lined drive out to the road, I stood in the doorway of the barn, pitchfork in one hand, staring after him.

The afternoon passed quietly, but monotonously, as did the following morning. It wasn't until Monday afternoon that my suspicions that something was up were confirmed. Herr Hinnemann, his secretary, and his head rider were meeting in the glass-fronted office that overlooked the indoor. I was riding a young horse so I was taking plenty of walk breaks. I could see them as they talked earnestly, studiously avoiding looking into the indoor arena where I circled below. Only Hinnemann glanced my way a couple times.

That evening while I was untacking my last horse, Julia marched in her efficient step down the aisle. She paused and looked at me. She looked so warm and clean. I felt like a ground-beholden soldier that sees a pilot wrapped in fur walking to his plane. Her head held high, Julia, it seemed, flew in the sky above the sludge and muck of normal barn life.

"Tik, please come to the office when all the work in the barn is done."

"Of course," I said quietly. I made myself meet her eyes.

For the last three weeks my motivation to sweep, muck, clean tack, and clip horses had been waning.

You're not here as a volunteer, I told myself. You're here to learn, and in exchange, to perform physical labor.

Shhh. I said to myself. Stop whining. Be patient.

And then, No! Stand up for yourself.

To muzzle the voices in my head, I concentrated on finishing with the horse, then cleaning the saddles and bridles, then sweeping.

Back in my room I gathered my thoughts, and quickly prepared myself for the discussion I expected by making some notes. I took my notebook with me.

In the office Julia sat at a desk, her hand around a steaming mug. Steffi stood, her arms crossed, not looking at me. Hinnemann was not there.

The whole meeting lasted less time than it took me to clean a stall, and with me talking just about as much. There was no preamble—Julia just jumped right in.

"You aren't good enough to be here," she said unemotionally. "And you aren't improving."

I looked at Steffi, who briefly made eye contact but remained silent. I waited.

"This is a *professional* stable," Julia continued. And then just to make her point clear she added: "We can't leave you alone on a horse for five minutes."

I said nothing. I felt myself turn inward and get in my own head, a weakness that admittedly often came far too close to self-pity for my liking. The only advantage, if I could call it that, was it meant a lot of potential arguments were avoided. I sat and looked at her, and kept my hands in my pockets, my notebook full of observations remaining closed on my lap. As Julia talked on, I studied her closely.

There was a certain light in her eyes. She was beautiful, like a bird. A falcon, maybe…or a hawk. Her mouth was still moving. Her lips glistened, and I wondered if she was wearing lipstick.

"Did you hear me?" she demanded to know.

I nodded.

Then she said, "It would be better if you left."

I nodded again.

She then offered me the chance to work until the end of the week.

"No," I said, speaking for the first time. "I'll leave tonight."

I left the office silently, then went to say goodbye to the other riders who were still chatting in the tack room. I forced myself to speak, to shake their hands. Back in my loft, I began packing my bags. I looked at the wall—white and uncluttered.

What now? I could go back to Canada, or I could stay in Europe through Christmas…perhaps longer.

When I run, especially any significant distance, there are many points along the way when I feel like giving up, like turning for home. *You don't need to run today…you ran yesterday! Take a break. Nobody will know!*

But *I* will know! I always say to myself, forcibly changing the tune in my head. You're being feeble.

Don't be soft!

You spineless wimp! Keep going!

I beat myself up because it feels weak to think about quitting. But as I argue with myself my feet keep moving—and that must count for something.

And so that day, although pained, tired, full of doubt, I kept putting one foot in front of the other.

With my bags half-packed next to me, I made a call to an acquaintance from a few years back—a fellow pentathlete from the Netherlands. Modern pentathlon was the sport Kelvin and I had both devoted a decade of our lives to. Invented at the same time, and by the same person, as the modern Olympics, it had five events, just like the five rings: running, fencing, shooting, swimming…and riding. Kelvin and I had kept in touch, and he knew I was in Germany.

"Kelvin!" I greeted him. "I'm thinking about going home to Vancouver…but I'm also thinking I should give Germany another shot. Can I come stay with you in Holland for a while and sort things out?"

"Of course!" he replied immediately. "Grab a train and come!"

Kelvin did not ask how long I needed to stay—which was perfect, because I did not know.

"What station should I come to?" My brain was already working through new alternative scenarios. Somehow I would salvage this experience.

"Arnhem," he replied. "Just let me know what time I should pick you up."

I walked to the train station, slowly reversing the path I'd eagerly taken to Dressurstall Krüsterhof only ten weeks before. I bought a ticket. I left Voerde in the dark. As the train rolled along I watched farms, fields, towns, tunnels, and graffiti come and go. I had stuck it out for two-and-a-half months for what? And why? Stubbornness? A hope that it would get better? A sense of responsibility? Definitely a desire to see my Grand Plan through. But now I was leaving, and not on good terms. My working student adventure seemed sadly, prematurely over.

But my mind was picking up my feet. One in front of the other. I would not quit. No, I thought. Nope! I would keep going.

This was just a new direction.

CHAPTER 6

A Silver Lining

Thousands of small white lights greeted me in Arnhem. A market bustled with people, their collars pulled up, hands in their pockets. The smell of sizzling dough caught my attention. *Olliebollen* came with raisins or apple bits inside and powdered sugar on top. I realized I had not eaten all day.

"One bag please."

The Dutchman was bundled up in a jacket and scarf. He removed his gloves to gather the sweet pastries and served them to me in a small white paper bag.

"*Danke*," I said, a tentative smile on my face for the first time in days.

I ate all of them in Kelvin's car on the way to his house.

As he drove, Kelvin explained that instead of exchanging gifts with his family for Christmas, they all wrote poems. My visit coincided with the holiday, so I found myself a not-unwilling participant. Over the next week my poem turned into an epic—sixteen stanzas long—and rhymed in the manner of Dr. Seuss. It was pleasant, distracting work when I needed it the most.

It was unusual to be away from my family for Christmas. And now that I was no longer at Herr Hinnemann's, the expectation back home was that I would return soon. But I became more adamant each day that I would stay in Europe until my previously scheduled return flight.

In the afternoons Kelvin and I would run six miles together, and in the evenings I found myself writing again—now about riding. *Gaitpost* had published a few of my articles, and I wanted to keep it going.

Hey! I thought when I saw an issue. That's *my* name in print!

And then I arranged to go back to Ingrid Klimke's barn. I would not have an official position, but I was welcome to come and learn, she said. I figured if I worked hard enough, and was polite and friendly, she wasn't likely to send me away.

I took the train back to Germany a week after New Year's. When I got to Ingrid's, I gave Eiren a big hug. We both had padded jackets on, so it was like two sumo wrestlers meeting.

"I'm staying with you, right?"

She grinned. "Yep."

I looked around happily. It was cold, but crisp, and the sun shone. Ingrid rode up to us and dismounted. Eiren took her horse, and I smiled shyly as I shook Ingrid's hand, telling her I would help however and wherever I could. Like a colt being weaned, I had been shut out of one world, but I was entering a new one.

Within a few days I knew Ingrid's stable was exactly what I had been seeking: A chance to learn in a positive atmosphere that encouraged questions and independence rather than obedience and anxiety. A stable that built professionalism and confidence, thus fostering loyalty.

I see two ways to build confidence in horses. One is to keep having positive, successful experiences. The second is to go through something difficult, but to come out okay on the other side. Perhaps it is the same for us.

Ingrid lived in Münster, Westfalia, a region I came to appreciate for its good beer and great horses. On weekends in the summer there were often ten horse shows, all within seventy miles of the city, yet I saw no sacrifice of quality for quantity. (The same went for the beer.)

Ingrid was everything I was looking for in a trainer: the best classical knowledge, passed on to her from her highly respected father; a deep compassion for and understanding of the horse, courtesy of a childhood caring for and riding all manner of horses and ponies; respect from her peers for her dedication and her open, honest manner with people; and experience in both dressage and eventing, including, at the time, three Olympic Games with a gold medal to show for it.

Most of all it was obvious Ingrid utterly enjoyed riding; she spread enthusiasm like confetti in the wind. I saw it every time she was on a horse—her concentration and focus shone from her face as she looked to her horse, then to the world, and the future, then back to her horse, always back to her horse. Her eyes glowed like a joyful child's, because play was her work.

On my second weekend in Münster, Ingrid went to a "really, really important and prestigious" dressage show (or so Eiren explained). There she ended up second to Isabell Werth (who, at the time, had been to four Olympics for her country), but what impressed me was a little footnote event at the show—something that wasn't printed in the official results.

Eiren regaled me with the story of how the night before the show, Ingrid was out working her top stallion when she overheard a group of grooms from other barns joking about the incompetence of dressage horses when it came to jumping.

Although dressage horses are bred for their gaits, and not their ability to jump, they are still capable of jumping, and many of them would do pretty well in a different career. It is usually a lack of training, not lack of athleticism or temperament, that results in their poor showing over obstacles. Of course, there is a big difference between a horse that can jump three feet, and a horse that can soar over five.

Ingrid, however, was one of the very few Grand Prix dressage riders who also competed over fences, and she wasn't going to let what she overheard go.

"My horse can jump," she said to the group.

The grooms knew who Ingrid was and were excited to see where her challenge might lead. This would be like an opera singer showing off her rapping skills. They eagerly—although somewhat nervously, considering the surroundings—dared her to jump a bale of hay.

"*One* bale?" she asked with a smile. "Put out two."

Her stallion cleared the jump with ease. And then the duo, who had now attracted a crowd, jumped it the other way as well. The grooms cheered.

At this moment a middle-aged fellow appeared, bundled up in a big red jacket and holding a beer (that likely hadn't been his first). In a tipsy German drawl he wagered she couldn't jump him, as well, if he lay across the bales of hay.

"I'm not sure if he was joking or not," Eiren admitted as she described the scene to me.

And maybe he wasn't sure either.

"No problem," Ingrid had replied coolly.

There was nothing skittish about Ingrid's horse as he approached the makeshift jump. The red jacket, and the man inside, were surprisingly still as the horse approached, and the pair easily jumped over him and landed lightly on the other side.

The crowd stood and brought their hands together, and as Eiren told me how it all ended, I cheered as well!

But Ingrid was not all guts n' glory. There was a bit of that, yes, but it complemented her very serious work ethic. In her day-to-day training, she was a relentless perfectionist. She carefully planned every season, every week, every day. She was structured yet flexible. She wrote her goals in concrete and her plans in sand. She surrounded herself with competent and enthusiastic help. She kept the number of horses at her stable manageable, between ten and fifteen, so that she could ride every horse and see to it that each was receiving the highest possible standard of care and training.

On my first day there I rode four horses. I was pretty sure it was more a chance for Ingrid to evaluate my riding than a compliment to my ability. I didn't let that knowledge deter me from relishing the chance to ride such athletic and competition-proven horses. My last ride of the day was on FRH Butt's Abraxxis, the eleven-year-old Hanoverian that had been her mount at the Beijing Olympics. "Braxxi" and Ingrid had placed fifth individually and won team gold, so this was surely the most accomplished horse I had ever ridden. I was flattered when I got the chance to ride him twice more that first week.

My scheduled return flight to British Columbia meant that I had only another two weeks at Ingrid's stable before I left Germany for good. While I perhaps could have stayed longer with Ingrid, I intended to stick to my original plan and work for other professionals in other places during the months ahead. I would return to Vancouver before heading to my next position. I was happy at Ingrid's, but I was also still unsure about what to make of my time at Hinnemann's. I still couldn't make sense of it: Had I acted spoiled or smart?

One Friday evening when I was feeling particularly pensive, Eiren and I were cooking potato pancakes and drinking beer when she asked what was wrong.

"Nothing," I replied, as is customary in such situations. She looked at me. Her dark hair fell over each cheek. Instead of brushing it back, she left it, framing her face.

"Tell me," she said.

I took a deep breath and a sip from my pint glass.

"I don't want to be a 'learning victim,'" I began. "I want to seize knowledge with both hands and take it. I don't want to be one of those people who wait for it to be handed to them. I know I should fight for it. But I don't think I fought hard enough, or maybe long enough, at Hinnemann's."

Eiren was quiet for a while. She flipped a pancake.

"There have been many nights when I have cried myself to sleep," she finally admitted. "Many nights where it was just so hard. And I didn't know if I was getting better. And I didn't know if it was worth it."

I looked at my beer, then back at her. At that moment I realized that although we were pretty much the same age, *she* was an adult. She had made peace with hardship, and moved past it, in a way I had not.

"This is a tough life," she went on, again flipping a pancake in the skillet. "I mean, horses are tough, and trying to be really good at something is tough, and when you combine the two...well, that's *damn* tough."

"I don't mind working for it. I feel like I've been blaming the fact that things didn't work out on Hinnemann, when maybe I should have done more."

Talking about this out loud, admitting my failings, was difficult, but Eiren made it easier. She was a good listener.

Eiren sat down at the kitchen table and ran her fingers through her hair. Our knees almost touched. I leaned back.

"It was *his* failure as a teacher," she said, "as much as it was yours as a student, that you were not learning or enjoying riding."

What she left unsaid was that I truly was not good enough yet to learn from Hinnemann. But I did not know that then.

CHAPTER 7

Every Answer Leads to More Questions

As Leonie Bramall had warned me, a working student position is hard to get. It's also maybe not the best way to learn to ride. It's not the most efficient way. And it's certainly not the easiest way. But for some people, it's the *only* way.

To become a *great* rider (not just a *good* rider) one must ride great horses. I've heard people say they have improved because they get on all the tough horses—the ones nobody else wants to ride. These people will become great at riding *those* kinds of horses.

Riding Grand Prix dressage requires a different skill set than starting colts, which is different from dealing with extreme behavioral problems. Often a Grand Prix rider is not good at starting youngsters or working with problem horses. And vice versa.

If you can't afford your own fleet of great horses to learn on (and most people can't), then you need to ride *somebody else's* great horses. That is, you need to become a working student.

Before I left for Germany, I heard it all: Instructors told me how tough it could be. Friends warned me that I would be treated like a slave. My mother counseled me about how to get the most out of my time. My dad's advice was: "Just don't mention the war!" (Have you watched *Fawlty Towers*?) I heard stories—some of success, but mostly of tears and brawls and early flights home.

I heard about the long days, the fancy horses, the spectacular horse shows, the cheap beer, the Autobahn, the cold winters.

It was all true—more or less.

A riding apprenticeship in Germany means twelve-hour days, or more, wearing long underwear all winter. It means starting work in the dark and finishing work in the dark. It means being replaceable. It means *feeling* replaceable. But it also means *knowledge*. At Hinnemann's, I saw horses learning piaffe and passage *every day*. At Ingrid Klimke's, I learned flying changes aboard Abraxxis, a horse that's worth at least half-a-million dollars. (Seriously!)

Although I didn't get as much formal instruction as I'd perhaps hoped for, every day I could learn by watching and learn by doing. And the more I learned, the more I realized how little I knew. I felt as if I were a high school student trying to stay afloat in a doctoral program. I was definitely in over my head. But every once in a while I would surface and look around and realize I wasn't just treading water, I was actually making a little headway.

One of the highlights at Ingrid's was being able to watch her jumping lesson. Her jumping coach arrived confident and prepared. He was slim with short brown hair, probably in his fifties—still young as far as equestrian coaching was concerned. Ingrid liked his matter-of-fact style. During her lesson I would set the jumps and ask him questions. His grasp of riding theory was impressive, and I saw the sense in everything he taught—that is, until he answered one question toward the end of one session.

He liked the rider to be in a slightly forward seat, thus allowing the horse to move more freely. He encouraged the rider to ask for more engagement from the horse when the horse was not working hard enough. Usually this is simply a matter of clearer communication, but it might also be the other half of training that is missing: motivation. Leg! His ideas on rider balance and its relationship to the horse's movement and balance reflected an inquisitive mind and an excellent eye.

And so I asked him if he could recommend any exercises for helping riders find a distance to a jump. Just like with a human long jumper or high jumper, the takeoff point for a big jump on horseback is vital to distance or height attained. My dad taught me to count "1-2-3-4-5" for each stride as I approached a jump. It helped me focus on slightly lengthening or shortening the stride length in order to get to the jump at the right spot. But I'd found that finding a distance was one of the hardest concepts to learn and to teach a student.

Other riders had different methods for finding a distance, most of them centered on the notion of paying attention to the rhythm of the horse's stride—for example, by counting "1-2, 1-2." Still others, including Ingrid, didn't count at all. They could just "see" a distance. To me, that ability was amazing and something I'd love to acquire. So I was curious what her coach thought.

"The *rider* should *never* find a distance," he said patiently. Instead, he explained, it was the *horse's* responsibility to find a distance. "Every horse can see a distance to a jump four strides away."

"And if he can't?" I asked.

"Well then, get a new horse."

I looked at him, quiet.

"The proof," he said, "can be found by watching a horse free-jump. Without a rider, a horse will always find a distance to a jump."

Assuming he meant a "good" distance, and not just any distance, it was all a little hard for me to believe. A good distance is usually about six feet out, although it depends on the height and type of jump. It is the distance that allows for the smoothest bascule to clear the fence. Hearing him was like listening to a passionate environmentalist lecture on conservation, then hearing him slip in that he was paid by the oil industry. It made me go back in my mind and replay everything he had said before. It made me question *all* his theories.

In a way I could see what he was getting at. If a horse, especially a green horse, attempted to clear an obstacle from an awkward distance, he might hit it if he got too close or land on it if he jumped from too far away. If the horse found a "deep spot" and hit the jump, then he might learn to rock back and lift his knees the next time, or shorten his stride in time to find that "sweet spot," where the takeoff was just right.

The more athletic the horse, the less he might care about finding a "bad spot," because he could clear the jump easily anyway.

When the rider stayed out of the way, it really shouldn't matter to the horse where he left from, as long as it didn't feel too awkward to *him*. When the rider caught the horse in the mouth, on the other hand, or lost her balance and landed on his back—well, that certainly worked to turn a horse off jumping.

What I found made a big difference to a horse learning to jump and to find a good spot was his level of anxiety. Lots of horses rushed toward an obstacle, and it was almost always because they were worried, not because they loved jumping.

Relaxation and understanding were two sides of the same coin. And they led to confidence. An unconfident horse, however, might start to rush or would jump flatly. Maybe even refuse.

With an experienced horse jumping at the Grand Prix level, a lack of confidence could be dangerous. Sometimes those jumps were as big as the horse! And what about a tight turn in a jump-off when the horse didn't even see the fence he was expected to clear until he was one stride away? In this scenario, could we still trust the horse to find his distance?

Ingrid's show-jumping coach did not have answers to these questions, but he still maintained, "It's my theory, and it's the best theory." I pondered it. Perhaps he was right—maybe it was all a matter of finding the right horse. I liked *his* confidence. Was such assuredness typical of the German mindset, or just typical of somebody who had studied horses a long time?

Ingrid Klimke was anything but typical. At thirty-eight with a six-year-old daughter (and a very supportive husband), she was competing at the highest levels of eventing and dressage. She was always presentable. I never heard her raise her voice, yet every word she spoke carried the weight of her family's dynasty. Her late father was perhaps the only person I would consider to be a better rider.

It would be years before I thought about the difference between *riding* a horse and *understanding* a horse. Or between *training* a horse and *showing* a horse. But these months in Germany provided the germ of such ideas, for Ingrid could do it all.

My last day at Ingrid's came too quickly. I had only been there a few weeks to replace what would have been my last month at Hinnemann's. I was sad to be leaving but had already made plans for where I was going next.

I was supposed to meet Ingrid for a final talk after the horses were all ridden. A "talk" such as this would make any guy nervous, but I had prepared notes and questions. I knew that this would be different than my final talk at Hinnemann's. There I had been nervous about how *wrong* it might go; this time I was nervous about how *well* it might go.

Maybe she will invite me back.

That thought comforted me—until Ingrid looked over at me and said, "It's nice out. Let's take the horses for a walk around the field and talk now."

I had thought we would meet in her office, maybe at lunch, maybe over a coffee. It was okay, though...I could roll with it. I would remember the important questions I'd written. I could jot down my thoughts on our conversation later. I was keeping notes in cheap, corner-store notebooks. Each one had a bright cover: red, or blue, or green. Like crayon colors.

Ingrid led me along a narrow footpath that separated one crop field from the next. The rows of brown dirt made a sad scene. The field and the path were both muddy, and in places I couldn't tell where one began and the other ended. Together with the gray sky they created a formless, colorless background.

I forgot almost all my questions immediately—they seeped from my brain just as the color had faded from our surroundings. And so I fell back onto the one thing at the forefront of my mind: the Big Question.

"Can I come work here again? In the future, I mean...maybe next year?" The words tumbled out as I tried to express my commitment without sounding like a lunatic. "When you have space...."

Right away I regretted it. I should have asked something less significant first. Maybe I had made a mistake. I waited.

"Right now, we already have a full staff for the year," Ingrid replied.

The gelding I was on was walking faster than hers, so I asked him to slow down, and he shook his head a little. I was looking more at Ingrid than where I was going; I kept a poker face.

"I think your idea to be a working student at different places, in different disciplines, is interesting," she went on, "and you would be welcome back here in the future."

I took a deep breath, from the ribs, like a horse that had been pacing the fence line and was finally allowed back to the barn.

"Thank you."

My relief was related to a sincere desire to come back, and it also was a boost to my confidence, which, frankly, needed it after my last "talk" at Hinnemann's.

"What are your plans next? Where are you going?" Her mare was keeping better pace now, and Ingrid was beside me.

"I have been talking to Karen and David O'Connor," I said. "That's where I'm headed."

"In Virginia?"

"They're in Middleburg, Virginia, for the summers, but they winter in Ocala, Florida, so I'll be going there." I slowed my mount once more to keep the horses in step.

"And what about a show jumper?" Ingrid asked. "Didn't you say you wanted to study with a jumper rider, too?"

I nodded and shared who my first choice would be. To my surprise, she said that she might have a connection who could get me a job there. And, in fact, she had worked for that same rider herself, once upon a time. That Ingrid Klimke was willing to vouch for me, and put my name forward to an internationally known rider, well, that was a compliment that meant a hell of a lot.

I smiled and thanked her again. We reached the end of the field and turned right, heading back again along another muddy track. With the "air cleared," in a way, I felt free to ask her other questions that came to mind, and they gave an odd, rifted rhythm to our conversation—each question unrelated to the previous one. It was like a game of Trivial Pursuit, and I kept switching topics: How often do you use cavalletti? At what age do you start piaffe? What do you look for in a young horse? Did you get to watch your dad compete a lot? What books do you recommend? Can you tell me about Herr Stecken?

Major Paul Stecken was Ingrid's dressage mentor, and she was more than willing to talk about him, his theories, and methods.

And as we walked along in our final ride together under overcast skies, I was happy to listen.

CHAPTER 8

Herr Stecken

Before I met Major Paul Stecken I saw a photograph of him taken during WWII. The edges had curled, but the image was still sharp. There were four bay horses, all the same height, and four military riders posing for the camera. The riders were wearing the cavalry outfits of the Third Reich. They looked young and proud, and they sat easily and confidently. (I wanted to ask what horses were doing in a war of tanks and planes and machine guns. But my dad's advice came to mind, and for better or for worse, the moment passed.) After the war, from 1950 to 1985, Herr Stecken managed the Westphalian Riding and Driving School in Münster. He had taken over the job from his father, Heinrich Stecken. During that time, he also helped Ingrid's father, Reiner Klimke, achieve international fame in the dressage arena.

Herr Stecken arrived late afternoon on a rainy day to coach Ingrid. I knew he would also stay late to give a group lesson to her working students. I really hoped I would be invited to join, so all morning I tried to be ready to get on any horse at any time in case I might be called up. Each time there was a job away from the barn I ran. I must have been a very strange sight, running erratically through the yard, dodging puddles on my way to the paddocks to fetch horses!

Seven or eight *bereiter* students took theory classes from Herr Stecken once a week, and I wished my German was good enough to get something out of them. Mostly we like things we're good at, but I have one exception: I'm not talented at languages, but strangely I enjoy trying to learn them. Given more time, I was sure I would pick up German, and Ingrid said Herr Stecken's riding theory was without equal. When she was writing her book, *Basic Training of the Young Horse*, Ingrid said she would often consult him. She could ask him anything. Just as an example, "Who invented the light seat?" and he could talk for an hour.

"He said," Ingrid explained with a smile, lowering her voice a little as if to vaguely impersonate him, "training with cavalletti and with it the 'light seat' was developed in about 1930 in Italy, whereas the 'forward seat,' which today is accepted as a matter of course, goes back even earlier to the Italian Captain Federico Caprilli. Caprilli recognized that horses are best able to balance themselves over obstacles, when, by bringing the upper part of his body forward, the rider takes his weight off his horse's back." Ingrid laughed, then in a lighter voice, went on. "Or something like that! I'd better check my notes when I get home before I talk to him again."

Even an Olympic gold-medalist had to be prepared for a lesson with Herr Stecken! He was ninety-two years old but had the eyes and intellect of someone fifty years younger. He was a gentleman. We never addressed him by his first name, or even just Stecken; to everybody I met he was always Herr Stecken.

Arriving back at the barn from my race to and from the paddocks, I noticed the horses just coming in from a school had wet mud splattered all over their legs, right up to their girths. More tack to clean, I thought. At that moment, Ingrid looked at me just before she dismounted: "Tik, you'll be riding Jazz Rubin in the lesson with Herr Stecken this afternoon."

"Thank you," I said, bowing slightly without thinking. I laughed at myself. I was being ridiculous.

I'd found all working students had different favorite chores. For some it was sweeping or feeding or dragging the arena. My favorite was mucking stalls. My least favorite: cleaning tack. But that day I smiled with each cheekpiece, browband, and bit that I cleaned.

Our lesson was in the indoor arena, and we began with a walk on a long rein. Then trot, long and low. A normal warm-up. For the canter we all went around the arena at the same time, adding in smaller canter circles twice on each long side. I don't remember what he said from that warm-up, so much as how he looked at us, and at our horses. Like he could see through us. Like a horse that can see into your heart.

After a short walk break we worked on riding serpentines.

"Do them more *loopy*!" Herr Stecken kept repeating.

What he wanted was less about going across the diagonal and more about paying attention to the changes of direction. The loops we were making started to look more and more like the line separating yin and yang. Loopy.

Late that evening, I overheard one of the grooms tell Eiren that Herr Stecken had told Ingrid I had good feel. Often a compliment received indirectly is more powerful than one told to your face, and that certainly was the case in this instance. A generous word here and there can provide motivation that carries you forward for months.

Years later, even though our paths had crossed only briefly, I was extremely sad to learn of Herr Stecken's death. It was in 2016; he was 100 years old.

CHAPTER 9

On Eventing (I)

I glanced down. I saw the sweat from my face fall on Sapphire's withers. It mixed with hers and slid to her shoulders. Her neck foamed where the reins rubbed against the hair. Drool from her lower lip fell, caught by the wind. We were two strides farther before it hit the ground. I was back in Canada, on Vancouver Island, in full gallop, home from Germany, and enjoying an intermission before heading to Ocala, Florida, to work with Karen and David O'Connor. I looked ahead the way a soccer player looks downfield before chipping the ball to a teammate.

Eventing. *Eventing*! So *this* is what it was. This was a thrilling and wild affair. My parents watched cautiously. It seemed they had hidden this great thing from me. *What? How?* Now they offered advice timidly. My friends didn't know where I was. But this was no fling; it was love. It snatched me from my home. It arrested yesterday's desires and replaced them with new purpose.

I had no idea where this sport might lead me. Would I end up living in Germany? Or maybe competing in Ontario or the Carolinas? But I was getting ahead of myself, and that was the one thing, perhaps the most important thing, I should not do in this situation. I smelled the air, fresh from the Pacific Ocean. Sapphire's hooves struck the ground like the thunder of timpani, and we galloped on.

I was halfway through my first course, wondering what I had been doing my whole life before now. I looked to the left—a cord of wood blocked my entrance to the forest. I continued on; my horse's legs flew in double-time, straight and true, and we turned to be perpendicular to the obstacle. And then we were up and over, and on a new trail. The trees rushed by! A blur. I knew they were evergreens, but they might have been fir or juniper or hemlock. The browns and greens blended together. We sped through; then we were out on the grass again.

The ground was firm, but not too firm. Dry, yet not too dry. Green as the emerald pastures of a picture book. I had no idea that footing like this was not just great—it was rare.

In my childhood, riding happened in a ring. Both my parents were my coaches. My mother showed me the joys and principles of riding as an amateur. My father explained the obligations and responsibilities of the professional. Although they had both evented themselves, they quit when my mom was expecting.

"Too dangerous," they explained when I was fourteen, "too many crushed bones."

"Yeah?" I had said.

"Too many shattered hearts. Eventing is like trying to outrun a train: eventually it'll catch up to you."

"Sure," I'd replied with a laugh. "But don't worry, I can leap tall buildings, too!" And I hurdled, and tripped, over the couch. The truth was, I was not really interested in eventing—at least not back then.

"You think I'm worried about *you*? No way!" my mother had said, shaking her head. "It's the horses. They don't deserve that."

Fifteen years after that conversation I found myself at my first event. And my parents were there to support me.

I sat on the wheel well of the trailer, my bare feet high on an upturned bucket. In my left hand I held a paper.

"What are you looking at?" my father asked me.

"Learning the dressage test…" I mumbled, my eyes staying on the list of instructions before me.

"You can probably have it called. I'll go find out." He turned and started walking off. "Be right back," he said over his shoulder.

My parents had not been involved in the eventing scene for twenty-five years. None of us even knew the rules. I looked at the paper in my hand.

My mother gave me a hard look.

"What?" I asked.

"You know what."

I didn't answer. I was trying to concentrate. I absentmindedly picked up a dressage whip.

"You should memorize the test," she said.

"Yeah," I agreed tepidly, tapping the whip against my leg.

When my mother had told me how to use a whip she'd compared it to a surgeon's scalpel.

"It has to be used *that* exactly," she had explained. "The whip can be used on a horse as hard as one horse will strike another, and it can be used as softly as a fly touching down. You should be able to tap an inch behind your leg or four inches behind it. And you should have that control with both hands."

When she talked about Reiner Klimke she talked as a Hindu might about Ganesh. *There are many gods, but this is my favorite!* She told me how Klimke warmed up for the Montreal Olympics without stirrups and only switched from a snaffle to a double bridle right before competing. And then she showed me the yellow-edged photos…of his youthful face and poised body…with only a snaffle bridle and no stirrups!

"You think Klimke had his tests called?" she demanded.

"Yeah!" My dad slid to a stop between us, excited. "He can have it called."

My mother turned to her husband.

"I was just telling Tik he needs to learn to memorize tests. If he doesn't start with the easy ones, it will just get harder and harder."

"I can have it called?" I repeated, to confirm.

"He should memorize it," my mother insisted.

"He can memorize the next one. No big deal."

"It's a matter of principle."

"You want him to win, don't you?"

"I'm right here." I stood up. "I can hear you."

The bickering continued after I left, but it was moot anyway. A dressage test lasted about five minutes and there might be thirty different maneuvers to do. For example: "Halt at X. Proceed in trot. E circle left. A canter…" Each letter marked a different spot in the arena. X was in the middle. Simply *remembering* the test was a task; combine that with *riding* the test at the same time, in front of a judge and audience, and it, well, it took some practice.

Although it was tempting to have the test read, I went ahead and rode it from memory. I went off course and the judges subtracted two from my score. But it didn't matter…not once I was on the cross-country course. Not when I was out there with a horse under me.

The dressage phase of eventing was a step up from the up-down, up-down, up-down, learning to post I had grown up with. But cross-country! It was *fast*! It was my heart in my mouth, tears in my eyes! It was my arteries working like pistons, throbbing in time with Sapphire's stride. Ba-BOOM. Ba-BOOM. Ba-BOOM!

And then there were the two water jumps, the first that left me behind, but the second that was smooth. My leg swung slightly forward, I landed in my heels, and I found my horse's mouth again. Below us the water splashed, cooling her chest, leaving a tiny rainbow in our wake. And then we were off.

We looked ahead. The Cowichan Valley rose up on my left. There was forest on my right. We rushed forward.

Spectators sat on the hill. They held dogs. They looked for photo ops. Sometimes they held their breath. I saw all these things, and I saw none of them. The stirrups held me high, out of my mare's way, but her breathing was more labored now.

The finish line came up. There were two flags marking it: red on the right, white on the left. I crossed through and forgot to glance at my watch. I was breathing hard, along with Sapphire. The stewards glanced at their clipboards. The vet was busy with other competitors. Sapphire put her head low, but her ears stayed pricked and forward. Someone took our photo. Later I would notice that in the picture, I was smiling.

In every sport there are those that finish with a sense of relief, and those that finish and wish it could have gone on longer. That first time I evented I felt no finish line at all—not the way a runner or a swimmer might. I just pulled up reluctantly. Sapphire and I walked a circle. We submitted ourselves to be examined. The veterinarian put her stethoscope against Sapphire's chest.

"Hmmm," she said, thinking. Then later she did it again, and this time said, "Okay. You are free to go."

I thanked her. Before we left I looked back at the course.

Like an addict I craved more.

CHAPTER 10

Ocala, Florida

L auren slowed her chestnut gelding to a walk and turned to look at me. She had to squint because of the glare. Behind her were 100 acres of rolling grassy hills with jumps, banks, and ditches scattered around. Behind me the sun was beginning its descent, tired after a day of baking the already brown grass.

The horses had just finished a quiet training gallop on the hill behind the barn. It was a bit more restrained than I was expecting, but the neck of Lauren's horse was still covered in a sweat like thick white ocean foam. And we were talking…about everything *except* horses.

"So you don't *believe* in evolution?" I asked again, trying to keep my voice neutral.

Lauren answered without sounding defensive at all: "If you are asking me if I believe that humans descended from monkeys, then no."

Lauren was one of David and Karen O'Connor's two full-time riders (the other was Hannah). Lauren had been with them almost four years. She came from the Midwest. At her high school, they had Drive-Your-Tractor-to-School Day. Classes were scheduled to begin a week *after* the start of hunting season. Lauren was intelligent and articulate, and she sure knew how to ride. She had recently been chosen to be part of the US Developing Riders Team coached by the English eventing icon Captain Mark Phillips. And she was Catholic.

I'd recently heard that more "fundamentalist" Christians had a derogatory term for more "moderate" Christians: They called them "Cafeteria Christians," meaning they picked and chose what they liked as they went down the line...they took a little of this, and a little of that—a portion of forgiveness, a scoop of love thy neighbor. They took whatever satisfied their hunger and quenched their thirst.

Sensible really, I thought. Instead of being an insult, Cafeteria Christian should be a compliment.

I was surprised when Lauren told me she was a creationist. I had always thought evolution was not a matter of faith, but a matter of fact. Before I met Lauren, creationists were like caricatures—alive only in my imagination. They lived in a different place—a land where they might speak a different language or have three eyes. And they existed in an earlier era, or at least before the age of government-sponsored education.

I asked Lauren, "How can you *not* believe in evolution? Do you believe dogs evolved from wolves? Do you believe the horse you are sitting on and zebras share a common ancestor? It's not such a big leap to believe all creatures have the same origins, is it?"

"But it's also not such a big leap to believe God created Heaven and Earth," she replied. "To me that makes a lot more sense. Really, it's *all* about faith. Not everything we are taught makes sense right away. But when you are ready, you understand."

Lauren had faith. Faith is something all religions share: humans' belief in something greater than themselves. And belief in the creation of man on the "Seventh Day" was just one part of her faith.

There was a lot to adjust to in Florida—even more so than in Germany. Everything from religion to the small nuances in the way the barn was run and the horses were ridden. In Germany, the culture, the government, the climate, I could understand. The cold—well, I'd been colder. At Hinnemann's I felt like an outsider, not because of the culture, but because of the personal relationships. In Florida, I got a taste of the South for the first time. Here there were billboards on I-95 that advertised guns ("Santa knows what you *really* want"), and Christianity ("Jesus is Lord! And you *know* it!"), and quoted Rand ("WHO IS JOHN GALT?")

Rand was worth reading, I acknowledged.

On the radio one morning the DJ quipped that Florida had more billboards than any other state. Hawaii had the least. It was easy to believe.

Here recycling was unusual, even quaint. Here there were no mountains—except those made of trash. Here the horse culture and the money that came along with it were growing right next to those who lived without cell phones or electricity. A 500-acre manicured estate with polo horses might be neighbor to a mobile home with a mule, three cows, and a llama living in the front yard. Here, *I* was the different one, different to both ends of the spectrum.

A few days later, Lauren decided it was time I learned some "natural horsemanship." The O'Connors started all their horses using methods similar to those taught by American horseman Pat Parelli, who had made his name in the eighties when he founded his school and his method. Parelli encouraged people to start building a relationship with a horse from the ground with a rope halter, rather than from the horse's back. The person often carried a stick with a string on one end, which was called a "Carrot Stick," "Savvy Stick," or "Horseman's Stick." Working with a horse from the ground might be called "groundwork" or "working on-line."

I was not sure how "natural horsemanship" was different than "horsemanship." Really, I was not even sure what "horsemanship" was. I had heard the word a lot, and even used it, but if I had been asked for a definition, my response would have been amateurish at best.

We took Mick, a giant gentle gray—who was only five and still dark-coated—to the round pen. I stood on the outside, leaning on the rail, where I was quickly covered in dust. But I couldn't take my eyes off Lauren and Mick. First Mick was sent around the edge of the round pen, where he loped lazily and kept one eye on Lauren. He would change direction when Lauren stepped back and pointed with her hand and arm in the new direction. Sometimes Mick was allowed to come into the center of the ring. Lauren explained the middle was the "neutral zone"—what that meant, I did not know. Watching this kind of groundwork for the first time was like watching a pair of birds flying in unison and trying to figure out which one turned first. Was it that one? Or *that* one? It was right there in front of me, it was happening, but I had no idea what had gone into it. I had no idea why it worked. I had a lot of questions.

She showed me four "yields": moving the horse's hindquarters away from pressure; moving his shoulders away from pressure; lowering his head into a position of trust; and asking him to back up. Each yield began with a signal from Lauren and was then followed by a form of pressure, but as the horse became more sensitive to her requests, the pressure was decreased, and the signals became subtler.

The "pressure" could be in the form of touch—her hand on his poll to ask him to lower his head. Or it could be something Mick saw, like the waving stick in front of him. The gentlest aid was communication. As Lauren increased the pressure it became motivation. The idea was that we could establish a form of communication with Mick. We didn't want him to back up just because we pushed him; we wanted him to *understand* to move over. A boulder will move if you push hard enough; that's not a partnership.

Lauren showed me how Mick would either stand still while she walked around the pen, or follow her, depending on her signal. Whatever she did, Mick was always aware of where she was and what she was doing. I'd been around horses and horse people most of my life, but this was the first time somebody had explained to me about body language—the horse's and mine. Lauren helped me see how the horse interpreted every move I made…or didn't make.

Lauren swung the stick and string in a circle over the horse's head and talked to me at the same time. I thought of how many horses would be scared. Mick watched her like a puppy.

"People say that when they are learning a new language and they start to dream in that language, then they know they're really getting it," she said. "It's the same thing with this. Once you get it, you start to see everything in terms of yields and lines of influence. It changes the whole way you look at situations with horses."

I nodded.

I assumed a "line of influence" was like a yield that extended though space. For example if I had a horse trotting around the round pen, and I stood offset to the center, that would "open" up one side of the pen and "close" the other. This was a lesson I had learned as a kid with our ducks and chickens. It was my job to herd them in for the night so the coyotes and raccoons would feast elsewhere. Sometimes I had friends help, but if they were not used to fowl they would always be in the wrong place at the wrong time, the birds would squawk and scatter, and it would be dark by the time we got them all in the safety of their cage.

Mick stood in the center of the ring, legs square, tail relaxed, eyelids drooping. Lauren walked halfway toward me. Mick stayed still, opening his eyes a bit wider and tracking her with them as she said, "A lot of people don't believe in this. They think it's hokey." And then she looked at me, waiting. It was my turn to say something.

"How could I *not* believe in it?" I replied, gesturing toward her and the gray horse. "It's right there in front of me. It's amazing! Of course it works! I just saw you do it. Anybody who just opens their eyes will *see* it and believe in it."

And then, thinking fast, I added, "...like evolution."

Lauren smiled.

I didn't really internalize at the time the colossal difference between *seeing* something and *understanding* something. It would be years before I understood what Lauren had done in that round pen—and a long road after that before I could do the same kind of work with a horse myself.

Lauren also gave me my first dressage lesson in Florida. I was riding Danny, another gray gelding, who had competed in the 2008 Beijing Paralympics.

Ingrid Klimke had taught me her dressage warm-up sequence only a month before, and it was still fresh and exciting in my mind. With horses it is important to do simple things well, to appreciate and be in awe of them. And indeed, I found that with my new knowledge, something as mundane as a warm-up *was* exciting!

And now I had a chance to put it into practice. Maybe show off a little.

This was how I understood Ingrid's system to work:

Step 1: A forward walk on a loose rein.

Step 2: "Long and low" at the trot and then canter, asking the horse to stretch down and use his back without his head ever coming behind the vertical. The canter could be in a forward seat in order to allow the horse's back to be as free and relaxed as possible.

Step 3: A short walk break, always forward and "on the buckle." Every horse should learn to walk "on the buckle." The buckle connected the two reins, so if I held it there, the reins were quite long. Most horses are more relaxed on a loose rein. But some are so anxious that if you walk on a long rein they become like a rock let loose at the top of a mountain. They speed up…and up. They go this way and that, that way and this, until they run out of steam, or are, through sheer force, slowed. These horses are anxious because of the rider, or the saddle, or the expectation of the lesson ahead, or a combination of many things. It may take a lot of patience and skill to get rid of that anxiety so they can learn to walk calmly "on the buckle."

After the warm up, the *real* work began. Some days in Germany, there wasn't any real work. We just warmed up, then cooled down. Or if there was work to be done with a horse, Ingrid or Eiren would get on and do it. I would watch. Or work and watch. I was happy to watch.

But I found that things were done a little differently at the O'Connors': Lauren asked me to start Danny in a frame right away. The idea was that the horse should first step more quickly behind, thus engaging the hindquarters, and then from *that* position, the horse would start to use his back. The horse's back would not relax until he was "in front of the leg" (forward) and "through" (being "through" is like being in "triple threat" in basketball or a crouch in ski racing—it is an athletic, supple position, all the way through the body). And then, later on in the session, the horse would be encouraged to trot long and low.

I was defensive. I thought, Why should it be different here? Ingrid Klimke gets great results with her system, and she wrote the book (literally) on correct training of the young horse.

I believed in Ingrid's system wholeheartedly, and although I had a hard time explaining why I thought it worked, I was still in no doubt that it did. I had seen it with my own eyes.

But I did what I was told. And Lauren's instructions worked. Danny softened up and started to engage more.

Of course, I wished I had Ingrid's book at hand from which to quote. When I had a chance later to look it up, I found it easily:

The most important aim at the beginning of a ridden session is loosening up the horse. It is only possible for a horse to remain in a correct outline with flowing movement while responding to the rider's aids if he is loose.

But then Lauren, who was standing in the middle of the sandy ring, said something that really struck me.

"All good trainers are trying to achieve the same thing. There are different paths to that goal. There are many ways to accomplish it. My advice to you is not to forget what you learned before but instead throw yourself wholeheartedly into the system in which you find yourself. Only with that total immersion can you hope to *really* figure out what someone is trying to teach you. And then, when you are home again, you can pick and choose what you liked about each trainer's methods."

She was right. I had come to learn, and if I was holding on to another system, then there was no point in my being here. I had to, at least while I was with the O'Connors, learn to let go and just *have faith* in this new system…just as I had come to have faith in the old one. Like Lauren said, I should take what appealed to me from each system.

I called it Cafeteria Riding.

CHAPTER 11

Working Student Position: Priceless

I was working in the driveway outside the barn when I met him, this giant of a man. The live oak leaves made a thick crinkly carpet on the dry grass, and I was toiling like a convict to turn them into orderly piles. Sweat trickled off my knuckles and stained the handle of the rake, but it was satisfying work.

Just past the barn and through a swampy grove of orange trees the Canadian National Eventing Team was riding. David O'Connor, my boss for the next few months, was their coach. I should have felt a kinship to them—this group of riders gathered here from all across my country—but I didn't. I hoped I would one day.

Most of them were too busy with horses or grooms or kids or dogs or fans to say hello. But Kyle Carter slammed the door of his pickup, his "Carter Eventing" logo prominently displayed on the side, and walked straight over to me. Kyle was well over six feet tall, and had the forearms of a prizefighter. I wondered what he wanted.

"Hi," he said, eyes laughing. (I later learned that his enthusiasm is rarely dampened. The only time I saw him without a smile was during his lesson with David, which I attributed to concentration rather than anything else.)

"I'm Kyle."

I knew, of course, but I wiped my hands on my shirt and shook his hand. "Tik."

"I've been reading your articles in *Gaitpost*," he said. "I was wondering when you were going to show up."

That caught me off guard, and I just stood there, weighing how best to respond. He was not the first one to say he had read my articles; I had been getting feedback for months. On one hand the reviews were mainly positive, but on the other, they were mostly from my mother. Also the majority of the *Gaitpost's* readership was in Canada, so nobody in Europe or the United States had mentioned them before.

Kyle tucked his riding helmet under his arm and went on in his friendly way: "After I read the second one, I told my wife there was *no way* you would last at Hinnemann's stable. I called it! We have working students as well, and you can always tell which ones aren't happy or don't get it." He paused, looking at me critically. "But you should know that there is so much you can learn just by being in an atmosphere of excellence like that."

Well, at least I knew *one* person was reading my articles.

And then Kyle, standing in his half-chaps, explained something I'd been struggling to understand.

"You know, in Europe, the forty-five-minute-lesson format is pretty uncommon. Instead they are always watching you. The trainer will say 'try a half-pass now,' or 'follow me over these cavalletti.' And although they rarely tell you when you are doing something *right*, they will for sure tell you when you are doing something *wrong*. That way, you learn to think for yourself."

I held the rake at my side. I nodded, feeling awkward.

Kyle went on: "It's mainly in North America that working students trade work for a structured lesson, where the trainer tells them what to do the whole time. That, my friend, is the difference between learning to be a *professional* and learning to be a *professional student!*"

"Thanks, Kyle," I said. I meant it. He certainly had given me something to think about.

There was a pause, and then he went off to chat with David, and I went back to raking.

CHAPTER 12

Uncomplicated

One Tuesday morning I woke up and announced to the empty RV I was living in, "I'm in Florida. I'm at David and Karen O'Connor's place! *Bada-bing. Bada-boom!*"

I turned the radio on. John Mayer greeted me, singing about past frustration and so-called problems.

I did a little dance.

Some days began like that; better ones ended like that. First on the agenda this day was I would finally get a chance to watch one of David's lessons. He was teaching Waylon Roberts, son of Canadian Olympian Ian Roberts, and one of the most talented young riders my home country had yet seen. Around the O'Connors' place, however, his shaggy brown hair and spectacles made him more famous as "Harry Potter"—he was a dead ringer. Waylon was one of those lucky few who looked more at home on a horse than on the ground.

I found David and Waylon in the dressage ring, which gave me a chance to sit in the shade—under a great live oak, out of the way—and watch. Live oaks were southern trees I hadn't experienced before. They had fantastic, thick, twisting trunks and branches that provided shade (and ideal backdrops for photos). They were called "live" oak or "evergreen" oak because they stayed green all winter.

The first twenty minutes I sat underneath that old tree David didn't say a single word. He slouched in his plastic chair, dusty cowboy hat pulled low, white sleeves rolled up, eyes like a cat watching a bird. He explained later that with the students he teaches regularly, he likes to just observe them for a while to see what they are working on, and to see if they are implementing what he taught them during their last lesson together. David's system combined the best of both worlds: Sometimes he let the rider just ride. But he was also ready to give one-on-one instruction at any moment.

In his lessons, David tried to understand first what the horse was thinking, then what the horse was doing. Finally he studied what the rider had to do with both those things.

It seemed to me that the ambition of all trainers, whatever discipline, was to create a "submissive" horse—that is, the rider should tell the horse what to do, and the correct reaction should be immediate. The rider should not have to physically or forcibly move the horse. Instead, they should become one, as if the rider is the brain, and the horse is the body: The neurons fire, the feet start to move.

Later on I changed this word "submissive" to "cooperative" in my mind. Instead of a motorcycle that could go zero to sixty in three-point-four seconds, I imagined dancing with a girl. How I would like her to move with me. How even though I might be leading, I would like to show *her* off. And how I wanted her to be my friend.

I now use "ask" instead of "tell." "Enthusiastic" instead of "excited." "Should," not "must." I prefer "usually" to "always," and I avoid "never."

Unfortunately, cooperation between horse and rider is often not the case. The wires get crossed, the tail swishes, the ears go back—the horse does not understand. The rider kicks or pulls. Both become frustrated or anxious, maybe even scared.

It was David who pointed out to me that instead of forcing the horse to understand our human vocabulary, we should learn to speak the language of the horse. That was why every horse at the O'Connors' was started in the round pen, learning to trust and respect, but also giving his handlers a chance to better understand him. Not just *him* in the way he moved, but *him* in the *heart* and in the *mind*.

Young horses were first ridden in only rope halters with horseman's sticks to steer. No bridle! The sticks were used beside the horse's head, not to hit, but to direct. The horses learned to move away from pressure. Or to be more precise, they learned what made pressure cease. They discovered that if they turned, the stick would disappear. They figured out that if they trotted, the legs at their sides would stop squeezing.

Beginning without a bit in the mouth allowed each horse to focus on going *forward*. A horse's gums, tongue, and lips are some of the most vulnerable parts of his body on a physical level but also and especially on an emotional level. If a horse makes a mistake as he moves and trips or falls, he is more likely to learn from the experience if the rider is not interfering. On the other hand, if he stumbles or crashes with a rider, particularly if the rider is unbalanced on the reins and catches him in the mouth with a bit, he is more likely to be anxious.

Anxiety, it should go without saying (but doesn't), is the enemy of learning.

For years David and Karen had a partnership with Pat Parelli and his wife Linda. There are videos that can be found online of the four of them co-presenting at horse expos around North America. In one David explains that so often we learn to *compete* before we learn to *ride* and we learn to *ride* before we learn to *understand* horses. In the video David is riding without a bridle. He's not doing anything profound, but there are only a handful of people in the world that can make something so uncomplicated *look* so uncomplicated.

The first few weeks of watching the O'Connors work with their horses was like reading *The Alchemist* for the first time. Many professionals understand horses, but few try to teach others how to understand them. Mostly we are taught how to control horses. Fewer instructors still truly inspire us to learn how horses *feel*. Riders lucky enough to acquire an understanding of how horses think usually do through "feel" or osmosis. But I was seeing that it *was* something that could be taught.

There are exceptions, but how a horse reacts to different situations can often be explained. A person's reactions to grief are commonly predicted by the acronym DABDA—denial, anger, bargaining, depression, acceptance. When horses encounter something new, they often go through predictable steps—fear, curiosity, playfulness or dominance, acceptance, indifference. When we don't understand this equine thought process we might take a horse that is scared of water and say, "Accept this!" But without giving him time to put his whiskers on it, and to be playful and paw the surface, we rarely achieve real acceptance. And that can come back to haunt us.

Hey, I thought after listening to David, this thing—this horse deal—this is about more than just riding. There is a bigger picture here, I can feel it. If I have a good bike I can ride it. I can learn to trust it. Learn to respect it. Maybe I can even love my bike. But my bike cannot learn to trust me back. Or respect me.

My bike cannot like me.

I started to think, Maybe this is what *horsemanship* is all about.

CHAPTER 13

Horses Are Optional

Frustration in a man is about as hard to miss as a horse at a dog show. It is even more obvious when the reins are in one hand and a whip in the other.

Karen had her back to the man and his horse; she was teaching a dressage lesson about 200 feet away. She casually pivoted, as if to stretch, and glanced over at the guy. She continued talking to her student, even as her eyes appraised the situation on the other side of her: "More inside leg! Good. Now across the diagonal."

I was trying to study dressage, but it was like learning art history, fascinating when I understood the nuances, even breathtaking, but also easy to lose focus when observing amateur work. (And even easier to be distracted when a battle waged in the background.)

Whipping a horse is not uncommon. In this case, it was because the gelding did not want to walk through a water jump. The horse was of medium build, chestnut-colored. It was late afternoon, and the lighting was soft, as it often is in Ocala at that time of day. Like the live oaks in the background, great for photography. Although I would not have wanted a photo of this pair. The man had been hitting the horse for so long I could have run a mile and back. There was stubbornness in the man's eyes, and the beating had taken on a tired rhythm: THWACK. Pause. THWACK. Pause. THWACK.

At first, the horse had fought every time the whip struck his hide. Eventually, he just stood there flinching. And now he was about four feet from the water's edge, not even cringing. Not blinking. His feet were still. His head was neither high nor low. His eyes neither alert nor closed.

For the first few minutes it had been strength against strength, but now the horse had gone inside himself. Now it was simply the ignorant beating the helpless, and I felt for both of them, but for the gelding more. I realized Karen had stopped talking. She looked composed but exuded an inner energy as she took out her phone and raised it to her ear. She may not have been ready to start a fight herself, but it appeared she wasn't going to stand down in the face of one, either.

"Drive the golf cart over to the water and tell him he has to go somewhere else if he is going to do that," I heard her say into the phone.

A pause, and then "Yes." She turned and looked at the man, finally she said calmly into her phone, "There are better ways."

Professionals try not to interfere in what others do with their horses. It's generally thought best to give another the benefit of the doubt. But everyone has his or her line, especially when it's on home turf. From the look of her, Karen was ready to draw her line—hard.

It was years later that I read an article on horseman Martin Black's website entitled "What About One Who Wants to Fight?" It perhaps summed up what I imagine Karen was thinking that afternoon:

The old myth of "not letting the horse get away with some-thing—staying there to finish what you started," has probably wrecked more horses and frustrated more horse people than anything. You don't win by fighting. You may win a battle, but in doing so, you lose the war. Many times, pride and ego get in a person's way here, and, when emotions take over good sense, you have already lost. When that happens, the best thing to do is to identify the situation as soon as possible, cut your losses and get out.

The man was asked to leave the property, and he did. I wouldn't argue with Karen either.

After the dressage lesson Karen was teaching had ended, I went back to the barn. I started sweeping the aisle. Sweeping is a great time to think, and so I did.

Should we have said more to the man who was hitting his horse? I wondered. Should Karen have reprimanded him? Embarrassed him? Reported him? If so, to whom?

Impossible, was my first thought. Then again, maybe not. But would it have helped? It might have treated the symptom, but it was ignorance that was the disease.

It is easy to criticize. But it is hard to see that we are all on our own journey with horses. Even now, we are all at different points. Sometimes we are "firm" with horses. But how "firm" is okay? When does "firm" change to "tough," and "tough" to "mean," and "mean" to "abuse"? It must be a spectrum, for I have never met two people with exactly the same idea of what is "firm" and what is not.

I did not know the answers to my questions that day as I swept. I knew that my ideas were evolving though. And they were changing because I was learning. And I was learning because I was inspired.

When I watched Karen pilot the small-but-mighty Theodore O'Connor, affectionately known by an adoring public as "Teddy," around the toughest cross-country course in North America, I was inspired. When I watched David ride his horse bridleless—wow! I got goosebumps.

I wanted to be able to do what they did. So maybe education was the pill we needed for ignorance. But inspiration was the prescription.

I was sweeping when Karen came down the aisle. She held her phone next to her ear. It was windy, and everything I swept kept blowing straight back into my eyes and nostrils.

With a hand over the receiver, and a smile tugging at the corners of her mouth, she whispered: "Why don't you start from the *other* end?"

Good idea. I walked down and restarted.

Karen continued talking, and then passed the phone to Max, her head groom. Max, raised in Massachusetts, schooled at Northeastern with a degree in sociology, began her career as an associate stockbroker. Each day at the office when she walked past a window that looked out over the parking lot, she would look into the distance and see where the land met the sky. One day she noticed that the light was gray-blue low down, near the horizon, and then a darker navy-blue above that; another day she saw how the crows played and fought for crumbs after somebody had dropped a sandwich. And each day she would ask herself the same question: "What am I doing here?"

Eventually she gave it all up—the money and the office—moved into a barn and was happy.

As Max took the phone from Karen, she pressed "speaker." Now I could hear the conversation, as well.

"I need some help. I'm coming to Rocking Horse with four horses, and the girl who has been helping me is sick."

"Sure, we got a guy. He's from—"

"A guy?" the voice interrupted.

"Yep. A Canadian," Max replied without hesitation, looking at me.

There was a pause on the line; then: "I don't want a *guy*. I want someone who will be *helpful*."

"That's all I can give you."

"How old is he?"

"Hmmm...twenty-six, I think." Max looked at me. "Tik, how old are you?"

"Twenty-seven," I said. My broom didn't miss a beat.

"Twenty-seven," she said into the phone.

"Oh my god. Are you on speaker phone? Can he hear me?"

"Yep," Max said, winking at me.

After she hung up Max asked me if I would go out to the Rocking Horse Horse Trials, near Altoona, and lend a friend a hand.

"Course," I said with a grin.

I borrowed the farm's old red pickup, pulling out as the sun arrived the next morning. The road to Altoona cut through the Ocala National Forest, where pines dominated, and only a few stands of the thick evergreen oaks had reached old age. The pines were sand pines, which do well with little water and lots of sun. Their cones can remain closed for years until fire burns the mature trees and opens them. They then reseed the burnt ground. Scattered along the edge of the road were a few dead armadillos, opossums, and a single red fox. It was interesting, my reactions to the road kill: I was drawn to look at the armadillos, perhaps since I'd never seen a live one; with the opossums, I remained detached; but with the fox, I had to look away. I hated to think of his life ending with a squeal of tires, sudden fear, and then the final *whump*. Perhaps he had not died quickly—a terrible murder!

The drive took about an hour and a half.

Parking at Rocking Horse was on the grass next to the temporary barns. As I got out of the truck I recognized a few of the more famous riders: Leslie Law with the British colors on his saddle pad. Darren Chiacchia with his stovepipe hat. Lauren and Karen were already there as well. But I knew I had a job to do, so I jogged toward the stalls where most of the out-of-town horses were staying.

I slowed down when I crossed paths with a horse, and then sped up again. I wasn't late, but the sun was up, the air crisp, and it felt fine to run—it had been a while. I went a little faster.

As I approached the stabling, I saw a young woman about my own age stop and look at me. She studied me a moment longer than was normal.

Maybe this is who I am looking for, I thought.

She looked away, but as I ran closer she peeked at me again. I studied her right back. She was shorter than me by about a head. She wore white breeches and a blue down jacket. I didn't know if white was supposed to be slimming, but no matter—she didn't need it. Her legs were as slender as a fawn's.

I was about forty feet from her when she spoke.

"Are you Tik?"

Bingo. I slowed a little but ran until I stood right in front of her. I wasn't sweating, but I was breathing hard. Up close I could see that she also wore a smile, one that was more in her eyes than her mouth. I introduced myself and impulsively gave her a hug. She did not resist. She smelled like fresh wood shavings and a little bit of horse. She stepped back and said nothing. She tilted her head slightly as if to say, "You're weird," but her eyes also said, "…and interesting."

I smiled and waited.

"Nice to meet you," she finally said. "I'm Sinead."

I was still smiling goofily. "Need some help?"

"Even if you just do the water buckets. Anything will help."

She started walking toward her horses' stalls. I followed slightly behind and to the side. A deferential position, as befits a groom.

Rocking Horse had permanent stables made out of wood. Sinead's horses, though, were in temporary stabling constructed out of two rectangular white tents, each big enough to cover at least a hundred stalls. The tents stood in a field, like twin forts, surrounded by cars, trucks, trailers, milling people…and horses. Each stall inside the tents was square, twelve feet wide, and there were *rows* of them. In the aisles between the rows, riders and grooms unpacked tack trunks and brushed their charges. The stall and aisle floors were simply the grass of the field.

Sinead's horses had arrived the night before, and so the grass in her stalls had been eaten down, and the floor was now covered with wood shavings. Besides the shavings, there was also manure.

That was my first task, then: cleaning stalls.

I quickly got involved in the easy, rhythmic Zen of mucking a stall. It was therapeutic to be absorbed in the repetitive motion of scooping and throwing, then leveling and smoothing the way a golfer might rake a sand trap. Next I emptied, scrubbed, and refilled the water buckets.

When it was time for one of the horses to compete I brushed him off, tacked him up, and held him while Sinead mounted. If she did not have another horse competing soon, I went and watched her ride. Otherwise, I stayed in the barn to get the next one brushed, put boots on him, and wait for her to return. When one horse finished, I hosed him off and walked him out. All Sinead's horses were sharing one bridle and one saddle, so between horses I had to readjust the cheekpieces and the noseband, and switch the bit. My fingers were not nimble at the best of times, and when I was in a hurry it felt like I had oven mitts where my hands used to be. More than once I dropped the bit, swearing under my breath, then chastising myself to hurry up and slow down at the same time.

During a break in the afternoon I sat on a bale of hay and leaned back against the stall. I could hear the horses chewing as I opened my book. In school, I had read mainly Canadian and British novels. Now I was catching up on American authors. Jim Harrison, famous for *Legends of the Fall*, also wrote a novella called *Revenge*:

He lived as a victim, albeit prosperous, of those dreams he built at age nineteen when all of us reach our zenith of idealistic non-sense. Nineteen is the age of the perfect foot soldier who will die without a murmur, his heart aflame with patriotism. Nineteen is the age at which the brain of a nascent poet in his rented room soars the highest, suffering gladly the assault of what he thinks is the god in him. Nineteen is the last year that a young woman will marry purely for love. And so on.

Words were important to me. I noticed them. For example, some people said, "I'm going to *train* my horse." Others declared, "I'm going to *work* my horse." A few offered, genially, "I'm going to *play* with my horse."

I wondered if the man beating his horse the day before would have proceeded in such a manner if he had in his mind that he was "playing," instead of "training" or "working."

In the United States, in Europe, in the United Kingdom, in this era, horses are optional (for the most part). There are certainly still some situations where there is no other choice than to use the horse as a partner in labor. There are still some places where horses are used for transportation or work or war. But for most of us today, certainly if we are reading this book, chances are, having horses is something we *choose*. So why not say "play"? Probably because, for some, it feels like it misses the mark on how seriously we take our equestrian sports and the accompanying lifestyle.

Horses usually do not get to choose who their human partners are. They also do not have words—at least not similar to our ver-bal language. From David I was learning to focus on how horses communicate through moving their bodies. And I was beginning to see the same subtleties in their language that we have in ours. I was becoming *more aware*. I was starting to understand the fifteen different ways a horse can say, "Back off!"

One way horses communicate through time is by sniffing smells left behind. Perhaps it is the only way? I considered the idea that when a horse stretches down and takes a whiff of day-old droppings, maybe that was like reading a short story for me. Not much annoys me as much as when I am halfway through reading a sentence and somebody interrupts me or takes my book away. Perhaps the horses I was training were irritated when they were "reading" something and I pulled them away.

Maybe I would let them sniff those paddock apples next time.

As I was sitting there thinking, with my book in my lap, I over-heard a conversation in the next aisle of the stabling.

"...and he seems nice."

"Well, he can carry water buckets, at least."

"What's he doing now?"

"I think he's reading a book."

Laughter. "A book? At a horse show?"

"Yep."

I frowned. I put my book down, brushed the hay off my pants, and stood up. They were right: No point reading somebody else's story when I should be living my own.

CHAPTER 14

"Hubris? Me?"

It was interesting to compare David O'Connor's method of training to Ingrid Klimke's and Johann Hinnemann's. Each was successful in his or her own right, but each had a particular spirit and style, and it was hard—occasionally embarrassing—to adjust from one to the other.

All of these trainers were winners—but there are many ways to be a winner. One evening I challenged myself to define each of them with only one word. It was an idea I got while trying to think of one word that defined a half-halt. The best I could come up with was *rebalancing*. A rebalancing physically, but also mentally, or maybe even emotionally. It could be subtle, like an extra breath to a swimmer before a turn. Or it could be dramatic, like a sharp word when I'm distracted—*Hey*!

David's word was *understanding*. He wanted to know how to shoe a horse, how to start a horse, how to ride Grand Prix. If he watched a reiner, he wanted to know how the discipline worked. As for getting "inside" a horse's mind, David said: "Monty Roberts trademarked 'Join-Up,' right? Pat Parelli has the 'Seven Games.' What I want is *The Look*. After that it's just circus tricks to me. I'm not going to teach a horse to get on a pedestal or lie down. I'm not going to stand on the back of a horse. It's *The Look* I want."

The Look was when a horse gave him two eyes, two ears, and seemed to be saying, "Okay, what are we going to do now?" Without that *Look*, a horse could be *made* to do many things…but without him ever really understanding, or learning, or improving.

Ingrid Klimke's way was *classical*, like the near-perfect concert pianist, who smiled, played from her heart, and seduced the audience into a standing ovation. She made the 30,000 hours of practice almost invisible. Ingrid had inherited a system from her dad, and she was expanding on it. She was writing books, producing videos, and speaking at international symposiums. She did not own a pair of draw reins—what I had observed was a go-to gadget for many trainers.

I doubted Ingrid would call herself a "natural horseman"—she didn't own a rope halter or Carrot Stick—but I would. Ingrid was about as natural with horses as an otter with waves.

I struggled with Mr. Hinnemann's word. *Professionalism* was the first that came to mind. His riding and training were technically superb, but when I compared his horses side by side in my mind with Ingrid's and the O'Connors', I realized how much the latter's horses were, well, more like horses: They nickered as I went by; they were calmer and happier in their turnout, because it was not unexpected. It was not any one thing, just a feeling; the distinct stitches in the fabric of stable life produce many different cloths.

I realized that my words of choice applied not only to the way these individuals treated horses but also to the way they treated their staff. An email I received from a woman I had never met before shook me up but also provided the impetus to clarify a problem that had been tumbling around in the back of my mind. She wrote to me after my second article was published in *Gaitpost*. It was a piece about my stay with Hinnemann.

I'm saddened by how much you seem not to understand what being a working student is about. In my experience, hubris is a typical male trait that often keeps men from getting the most of their time as working students. It's such a shame that you weren't able to maximize such phenomenal opportunities. I would love to see you write an article reflecting back on your experiences a few months after your return home as this, in my experience, tends to be when you finally "get it," once you're able to get over the abusive aspect.

Since now I was a few months removed from Germany, I could do as she asked. In one respect, she was right, of course: What I had experienced *were* once-in-a-lifetime opportunities. A trainer did not have to be my best friend to be talented and knowledgeable, even phenomenal. Perhaps a more reserved, professional trainer was even better than one who became close and comfortable. When relationships are clearly defined, there is less reason for arguments or angst.

Deep within, however, I felt that greater empathy for people and horses did not take away from a trainer's greatness—rather it made the trainer *greater*.

David and Karen O'Connor were proving to me, in living color, that treating others with kindness was more rewarding in the long run. Respect fostered loyalty and hard work. Abuse (not my word, but the one used by the woman who sent the email) on the other hand, created discontent and unfaithfulness. It could even have the ironic effect of creating dependency through weakness. Abuse is not something anyone should have to "get over."

When I first read the email I thought, Hubris? Me?

It is often easier to see and evaluate emotions in someone else— we are so close to our own! So I decided I would reserve judgment. This lady might be right. But experience proved to be on my side, because I did find other places where learning and hard work were fair, even fun. I knew that it was a fine path to tread between having the fortitude to see something through and quitting a dead-end endeavor too late.

My email critic had obviously had firsthand experience being a working student, though, for she was right…as the months and the years went by, I looked back at my initial time in Germany differently. Frustration gave way to a wry pride. I had survived it! And simply by surviving I had learned something I would not trade.

I knew that what I saw of Hinnemann's stable was only a snapshot of life there, that others would surely have different experiences. My writing, my articles, were never meant to be a definitive look at horse people and their training methods.

They were only meant to be my story.

CHAPTER 15

I Love You,
Karen O'Connor!

A "platinum" sponsorship package for the Kentucky Three-Day Event at the Kentucky Horse Park in Lexington cost $20,000. The *cheapest* sponsorship package, "bronze," was $6,000. Both included grilled vegetables, sautéed snap peas, chicken paninis, tomato-and-herb soup, organic spinach salad, and an open bar all four days of competition, along with a view of a large-screen television running with the live feed of the dressage, cross-country, and show jumping phases. Access to the sponsors' tent also included an outside viewing area, which was crowded with fashionable young ladies and gentlemen, sporting Prada, Ray Ban, and Maui Jim.

Eventing is a test. At any level it is a test not for the faint of heart. Like racing cars or underwater spelunking, if something goes wrong death is a possibility. But done *well*.... Done *well*, well, it's Jack Reacher starting a fight, Kurt Vonnegut alone in a room with a typewriter, Michael Jordan getting his hands on the ball with six seconds left.

In the world of eventing a four-star competition is traditionally the highest—many say it is even harder than the Olympics. There are six four-star events per year but only one in North America. (The others are in France, Germany, Australia, with one each, and England, with two.)

This competition was a four-star. And it was my first time attending one.

I had a frosty glass of Belgian beer in one hand, a rum and coke in the other, and I was wearing a grin very similar to Germany's Bettina Hoy (who had just scored a "28" in dressage and was leading the world in the first phase by fourteen points) when I saw Karen.

"How did you get in here?" she asked, looking at me in surprise.

"Through the kitchen, in the back," I replied, having absolutely no idea whether she would think this was funny or brave or rude. Perhaps if I had not already had two rum and cokes, with lime, I would have had a better idea of how she would react.

Karen must have come straight from the trade fair where she and David had been scheduled to sign autographs at the *Practical Horseman*—the most popular English riding magazine in the United States—booth. I had walked by two hours before and seen the line of eager kids and patient parents, stretching and twisting and blocking traffic. I knew the O'Connors had fans, but the atmosphere was more like J.K. Rowling signing books at Universal Studios than a couple of riders at a horse show. Most of the young, aspiring riders held magazines or books to be signed—Karen and David's book *Life in the Galloping Lane*, a chronicle of their experiences and success, had been released not so long before. I recognized the blue-and-green cover because I had my own dog-eared copy.

Karen was standing with a small group, but now she stepped away from them and looked at me. She wore a blue shirt, gold rings in her ears, and a poker face. I stood still. The last few months with the O'Connors tumbled through my mind.

Throughout my stay with them, I had retained a confidence in my riding that was not always justified by reality. In my first jumping lesson with David—on Danny, one of his favorite horses—I crashed through an oxer, lost my stirrups, and landed in front of the saddle, up on the horse's neck. I could have reached down and grabbed Danny's ears if I wanted to. David did not say anything; he simply lowered the jump, and said, "Come again." However, it would be a long time before he had me reattempt that height.

Karen, on the other hand, said exactly what was on her mind. When we were schooling at a neighbor's farm one weekend, I was riding Danny (who was quickly becoming one of *my* favorite horses) at a walk when Karen slowed her horse beside me and asked me how he was doing.

"Perfect!" I said.

"Perfect. *Perfect*? What do you mean?" She scowled. "People are way too quick to use the word *perfect*."

"He is fairly good," I quickly corrected myself. I kept walking Danny and now Karen walked beside me. We stopped by the water jump, in the shade of two large palm trees, and watched a few other riders and horses splash through.

"*Perfect* is way too often used," she repeated, as we watched. She spoke now with the voice of a teacher. "People just throw it around, sort of like the words 'I love you.' Now, tell me truthfully, *how* is he?"

"He is forward and sound, and very well behaved," I answered.

She was right. Unless I meant it, perfect was a lazy word.

Then there were two days in April when I could not do anything right. They were minor issues, but when taken together, they earned me a stern lecture from Karen on the importance of *horsemanship*. Horsemanship was a concept that I was beginning—only beginning—to grasp.

The first incident was the time I sat down on the grass to watch a horse being shown to a potential buyer and spooked him (the horse, not the buyer). Many horses might shy at a person sitting in an unexpected place.

Then there was the time I led a horse out of the barn and almost straight into another one that was supposed to be jogging for a veterinary evaluation but was, without my help, already rearing and causing havoc.

There was also the time I was cleaning stalls and didn't notice a cut on a horse's knee. These mistakes, luckily, were neither severe nor tragic. (Missing the cut on the knee the first time around did cost an unnecessary second vet call down the line, however.) But it was made very clear to me that in dealing with horses, it is not enough to be alert and attentive ninety-nine percent of the time.

It was Karen who made me take a deeper look at what horsemanship *means*. I received a lecture after my third egregious error (the cut on the knee) and these were the notes I took that night:

Horsemanship is more than riding. More than horse care. It is not about doing flying changes or learning to braid, although it may include those things. Horsemanship is an almost indefinable ability to understand and be aware of horses. Just as some musicians can hear and understand written music before it is played, so a horseman can predict how horses will act in certain circumstances. Horsemen realize that all horses react in certain predictable ways, and yet every horse is unique. Great horsemen have fewer accidents, more trust from their animals, and ultimately, greater success.

After my not-exactly-pleasant talk with Karen I decided to go clean tack—a relatively harmless task that was not my favorite, but that day I found it soothing because the tack room was cool and quiet, while outside was hot and humid and sweaty. I grabbed the first bridle from a group of eight or nine that hung on a four-prong hook, descending from the ceiling, and started the first step to proper cleaning with a wet sponge. I was still hoping for a few minutes to myself when Karen and a few other riders entered the tack room, also seeking respite from the heat and humidity. It was too late to leave, so I just stayed quiet and wished I was a little smaller. (I am six feet tall, 180 pounds…not a giant, but certainly as an eventer taller and bigger than most.) Karen looked at me and joked about something. I must have looked back in complete shock because she then laughed and said, in front of everyone, "What? Can't I be nice to you after I'm mean?"

"I guess you can," was all I could come up with. But a cool wash of relief swept through me, and with it my confidence began to return.

Some trainers have a structure they use for every horse, but Karen believed training a horse was like creating a painting: every painting follows certain broad ideas and goals, yet each one has its own unique path to that end.

Karen had a way of explaining and simplifying concepts that just worked for me. In my first lesson with her, she taught me the four cross-country positions (galloping, preparation, jumping, and drop) and the four rider responsibilities (line of direction, speed, balance, and rhythm). She described how, by standing in the stirrups at a gallop, I could help the horse feel the change in balance and slight increase in wind resistance, which signaled him to slow down. She taught me how my feet could be placed slightly farther forward on the stirrup and how the stirrup leather should remain perpendicular to the ground, even over jumps and down banks.

Until that point, I had always simply assumed that the cross-country phase of eventing was a faster, longer version of show jumping. Now my whole body position began to change…and with it, my mindset. I acquired the ability to set up for even the biggest jumps. I did not do everything smoothly the first time, but by the second or third attempt it started to feel pretty good. I found I had more skill than experience. What that meant was I could do what I was *told*, but I had not figured out for myself when to do what.

I wondered if hearing a difficult truth was out of everybody's comfort zone, or if it was possible to mature enough that eventually one could be swallowed and digested easily. Karen, at least, had a way of balancing her tough talks with a laugh later on. As I stood in front of her that day in Kentucky with a drink in each hand, I didn't know which was coming.

I *did* think she should really have been out competing and not in that bar at all.

Karen had more aptitude and experience than most, but she did not have a horse for the Kentucky Three-Day Event the year I was her working student. The year before she had *five* horses qualified. Karen had won the event three times in the nineties. (David had also won it three times.) But horse sports cause a lot of wear and tear on horses and riders, and it was not unheard of for a rider to go from having a large string of competition-ready horses to none. I imagined Karen must be feeling like a wallflower, but between coaching other athletes, participating in presentations, and making time to meet some of the younger athletes and fans who had come to watch, she seemed to be making the best of it.

By then I knew that Karen was one of the most honest people I had ever met. And so I should not have been surprised in the sponsor tent that day when she looked me straight in the eye and said simply, "Bad form!"

The rum made it a little hard for me to realize she was actually serious, and although my stomach turned over as it began to register, my smile remained a moment longer than it should have.

Karen glanced at my drinks and then looked back at me.

"Really bad form."

I stood awkwardly next to her table, frozen, unable to decide whether to apologize or just silently fade toward the nearest exit. Karen sat for a moment with her friends and sponsors watching the mega-screen, then turned back to me after the next rider had finished her test. I was sweating and uncomfortable.

She smiled and said, "Well, I guess your excuse is that you're from Canada. You better sit down and join us!"

I could feel my pulse in the palm of my hand that was holding the beer. I sat down on the very edge of one of the empty chairs and stared at the television, not really seeing anything. Nobody paid much attention when I found a moment to slip away a couple minutes later.

I did not go into the sponsors' tent again.

Later I remembered how after my first cross-country lesson with Karen, I had hosed off Danny, cleaned my tack, and returned to a chore I'd been earlier charged with: raking leaves. I kept my mind occupied as I raked by replaying the lesson over and over again in my head. I could feel my body lean back and my legs go forward as Danny dropped into the water. I again felt myself slip the reins and then gather them again as Danny balanced himself underneath me. The five strides on a bending line to the skinny, slight opening left hand. Land, balance, go forward.... I was so involved in reliving the session I did not realize Karen was approaching me in her golf cart until she was already beside me. She rolled to a stop and looked me in the eye.

"Great job today!"

I looked at her, surprised. I said nothing.

"Tik, I think you may have found your destiny," she said matter-of-factly, and then drove off.

I hoped she was talking about my riding and not the orderly piles of brown leaves I had left in my wake. Just like Karen, I already knew I would rather be riding around the Kentucky Three-Day than watching it on the mega-screen. However, I realized that those few minutes of riding in the international arena or around the massively challenging four-star course, beneath the watchful eyes and tanned faces of the sponsors in the white tent, were not what this year was about. Instead, I was learning the 10,000 details that preceded that point.

After the Kentucky Three-Day, I drove with Hannah and two of Karen's horses back to Middleburg, Virginia, the summer home of the O'Connor Event Team. The farm overlooked the Blue Ridge Mountains. While the Rocky Mountains back home in Canada beat them in height any day of the week, there was no denying the *class* of those hills. The O'Connors' cross-country course was called "the playground," and it was one. I had a few more days with David and Karen before I went home to prepare the next stage of my working student plan: hooking up with a show jumper.

I just had to figure out with *which* show jumper.

CHAPTER 16

Cutting in with Captain Canada

Anybody can sit *on* a horse. A *good* rider sits *into and with* the horse. A *great* rider becomes, in terms of balance, communication, and harmony, seemingly an actual *part* of his horse.

The great rider anticipates not only which shadow his horse will shy at but in which direction he will do so. And the rider knows this without conscious thought. He becomes a brain that is nestled just behind the withers, moving in concert with his mount just as driftwood moves up and down with rolling waves.

The calves, the heels, the hands are capable of great strength if needed, as they sometimes are, but in the end they become simply aids, transferring signals from the great rider to his horse the same way the brain fires messages along the neural cables to the muscles. They never force, they simply direct. They ask. "Could we?"

It is a great thing to see this.

I watched Ian Millar compete at Spruce Meadows in Calgary in June. Spruce Meadows is an outdoor tournament, with many arenas, demonstrations, competitions, shows, bars, restaurants, and shopping. It is Disneyland for the fan of show jumping. I waited for three days for a chance to talk to him, as I wanted to give him my résumé. Having observed his riding ritual over several days, the only place I knew I would find him was in the competition ring, and each time he came out of a class I was now aware a dance would begin: Millar would hand his horse to his groom—with a smile and a pat, regardless of how he did in the class—then turn and talk with the reporters, the sponsors, the fans. He would lead them around the ringside sponsors' tent, before ending in the parking lot where he would get on his motorcycle. The roar of the engine would finally silence the gaggle of followers. A wave, a smile, and he was gone.

Somehow I had to find a way to cut in.

Two days before I was due to leave the show, I wriggled my way through the crowd and thrust my résumé in front of him just as he was starting his bike.

"Here," I said. "I was wondering, if, maybe, you might have an opening for a working student."

He glanced at the sheet of paper.

"Tik Maynard," he read out loud. He looked further down the page. "You worked for Ingrid Klimke? Great. I have so much respect for her family."

"I did."

Ingrid had been one of the people who had said how much I could learn from Millar. To a Canadian, however, that would often go without saying. Millar rose to fame with a horse called Big Ben— together they won forty Grand Prix titles. Big Ben was long gone, but Millar—known by the press as "Captain Canada"—had managed to find horse after horse that could jump, and the year before, in Hong Kong, he had just competed in his ninth Olympics.

Yes, his *ninth*!

Ingrid had spent a while as a working student for Millar. She had flown to Ontario in the summers, traveling down the East Coast with him, learning what it was like to compete on the Grand Prix circuit in North America. Sometimes she groomed, sometimes she rode, sometimes she walked courses with him. Before I left Germany, Ingrid had even said she would help me get a job with Millar if I wanted, but I had never followed up with her; I was nervous about taking too much of her time, of becoming an irritant or too assuming. And I thought I could get the job on my own.

"Ingrid was amazing," I said, looking Millar in the eye. "I would love to work at a show jumping stable, too."

"Well, I can't say one way or another. My daughter is in charge of hiring. I'll pass this along to her."

He folded the written record of my work history four times, unevenly, and put it in his breeches pocket.

The next day I went to the show with one mission: find Ian Millar's daughter, Amy, and re-present my résumé.

Amy, her brother Jonathan, and their father ran Millar-Brooke Farm, in Ontario. They had 650 acres of land just outside Perth, including rings, stables, woods, fields, trails, and multiple homes. I had the feeling that a job—back home in Canada, even—with Ian Millar would be a great way to round out my stint as a working student.

I knew what Amy looked like and I had often seen her ride. She and Jonathan both rode at the international level. Amy was blonde, slim, a little shorter than me, a few years older than me. Statistically probably a pretty common description of riders at Spruce Meadows that year, but by this time I had found where their horses were stabled, so the search was much easier.

The first time I went by she was studying an entry list and talking with another, younger, lady. Both wore beige riding pants, and their tall boots gleamed. After introducing myself I asked if I could chat with her about a working student position.

"I'm really busy right now," she said.

The next morning began crisp and cool, and I arrived at the show grounds as the queues for morning coffee began. I walked past the lines and headed for the Millar-Brooke stabling, which took up one end of a long "barn." When stalls were rented at this show, they were barren: There was industrial steel for the frame, plain unpainted wood for the walls and door, and an open roof above. All this was covered by a large white tent. On the floor were rubber mats. After adding shavings to the horse's stall, and buckets for feed and water, it is common practice at jumper shows to decorate the area of stabling you rent. Mulch, flowers, wicker chairs and tables are arranged. Sometimes even artwork is added to dress the area up. Visitors are impressed, and the riders feel more at home.

Amy had a helmet in one hand and what looked like a hot drink in the other. Behind her a girl was carrying a saddle. The way Amy moved was purposeful, like a cat heading to her favorite stalking grounds. I could tell she was getting ready to ride. I wasn't surprised when she saw me and immediately said, "Good morning. I can't talk now."

I nodded. I thought about just offering to help for the day, but it seemed like they had everything under control.

"I'll catch you later," I said, turning to go. "Thanks!"

After a morning of watching horses in the warm-up rings, I decided to try again. I would go back as many times as it took. The job was not going to get itself.

When the sun was high above I again stopped by their section of stabling, this time catching Amy at lunch.

Perfect, I thought. Then I laughed to myself and changed the word: Convenient.

She was sitting down and let me talk. I explained I wanted to come to Millar-Brooke Farm. I wanted to ride with her dad.

"And you," I added. "And your brother."

Amy asked if I had video of my riding. I did. She said she would like her brother to take a look before they decided. And right then he came around the corner.

Convenient. Again.

Jonathan was built tall, six-foot-four, and slim, like his sister.

I showed him a short video of myself riding around a show jumping course on a horse of my dad's—the mare we called Sapphire.

"But not McLain Ward's Sapphire," I added, referring to one of the most famous jumping horses in the world.

Jonathan nodded as if to say, "Of course."

"Looks good," he said. But he was not about to be pressured when I asked him about a working student position. "Let me think about it. One of us will give you a call in a month or so."

"Thank you, Jonathan." I shook his hand. "Thank you, Amy." I shook hers. Both good handshakes. Firm.

One month later, to the day, I got the call. Amy left a descriptive message, informing me where and when I should arrive to assume my duties. Her tone was young and jovial, but it was also a voice that was used to giving orders, to taking charge. She had no idea that I would listen to her message three times before handing the phone to my dad. He listened to it a few times himself, smiling.

CHAPTER 17

One Day with Ian Millar

I was to meet Ian Millar in September, at Spruce Meadows, at the Masters Tournament. So I had six weeks downtime to ride Sapphire and TJ, my dad's horses; to run on the shaded trails that snaked through woods of cedar, hemlock, and fir in Pacific Spirit Park; and to catch up with friends. Being at home I was also quickly drawn up in my family's life, which was full and busy.

The plan was to groom for Millar Wednesday through Sunday at the Masters, then board a flight for Ontario to stay at his home base for another six months. I packed one suitcase with winter clothes—sweaters, jackets, long underwear—and another with riding clothes and casual wear. I shined my boots. I shined my spurs, as well. I cleaned my helmet. I ordered new riding pants. I bought more boot polish. I had read *Because Every Round Counts* by George Morris, and I was paying more attention to such details. Also, while my determination had paid off in getting the job, I knew I would have to be vigilant to keep it.

Millar had two horses with him. They flew out from Ontario for the week. I was enveloped into his fold before my eyes even adjusted to the low light in the barn. Christy, a quiet Kiwi who was educated as a teacher but had worked with horses her whole life, took me through the feeding schedule. We started with supplements: "This is for the blood cells...this is to help the blood flow...this is Vitamin E..." I remembered the first three, but quickly lost track of the rest. By the time Christy measured out the last dose, my palms were sweaty.

I thought back to some advice I had been given before I headed off on this leg of my journey.

Horseman Jonathan Field lived almost two hours from me, but spending time with him was always worth the drive. I had met Jonathan a few years previously and had been instantly impressed. He had learned from renowned horsemen like Ronnie Willis, Craig Johnson, and Ray Hunt. He had spent close to a decade studying with Pat Parelli. Jonathan had the sense of a scientist and the soul of a saint. He told me, "Listen to Ian Millar. He is a master, a horseman. His horses always go truly forward, and they are truly soft."

Moreover, Millar also had the ingredients that determine what it means to be successful in the horse business: horsemanship, proven performance, business savvy, and a flair for marketing.

Of course it depends what the business model is. A teacher or clinician does not need proven performance in the ring (although it helps with marketing). He needs the ability to communicate. And to not confuse.

About marketing Jonathan reminded me in his playful, joking way, "There are lots of great horsemen out there, but if you can't market yourself, you will always be a 'poor' horseman."

Over the years, other trainers have told me their formulas.

George Morris explained in a clinic what it takes to win: "First is ambition. Ambition! Second is emotional control. I'm tough, but I never lose my temper with a horse. Third is management. Be meticulous. When McLain Ward wins, it is no accident. He is meticulous. Fourth is selection. Get the best horse you can. Last is talent. *Talent is last*. Every country has talent. But not every country wins. Talent is last."

Pat Parelli, over sushi and sake, in Ocala, on training horses: "Strong legs, soft hands, and willpower."

Ernest Shackleton, that explorer and leader of men, wrote about the qualities he valued in recruits for his polar expeditions: "First, optimism; second, patience; third, physical endurance; fourth, idealism; fifth and last, courage."

It is interesting that he puts them in this order, and especially interesting that he puts optimism first. Hope is as necessary as water for riders to continue their journey.

Above all, the first quality *I* want to see in a trainer is joy. I want to hear him say, "How does *that* work? How can we share this with the horse world?" David O'Connor has that kind of passion when he talks about horses. He speaks from the heart:

> *This is about the world of possibilities with horses! All of what you've seen so far is about communication. The art of riding is about communication!*

When Millar mounted for his second class that day, I followed him to the warm-up arena. Although there were lots of tents and distractions for the spectators, there were also special paths for the horses. When we got to the arena he didn't really need assistance—he had Christy to set the rails—but I wanted to be there. I wanted to see how he prepared: how long he walked, how he stretched the horse, what kind of jumps he used. I wanted to see his pregame rituals.

He dismounted after the class and handed me his horse. I walked the horse until his sweat was dry. I took the studs, which helped him grip the turf while on course, out of his shoes.

I was walking the horse again when Millar called me over.

He stood off in a corner with Christy at his side. I eyeballed the horse beside me. Was his blanket not straight? Should his boots be off already? What had I done wrong?

"What's this I hear about you writing articles for a magazine?"

"Oh." I swallowed. "I wrote a few articles for a magazine back home. *Gaitpost*. It's based out of BC."

"I know it. We subscribe to it, actually."

Millar stood, arms crossed. Stern but not even close to losing his temper. Christy seemed neither interested, nor embarrassed, so far. Just indifferent. The horse stood quietly, his ears going first toward Millar, then toward the path where a family with a stroller walked by, then back to Millar.

"So…" I began, deciding to try a smile and a casual nonchalance in spinning what obviously was an issue. "I wrote about my experiences as a working student so far…"

Well, it was not exactly a secret. Honestly, I didn't think anybody would care. I was always careful about what I wrote, trying to err on the side of caution. Affairs and scandals were not my business—they might, as Steinbeck wrote, "be perfectly acceptable as confirmed gossip, but in print the protagonists might be inclined to consider the histories libelous, and they surely are."

Millar took a step back and leaned against the railing. His eyebrows were raised. Christy was still silent. The horse had lowered his head, and his tongue was out, feeling his lips like he had just realized he had them.

"I wish you had told me before that you were writing about your experiences. How many articles have you written?"

"Nine. *Gaitpost* published eight of them," I replied, caught between pride in my accomplishment and awareness that this was not making him happy.

"Nine. Can you believe that?" Millar looked at Christy.

She didn't say anything, but she turned subtly away from me. No help there.

Millar turned back to me.

"You know, I like you, Tik."

I nodded.

"I just don't know if I can do it. It would be like inviting the paparazzi into my bedroom."

Families, couples, a Great Dane, continued to walk by behind him. He was composed, but I imagined it would take a lot for him to ruffle.

"Well, if you hire me I won't write anything," I replied quickly. I looked him in the eye. I meant it. "Maybe I could sign something stating that," I offered.

Millar turned to Christy: "What would you do?" Then he smiled and laughed before she could answer. "You would fire him, wouldn't you?"

He turned back to me, his composure and his smile solid again. "I'll tell you what. I'll think about it."

Back at the barn there was still tack to clean, horses to feed, stalls to muck. But the stable seemed suddenly darker, and smaller, more cramped. I offered to graze the horses. I caught the first one in silence. He put his head down obediently and let me slip the leather halter over his ears. Outside I thought about something else I had learned from Jonathan Field. Once a horse learns something, whether productive or destructive, that memory is there forever. But horses are always learning, they are always curious. A good horseman had to be the same way. He could not say, "There, I've done it. I taught him, and now I can rest." No. A horseman must always be creating, building, learning, and teaching.

I heard an engine approach, then stop. Silence, broken only by a horse's kick against the stall wall. The camaraderie I had shared with Christy only a few hours before was already gone. A minute later Millar walked into the barn. He wore jeans and a white cowboy hat.

He put his hand on my shoulder. I looked up at him.

"I just can't do it."

"Do what?" I almost felt sorry for him.

"I just can't take the chance with you. I'm sorry."

I nodded. "Okay."

I had to go past him to get my backpack in the tack room. He stepped out of my way and apologized. I took a breath, fumbled the groom's pass off from around my neck, and held it out to him.

"Why don't you keep it," he said.

The next day, back in Vancouver, I hung the pass on the mirror in my parents' guestroom. My old room. My new room again. The sun cut a dagger through my curtains. It hit the pass like a spotlight. I saw my photo staring back at me. For one day I had worked for Ian Millar.

Ian Millar was a great rider. He had the uncommon combination of drive and focus, patience and guts. Even as he completed his ninth Olympics in 2008 and gray hairs sprouted out from underneath his helmet, he was still a rare competitor. Everyone knew that.

My first thought was to be defensive. But seeing as this was the second time I was fired in as many years, I recognized maybe I should be looking *in* more, instead of *out*.

I began sending out résumés again. I checked the ads on yardandgroom.com. There was a rider position available in Maryland. A groom wanted in England. An instructor was needed in Riyadh. I clicked on the link to the website. Riyadh: the capital of Saudi Arabia. I didn't know if I would apply. I was a hungry dog, stomach thin, searching high and low for food. I knew that if I did find a new job, I would be sure to mention right out of the box that I would like to write about it.

I clicked on the next available position, and then the next.

CHAPTER 18

And Now for Something Completely Different

My dad cantered along next to me. He was on the big grumpy gelding TJ, and I was on Amadeus, a Lipizzaner, who was struggling to keep up. The track at the riding club was easily wide enough for both of us, and the footing was excellent; the rainy days were still ahead. Since the horse properties in Vancouver were often only an acre, most of the riders were members of the local riding club, where there was a track, dressage rings, jumping rings, an indoor arena, and a grass field.

My dad looked at me, and I knew he was going to say something ridiculous. It was his eyes—bright and curious—that gave away his enthusiasm. And he *always* asked the most *obvious* questions when he was enthused. It drove me crazy.

"If you can't work for Ian Millar, do you want to stay here over the winter?"

I spurred Amadeus on, trying to keep up.

"I think I want to get away. I talked to a guy on the phone today who said I could come down and apprentice for him."

"Why don't you go to England and work for an eventer? Didn't you have a job offer from William Fox-Pitt?"

I looked at my dad. He was standing lightly in the stirrups, letting the horse roll along smoothly below him. He *knew* I had just finished working for the O'Connors. And, yes, I did meet William Fox-Pitt. We had sat down together at the Kentucky Three-Day and discussed the possibility of me crossing the Atlantic again to work with him. Sinead, the woman who I had cleaned buckets for that one day at Rocking Horse while working for the O'Connors, had kept in touch. She had set up the meeting.

"You remember, Dad—I told him no, because I decided to go to Ian Millar instead. England did sound fun though, especially since he said we might go foxhunting."

"If you are serious about eventing, you really should go to England. Badminton and Burghley, the most famous events in the world, are there!"

"He's hired somebody else, I'm sure," I replied, continuing to leg Amadeus along. "Besides, I want to learn to ride Western and check out some more natural horsemanship."

I had told him all this already. It seemed like our relationship was at its best when I was just getting home or just leaving. I always missed him when I was *away*.

"How many horses do you think he has?" he asked.

"Fox-Pitt? About twenty, probably. But he already has a rider now."

We were galloping; I was leaning over the withers and really urging Amadeus forward. The footfalls of the two horses combined into a steady drum roll beneath us.

"You know," my dad yelled over the sound, "all good horse people use principles of 'natural horsemanship.' You don't need to specialize in it to benefit from learning to use body language with horses."

He was right. I did not really care for the word "natural" either. *Natural* horsemanship reminded me of advertisements I saw promoting *wholesome* food or *real* sugar. At what point did we start to advertise the "specialness" of things that used to be simply expected? Perhaps "natural horsemanship" should be known as just "horsemanship." On the other hand, as horsemanship changed from a way of being to a discipline and an industry unto itself, maybe we *needed* a qualifying word to make it stand out.

Honestly, it still wasn't clear to me that I even understood what "horsemanship" really was. My working definition: A way to communicate what the human wants in a way the horse understands. I had been using "natural horsemanship" interchangeably with "working with the horse from the ground," in contrast to what you might do as a rider on his back. But I did not know if that was right either. "Groundwork," as people called it, seemed to be its own discipline—while this idea of natural horsemanship crossed *all* disciplines. Groundwork was for some an *end in itself*, and for others, like the O'Connors, a *means to an end*: a way to teach, or cajole, an unsure horse to jump into water or encourage an insensitive horse to leg-yield.

Groundwork appealed to me right away, just the way dressage appeals to some people and jumping to others. But even as I grew even more convinced of its value, I tried never to judge others if their interest in it lagged behind mine.

The reason I felt natural horsemanship was not more popular with English riders was that few top competitors in English disciplines used it, with fewer still pitching it as a valuable tool. I predicted that was all going to change. In the future, riders were going to learn from all different disciplines. Anky van Grunsven, eight-time Olympic medalist in dressage, was already improving her riding by applying lessons she learned while reining. (In 2010 she competed at the World Equestrian Games in Lexington, Kentucky, in the Western discipline of reining.)

My dad, still beside me, and still going strong, tried one more time.

"At least consider going to Fox-Pitt's."

"Come on, Dad!" I replied, frustrated. "I want to get away, see the world. I want to do something *different!*"

Did I have to spell it out?

My dad slowed TJ to a trot.

"You could always try a show jumper in the United States," he tried. "What about Anne Kursinski? Or Beezie Madden?"

I kept my leg on. A slow canter for Amadeus was the same speed as a fast trot for TJ. Yes, my plan had been to go to a show jumper, but now that plan was going on hold.

"Listen...I want to do something *really* different. Something extraordinary. I don't care if people think it's bizarre."

He looked at me, but said nothing. My dad looked at home on a horse. I wondered if I ever would.

"Dad," I continued, "I'm constantly being inspired by other people. I love watching top riding! But I think there is more. What if my idea of getting along with a horse is only a fraction of what is possible in a partnership?"

Southlands used to look big to me, then Vancouver seemed immense...now I looked around the world and saw bigger opportunities. Then again, there were people who studied the stars, and that made it all seem small again.

I had sent an email of introduction to Monty Roberts, known by many as the author of *New York Times* Best Seller *The Man Who Listens to Horses* and the first person to bring natural horsemanship to the attention of the general public. I hadn't had a response. A show jumping position would be the easy way forward. It was still the realm I knew the best. Yet, each day I grew more certain that I had a more unusual path ahead of me. A trail that had been little used. What it was, where it led, I was not sure.

So I waited. And I wrote.

"Write about the tough experiences but don't publish them," my mother told me.

"People want to hear about the good times!" my brother said.

"You're never going to get any sponsors if you write about being dismissed and fired," my father warned.

"Don't burn any bridges," they all insisted.

It turned out they were more right than they knew. *Gaitpost* had decided to stop publishing my articles. They felt my most recent piece, "One Day with Ian Millar," was not suitable. They wanted to give other riders a chance to write.

Fair enough, I thought. But I was surprised. And rejection always stings.

My wandering thoughts meant TJ was getting ahead of us again, so I shook myself back to the present and urged Amadeus on one more time. I kept getting left behind today, and I was getting left behind in life. It was tiring, following. I wanted that caffeine-like jolt that comes from forging ahead despite any obstacle. What was it Bonhoeffer said?

The mature man will decide for himself, while the weaker man will choose between options that have been laid out.

It was time to tell my father what I was setting up. Amadeus and I caught the other horse and rider as we rounded the bend in the half-mile track.

"Dad, slow up a minute," I said, breathing a bit heavily, carefully choosing the best way to begin explaining my new plan. "I just got off the phone with a cowboy in Texas."

My dad didn't respond.

"I want to go there."

"What?"

"Texas, Dad. Loving, Texas."

Loving, Texas, was cattle country. Northwest of Fort Worth and almost directly south of Wichita Falls. On Google Maps I had found a post office and the Loving Baptist Church...and that was about it. Also, apparently, in Loving, was the Bruce Logan Foundation Station. *That* was my intended destination.

"And how is *Texas* going to improve your riding?" my dad asked, as he once again slowed to a trot. To the side of the track was a stand of birch. Birch trees were rare in Vancouver, and I appreciated their creamy bark on every lap.

"It's not about improving my riding. It's about cutting and colt starting."

It was hard to put it into words. I wanted to not only *go somewhere new*, but to *learn something new*. Animals have a destiny—birds to fly, fish to swim—and while mine might not be pre-written, this was one of those cases that made me wonder. I thought back to when David O'Connor had told me he had spent some time riding cutting horses and learning natural horsemanship.

"So," my dad said, finally slowing TJ to a walk. "Who is this cowboy?"

I told him what I knew—admittedly not a lot.

"He has a ranch, spent a few years learning from Pat Parelli and Ronnie Willis, and he starts horses and gives clinics. I think he competes in cutting, as well."

"Does he compete in reining?"

Because of its inclusion as an FEI sport and its growing international popularity, reining was better known in English-riding circles than other Western sports. It was also a sport that required more tact, and subtlety, than most rodeo events.

"I don't know. I've told you all I know."

We were walking past the cross-country area at our riding club. It was small and seemed to be getting smaller as more room was given over to rectangular arenas. I was tiring of riding in a box.

"How did you hear about him?"

"Jonathan Field."

Even after what happened with Ian Millar—for I knew what happened was my fault, not Millar's—a Jonathan recommendation counted for a lot with me.

My dad turned TJ around, heading back the way we came. Amadeus pinned his ears back and made to follow. But my dad was off, and I was left behind again. I let the reins out and settled into the stirrups in a smoothly accelerating canter. I thought about Texas: cutting, colt-starting, working cattle.

My dad looked back over his shoulder and yelled, "Well, if it's what you want to do, go for it!"

I smiled.

And then, as he turned forward again, "Hope you last more than one day."

CHAPTER 19

Loving, Texas

I ripped a square of paper towel off the roll beside the sink—dishes overflowed onto the counter—and folded it in half to form a pincer between my thumb and forefinger. The satiated tick was still as I picked it up from where it fell off the dog. Its body was smooth and spherical as I rolled it between my fingers, smaller than a pea. I palpated it a couple times. Its texture reminded me of a paintball, or a fresh egg after someone had peeled away the shell, leaving only the thin membrane that sealed the yolk and white inside.

"Are you going to squish it?" Rhiannon asked while petting the dog.

"I guess," I said and looked at her as I continued to roll the ball around between my fingers.

Rhiannon was young and enthusiastic: She didn't take *no crap from no one.* Although, *just this once,* she was content to let the job go to a man. She said *man* with all the scorn an English teenager can muster. "That's not a job for a *lady.*"

"I like your accent," I replied.

Living in the backcountry and rising with the sun was tough and lonely work, whether man or lady, but Rhiannon was following the horizon. She had Gone West, and her calloused hands and sun-bleached hair no longer fit the model of a girl born on the northern island of Shetland and raised in Cumbria.

"Go on then!" she insisted.

And so I squeezed it. It burst easily, and when I looked inside the paper towel, I saw the remains of my arachnicide: a splotch of dark crimson, about the size of a quarter.

"Time to start the day," I said, as I threw the paper towel, and tick, in the garbage and clomped down the steps of the trailer, Pop-Tart in hand. Bruce Logan, Rhiannon, and I saddled the horses and rode out. The dogs—Cougar, Cutter, Beau, Turtle, and Dottie—followed.

The Western saddle had not taken long to get used to, and we were now trotting along the east fence line, heading out of the "Close 600" and into the "Southern 3000" to check on the cattle and look for buffalo. At least, *I* was looking for buffalo. And deer and coyotes and wild hogs. And turtles. There were probably box turtles, which, if moved, are said to wander aimlessly, their houses on their backs, looking for something they recognize. As for many, a house is not the same as home. These lost turtles keep searching, stressed, until they die.

All of these animals could be found on the range somewhere in the maze of oak and mesquite, often near water holes.

At the bluffs we let the horses pick their way up, shale breaking and rolling underfoot. Bruce led, but he was ready with advice if I needed it.

"Tik, with that two-year-old you're on, let him feel his way, but be ready to support him if he needs it."

Bruce was also on a young horse and was riding ahead of me, somehow finding a path through the dry skeletal scrub, which grabbed the stirrups and twisted around my legs. He didn't look back to see if I was still there, but he continued explaining: "Keep the horse between your legs and hands. If you want to go right, use your left leg and open your right one. The horse needs somewhere to go, and when you take your right leg off, he should go *toward* it. If he doesn't, *then* use the reins."

I remembered the first time I met Bruce—last week—while he was competing in a colt-starting competition in Canada. I caught up with him between rounds and asked him if I should bring my English riding pants, boots, and helmet when I headed for his base in Texas the following week.

Bruce had eyed me up and down, taking in my North Face vest and sneakers, and said, "I don't think you'll need them. We run a pretty simple operation. Jeans and boots are all you'll need."

But then he couldn't resist adding, the tiniest gleam in his eyes: "But bring whatever you're most comfortable in."

English riders seldom wear jeans and cowboy boots—it can look contrived. Western riders wear breeches and tall boots even less—they wouldn't be caught dead in them! But I would have been happy to slip into some Wranglers. There was a part of me that whispered, *I should have been a cowboy.*

At the top of the bluffs, I surveyed the rocky, lilting landscape. Somewhere the cattle were grazing, and I was going to spot them. I was wearing a button-down shirt and a borrowed cap with *STIHL 4-MIX* printed on the front. It fit a little tight but kept the glare out of my eyes. The sun formed an aura around Bruce. In his silhouette, his wide-brim hat seemed as much a part of him as his arms or hands. I squinted and noticed his lariat at the ready, looping around the horn and falling partly over his thigh, a bright white circle that stood out against the bay horse and brown saddle, even with the sun behind him.

For the most part we were quiet and happy to be. But I also had questions. I asked him how he had met Jonathan Field.

"At Pat's."

I asked him who had taught him.

"Well, let me think," he said, as he led the way down a new trail. "I spent a good five years with Pat Parelli. Craig Johnson taught me reining. My biggest influence? Probably Ronnie Willis. Either him or my father, I guess."

I was becoming more interested in who had taught whom. And patterns were starting to emerge. There were certain men—and they were mostly men—who may or may not have competed at a high level, but what they were really known for was influencing the next generation of trainers.

In show jumping, in the United States, it was George Morris.

Craig Johnson was known for teaching his reining techniques. And winning. He won like Stephen King wrote—often and without apology.

Pat Parelli: I might bet more people have heard of Parelli than any other horseman in history. He crossed disciplines, countries, and languages. He was an inspiring speaker, but when I watched his demonstrations I learned just as much with the video on mute. His body language was as clear and interesting as a mime's.

And who did Parelli learn from? Well, some from Ray Hunt and Tom Dorrance—the two men who are said to have begun the "natural horsemanship movement" in the United States, but also from Ronnie Willis. Willis was a sort of in-between man. He passed away in 2003, in his sleep. I would never get to meet him. But there were still interviews out there for those, like me, who searched. The way Willis talked about horses…he *got* them. He understood them in the easy way some people just *get* music, or math, or cooking.

The way he (a horse) learns is, number one from confidence, then understanding, then the achievement, the result.

Bruce picked his way amongst the mesquite and seemed content to talk more about his mentors. He had taken what he wanted from each of them and made it his own, and now he was passing it on. Paying it forward and having fun doing it.

The horse I rode, a black Quarter Horse, tentatively started up a short bank after Bruce, rocked back on his hocks, and then scrambled up the steepest part, almost brushing me off on the branches of an oak. I let the reins slip loose and gave him his head, rubbing his neck as he rested at the top. The dogs rushed on ahead.

We walked on, picking our way among the rocks, Bruce first, Rhiannon now second, and I brought up the rear. That was when we saw the bull. The horses were instantly on edge. They stopped, backed up, pricked their ears, tensed their shoulders. I stared at him, hidden slightly behind the canopy of a dying oak, and he stared right back. He was the only bull in this section. He had thirty cows to service; if there were any more than that he wouldn't be able to manage—a second bull would be necessary.

He was a fine bull; the biggest I had ever seen. Red coat, white longhorns, and a meaty face with a blaze.

"They are all completely grass fed, right up until the end," Bruce said, pulling his hat down lower. "That bull has an important job to do."

We started off again at a trot, the most efficient gait for riding long distances, and after another mile we came to a second fence. At the gate, Bruce dismounted to open it while the dogs galloped underneath and took off after a deer. I watched Bruce place his foot in the stirrup, grab the pommel, and swing himself up. But as he did, his horse stepped forward. Maybe Bruce's weight shifted, or the horse reacted to the dogs, or maybe the horse was impatient to get back to the barn. The reason could have been one of many, but the reaction was unacceptable.

Bruce pulled on the reins and shifted his weight back, backing the horse up three paces. The horse threw his head, so Bruce backed him up again. He jabbed once with his spur. The horse stepped back awkwardly another step, tired of this game now, then he was still, and he lowered his head. Bruce immediately lowered his hands; they went soft, and he let his horse stand. Then he got off, rubbed his horse's neck, and remounted quietly. The horse stood still.

"If you make a mistake, they'll probably forgive you. But if you are unfair, they might not," he explained. "I'm firm, but I'm fair. Sometimes you have to go through fire before they get it. But if I stop before that point, I'm teaching him that it's okay to act up, that he's right and I'm wrong."

I nodded in answer, but Bruce was already looking ahead, scouting the best route through the brush.

What Bruce meant is, with horses, honesty and consistency are key. Your expectations must be understandable and logical. If I walked up to you and offered my hand as if to shake yours, you might extend your hand. But what if I then looked you in the eye, winked, and slapped you across the face?

I followed Bruce again. We were out there to check on the cattle. We were out there to check on the fence lines. More than anything we were out there to give these horses a ride. The horse I was on was nervous at the start, but now he started to relax, and as often happened, just as he began to focus, he also began tiring, feeling the effects of my weight and that of the saddle, which was probably close to twenty-five pounds. And so after an hour we started heading back. We did see more cattle, and more fences. And then, suddenly...four buffalo! All in a row, looking at us.

"Hey, Rhiannon," I said as her horse stopped beside mine, his head high, his eyes and ears fixed on the ungulates.

"Yes." She didn't look at me. I was sure her heart rate was up, and I could see her horse's was. His muscles were taut. His feet were still, but his legs trembled, like he was shivering. He was ready to bolt!

"What did the dad buffalo say to his kid when he left?"

"What?" she responded, never turning her head.

"Bye, Son."

Bruce gave the tiniest smile.

"That's not funny," Rhiannon snapped, but I saw her body relax a little. And then so did her horse. We let him settle, and then turned to go around the small group of buffalo. There used to, I thought, not so long ago, be more buffalo than people in this country. What a change. What a shame.

An hour later we arrived back at the barn and dismounted. As we untacked the horses and turned them out for the night, Bruce told us the plan for the next day.

"Early start. The cattle in the Close 600 need to be brought in so the young ones can be weaned."

This was a rare year—every cow in that group had a calf, and the calves followed their mothers with dogged perseverance. Once the calves were weaned, they could be used to practice cutting.

Cutting is a sport born of necessity. Horses are ridden into a group of cattle and taught to separate one that might need doctoring or branding. Quarter Horses get their name from quarter-mile races, for which they are the fastest breed in the world. They are versatile and friendly. Today many of them make their living moving cattle—a job where they can learn to be responsible for their work.

I was learning to think more like a horse, learning to have a softer, wider vision. Learning to look and beware. But I was also trying to get the horses to think more like *us*. Could they become more focused on one thing? Could they learn to think first and react second? Learn to trust, not run?

"Horses work better when they have a job to do," Bruce said as he took his lasso off his saddle and threw it on the bed of his truck next to his welding equipment. I smiled at the sight. You never know when you'll need that.

I looked over at Rhiannon, offering, "If you feed, I'll do the stalls."
"Deal," she said.

As I picked up the pitchfork I looked around. The dogs' tongues
were out, and their heads were low. Flies stole sweat from the backs
of the horses, now drinking and rolling in a large corral. The saddles
were put away neatly, but they were not oiled. What's a little bit of
scuff? Rhiannon smiled at me. And behind her dust rose from the
road as Bruce's pickup faded into the distance.

In the evening, chores done, Rhiannon and I walked back to the
trailer where we slept. I grabbed a Coors Light and Rhiannon headed
for the shower. I hadn't brought my English boots or breeches, and I
knew now I wouldn't want them. I definitely wouldn't *need* them. In
the background crickets chirped, coyotes howled. It was a place that
put the color back into those black-and-white expressions of old:

Hold your horses. Strong as an ox! Wily as a fox. Frisky as a
filly. Don't look a gift horse in the mouth. Grab the bull by the
horns! He's as fat as a tick.

Or…

…as useful as a bull with tits.

Life was simple here. Every job had a purpose; every animal had
a use. People and horses were similar in that regard: purpose brought
out the best in them. I sat down on the sofa, pen and notebook in
hand, and wrote:

I flew east to get here, but this is the West. This is the frontier. This
is the country of purpose. Or was. How much longer will people
like Bruce, in his dusty cowboy hat, be around to show us the way?

When I finished, it was time for bed, but instead I put on my jacket. I had time to walk and stretch my legs. I stopped just outside the trailer. I could see the barn, a few hundred yards away, even from where I stood. I glanced down and could see the path clearly, every rock. And when I looked up, I saw millions of stars lighting the night, from one horizon all the way to the other. Then there was the moon: almost full and so bright I cast a shadow. It was night, but it was the lightest night I'd ever seen.

CHAPTER 20

"This Is a Lot Different Than Roping Cattle"

From where I sat—the passenger seat of the Ram 3500—the horse was black, possibly dark bay, about sixteen hands, and seemed curious enough. He trotted to the center of the corral, which was about fifty by a hundred feet, pushed his nose up, sniffed the air, and looked out at us.

On the drive Bruce explained that he was to take this horse on for ninety days and start him. The owner, a cattleman, apparently by inclination more than need, wanted a new ranch horse.

"He's four," Bruce told me, "and he's lived out most of his life. This will be all new to him."

I glanced over at Bruce. He was taller and heavier than myself, but not by much. He was an athlete, from a family of Texan athletes. Football was his sport. His father, Jerry, played ten seasons as a safety in the NFL, and helped the Baltimore Colts win Super Bowl V. Bruce wore a blue denim jacket and a neck scarf. His hair was short and neat and graying—and seldom seen because the cowboy hat rarely came off. We drove another fifteen minutes. He was comfortable with the silence, and I was determined to not always talk first.

We parked. The view from our parking spot was of grasslands on the right and the Jacksboro High School football stadium, dropped, it seemed, like an old fort, on the left. Bruce chatted with the horse's owner, a middle-aged man whose paunch was hiding underneath a Dallas Cowboys jacket. The guy handed Bruce a slip of paper. Bruce glanced at it and slipped it into his pocket. After a minute more they shook hands, and Bruce returned to the truck.

"Hey, Tik. Grab the halter and my rope. Let's go!"

The rope halter was in the backseat, and the lasso was lying on the bed of the truck, immediately behind the cab. It was a forty-foot polypropylene rope, worn soft as leather.

Bruce was already heading for the gate, and I put a hand on the fence and swung over to catch up. We stood together in the middle of the pen while the owner watched from outside the corral. Bruce looked at the horse and spoke to me in a low voice: "That boy. He ain't four. That bill of sale his owner showed me says he was born in 2003. He's six."

I studied the horse. From close up I could see a narrow stripe that started between his eyes and stretched slowly out into a snip that separated his busy nostrils.

"I figure it don't really change much. Just that the buck on a full-growner is bigger. We'll be a bit more careful."

Bruce stood organizing his rope and letting the horse get used to our presence, then yelled over to the guy where he was leaning against the fence, "He's gelded, right?"

"I s'pose so. Check his papers," the man yelled back. Bruce took out the paper in his pocket, confirming the horse was indeed gelded. A gelding would be less likely to be distracted or aggressive. He would be easier to work around. Not *easy*…just, on average, *easier*.

We started walking toward the horse, Bruce explaining the plan to me.

"We'll get closer, slowly, just a few steps at a time. If he moves *at all*, we stop."

"Okay." I kept my eyes on the horse. I held the halter and a short rope in my hand. Bruce held the lasso in his.

"Watch his feet. When they are still, we move forward another step."

I realized what was happening. Our two bodies were creating a human wall that would, in a few more steps, corner the gelding. The closer we got, the slower we went. The last few feet we moved only inches at a time.

When I was close enough, I reached out and slowly touched the horse. He faced the corner, and I stood by his hip, rubbing him. Bruce stood by the opposite hip blocking the horse's escape and watching me. He was just out of kicking range. I moved up and rubbed the horse's shoulder, but as I did, he pinned his ears back and turned his head away from me. So I took a step back. I stood again just behind the shoulder. Then Bruce asked me to see if I could put a rope around his neck. I nodded. I reached a hand forward and rubbed the horse's withers. Slowly, easily, I let the rope that was attached to the rope halter fall around his neck.

Then I grabbed the lead rope at both ends. But I didn't leave enough slack. I found I didn't have any play in the rope, and therefore, no leverage. The horse spun on his hindquarters and ran back, splitting the space between us.

"I would have done that a little differently," Bruce said, as he shook his head. "I would have gone slower. It's not a race. And when you do get the rope around his neck, make sure you leave out more slack."

I nodded. The horse kicked out as he cantered away from us.

"Right now we just have to catch him," he continued. "One try with the halter is enough. We just want to get him out of here as calmly as possible. It should be whatever is easiest for the horse. Later, when he's settled in at my place, we can start with the real work."

The gelding was now at the far end of the ring, looking straight back at us. One ear was forward and one back, then they switched. But both eyes never left us.

Bruce went to the middle of the corral where he had left his rope and picked it up. "How we get him in the trailer now depends a lot on what kind of space he's in. With this size here, the lasso might work best."

He let the rope slide through the honda knot, creating a cylindrical loop a couple of yards in diameter.

"If you keep him at this end, I'll see if I can throw this over him."

"Sure, no problem," I said, but I was a little skeptical, both of Bruce throwing the loop over the horse, and of this being the best tactic to take in order to quietly catch him.

Bruce walked down the middle of the corral, directly at the gelding. The lasso knocked against his thigh as he moved. He stopped about fifteen feet from the horse. I stood on the left side of the ring, so that if the horse moved we knew it would be to the right. Bruce brought his lasso into a slow swing over his head. There are many kinds of throws, and I had learned three: the overhand, the houlihan, and the backhand. Bruce was planning a simple overhand. The horse saw the rope move and bolted down the fence. Bruce didn't hesitate. Once more the lasso went behind the man's back, picking up speed, before leaving his hands and moving, slowly it seemed, toward the fence, slightly ahead of the gelding. The horse galloped on—straight into the trap. As the rope settled around his neck, his speed and momentum tightened it, but he continued down the fence.

Time seemed to speed up. Bruce madly played out rope, letting the horse gallop, giving him a chance to feel the rope and the easy tension in it. I tried to stand out of the way behind Bruce. He let the horse circle the corral twice and settle.

"This is a lot different than roping cattle!" Bruce yelled to me.

I thought back to the afternoon when he had taught me how to rope. Bruce showed me the simple overhand first, then the backhand from different angles, and finally the houlihan. He demonstrated the scoop toss and del viento, but I stuck with the basics. I learned how to switch from the backhand to the hula, but how it's impossible to go from the hula to the backhand. He showed me how the scoop toss soars into the air like a dove freed from your hand, returning to the earth in a deadfall, until suddenly, when the calf steps into the trap, you pull on the rope, and the scene unfolds in double time, the rope quickly, suddenly, ferociously alive.

After that lesson, when Bruce had left, I had kept practicing. It was hard enough on the ground; I couldn't imagine riding at the same time. But I liked the feel of the rope in my hands and set up a bale of hay on its end, playing with the different roping shots until dark.

"Tik," Bruce said, breathing hard now, "I don't call this 'natural horsemanship.' Once he's got that rope around his neck, or a halter on his head, that ain't 'natural' anymore."

The horse turned his head to the outside of the corral, looking to get away from the tension he felt encircling his neck. Sweat glistened along his flanks. He broke into a trot. Bruce was watching, ready to release the tension as soon as the horse took one step toward us.

"Look at it this way," he said, gesturing to the left with his head while managing the rope. "Over here are the 'natural horsemen.' And often there is nothing *natural* about what they do. And over there," he nodded to the right, "are the, well, whatever the opposite is—the people who don't take into account the horse and what its capabilities and tendencies are." Bruce paused for a second, thinking. "There are lots of those guys, I guess. In the middle, though, are the horsemen."

To Bruce Logan, a horseman was a person who could balance the need for performance with the understanding of how the horse's mind and body work. Everyone has a different idea of what "performance" is. A circus trainer's horse has to perform tricks. A jumper rider's horse has to jump. A cowboy's horse has to work. For professionals, the horse is what puts food on the table. For amateurs, horses are a hobby rather than a way to make a living, and then what is required in terms of "performance" can be vague.

The gelding took a step toward us, his eye calmer now, and as he did Bruce relaxed, and the rope went slack. The horse knew he was caught.

He settled quickly, and I smoothly slipped the halter on him. I led him with two ropes to the trailer, one attached to the halter and one to the lasso around his neck. Bruce followed behind, encouraging the gelding forward, still talking.

"Anybody can rope a horse. It's what you do *after* that's important. Do you let him run with it and get used to it, or do you jerk him up, try to stop him right away? Can you give him the time he needs? Or are you in a hurry?"

As the horse stepped up into the trailer, and into a new future, the owner walked over to us.

"That was easy," he said, resting his hands on his stomach. "I thought we'd have to chase him down the chute."

Bruce didn't say anything.

The man continued: "You think he'll be ready in a month? I've got some cattle that need bringing in."

"Well now," Bruce said, then thought for a second. "I don't know. Depends on how things go, but I'd like to keep him for ninety days. A solid start, you know? Give him some time to get confident. It's not a race."

On my first day in Texas Bruce had told me, "I want a horse to think and enjoy his job. If we have a problem, I want to *fix* it, not just manage it. Horses are like people, they learn more if they make mistakes. If I always micromanage situations, the horse will eventually either rebel or lose interest. I want a horse that has personality, and I want him to show it when he performs."

This is a theory that can be transferred to any situation, any discipline, any relationship. David O'Connor showed me how it applied on the cross-country course in Florida, and Ingrid Klimke demonstrated it in her indoor in Münster. I again imagined that relationship akin to dance partners: one leads, one follows. One's role is to show off the athleticism and personality of the other—a partner who won't be forced, but must be *led*. Dancing is fast and slow; it is playful and boastful; it is confident and humble…but it isn't a race.

The horse's owner didn't seem totally convinced, but Bruce shook his hand and latched the trailer. I saw the man still standing, watching us leave, hands in his pockets, the football stadium behind him, as we drove off.

CHAPTER 21

On Cutting

One Tuesday I watched a dozen calves trot into the arena. The walls of Bruce's arena were framed with metal pipes and filled in with wooden slats. A mosaic of shape, size, and color—brown, dun, chestnut, rust, white, and black—slowly settled in front of the back wall. Bruce's stallion Joker flung his head as the two of them stood by the gate, getting the worst of the dust.

I was riding Three-Sixty, a two-year-old filly. She was a Quarter Horse, and a wonderful rich chestnut color. Rhiannon was atop a young Quarter Horse gelding named Abra. The four of us would be turning back the calves for Bruce. I looked over at the calves as they straggled in. The last few stumbled into a canter, then forgot to stop before entering the herd. Commotion and fear rippled out from the crash site.

Rhiannon took her reins in two hands and looked over at me.

"You ever do this before?" she asked.

"Nope."

"The herd stays on the back wall. Bruce walks through them and separates a calf. Once that calf is isolated, Joker goes to work. His job is to keep the calf from getting back to the herd. Cutting. It's pretty straightforward."

Rhiannon took up a position about forty feet from the calves. I followed her lead and nudged my mare forward so we were facing the calves, too, about twenty feet from Rhiannon and Abra. We were about a third of the way up the ring, with the herd on the back wall, and Bruce between us.

"What do we do?" I asked.

"We stop the calf that Bruce is working from running to the other end of the arena. We turn it back. We're the 'turn-backers.'"

"Sounds easy enough." I looked over at her, squinting to keep the sun out of my eyes. Rhiannon looked right back at me.

"It's not," she said flatly. And then, "Get ready!"

I looked back at the calves. Bruce was now in the middle of them; they bumped and pushed to get away from him. Although Joker was small, I could see his shoulders above the herd. Bruce singled out a calf that he thought would "work" for him. A calf that "works" is one that doesn't ignore the horses, but also doesn't run away. Bruce wanted him to try to get back to the herd just hard enough to give Joker a workout.

Bruce slowly drove the calf forward. The others in the herd moved with the chosen calf at first, but one at a time they separated, flocking back together behind the horse and rider.

The calf, brown with a white face, was now isolated. It faced Bruce and Joker—the only things separating it from the safety that numbers provide. The calf ran to the left, thinking it would skip around Bruce, eyes wide and unsuspecting.

And that's when Joker went to work. He lowered his hindquarters. His back pushed the saddle up. His head went down. He was transformed from an animal that was calmly listening to his rider, to being let loose. This was his moment, and he knew his job. The tempo doubled, and I found I could not *not* watch as Joker tracked the cow. Bruce sat deep in the saddle, his legs slipping momentarily forward as Joker pivoted on his haunches. One canter stride and Joker was parallel to the calf, blocking its return. The calf, eyes larger now, and watery, too, turned the other way. I heard the slap of hooves on sand as Joker turned in time with the calf, again and again. His ears were pointed, his nostrils had picked up the scent. The game was *on*. In no other equestrian pursuit is the ability of the horse to think for himself so necessary and so apparent.

The calf finally turned tail on Bruce and Joker, looking for escape, looking for a way past Rhiannon.

SLAP-SLAP-SLAP went Rhiannon's hand on her thigh.

"HEY-HEY-HEY-HEY!" she shouted at the calf, pushing it back toward Joker.

The calf turned then and trotted my way. Its knobby knees moved quickly. Suddenly it ran toward the fence. I rode parallel to it, trying to block its escape, but it cut in front of me and headed up the fence line, away from the herd, away from Bruce and Joker, and away from me.

I looked back at Bruce, unsure. Should I go after the calf or turn back to the herd?

"Tik!" he shouted. "Go bring that one back. That's a good calf."

I took Three-Sixty down the arena, past the calf, turned the mare so we faced the calf, then pushed it back down to the herd. But Bruce was already scanning for a new one.

"Hey, Rhiannon…a 'good calf'…what's that mean?" I asked as I stopped near her and reined back a step.

"It means it knows how to 'work.'"

"But it escaped."

She continued watching Bruce and Joker and the calves, not even turning her head my way.

"That's because we screwed up."

The sun was high in the sky, and the wind was picking up. I

should have worn a sweater. I pulled my hat down lower, trying to keep the wind and sun out of my eyes while Bruce walked through the herd, taking his time to find another "good calf."

That morning, I realized, was exactly one year since I left Hinnemann's stable. I wondered if I should do something to mark the occasion. But it was hard to go out for a drink in a dry county. And what did I have to celebrate anyway?

Time was giving me perspective on my stay with Herr Hinnemann, but I still had more questions than answers. Why did I stay as long as I did when I was unhappy? Should I have stayed *even though* I was unhappy? Would I have had the courage to leave his stable if I hadn't been dismissed?

It's a curious thing: Sometimes it takes more guts to quit a job, no matter how unsatisfying it is, than to stick with it.

Three months before, after returning home from Spruce Meadows, I had found myself in a familiar situation: out of a job, back at home, with no plan. I sort of looked around for work and an apartment to rent. Maybe it was time to get a real job…maybe a career, I thought. That same day my friend Eiren sent me a message from Germany:

> You have to finish this, Tik, or it will forever haunt your soul. Forever. Go back and re-read your articles. There is plenty of time to be at home without a plan. You can do that anytime. When you're thirty, thirty-five, and even forty. I'm sure you can do this. But as you get older, it gets harder and harder to head out and experience adventures.

"Tik?" Rhiannon's voice cut into my thoughts.

I looked up. Joker was rating a new calf as it confidently strolled across the width of the arena. It was a strange-looking baby, all black, and its withers were bony, its legs slightly longer than normal. It trotted lazily in front of Bruce, a look of calmness in its eye, and then it stopped and peed. It stood there facing Joker as it finished its business. Some might think this calf dim-witted, seeing its behavior. But perhaps the opposite was true—maybe this calf made up its own mind about things. Often when animals do not do what we want them to do, we call them lazy or stupid or difficult, but these same characteristics in people we call independent or creative or courageous. Bruce let the black calf return to the herd, looking for a new candidate.

This time Bruce made a shallow cut and isolated a chocolate-brown calf with white legs and face. This was a calf that *worked*. Really *worked!* It was desperate in its attempts to get away from Joker, and within half a minute it was looking to get past Rhiannon and me. It ran parallel to Rhiannon, then cut in between us without warning.

Behind Rhiannon, I saw Bruce shaking his head.

"Go get it! I want to work that calf again!"

As I trotted off down the arena I heard him yell to Rhiannon: "Every time a calf gets away like that he learns something, and that's a good calf."

He meant, I assumed, that every time the calf got past us, he would be more likely to try to do the same thing the next time. Bruce wanted a calf that would stay and work, not one that would cut and run.

That day in my parents' kitchen more than a year ago, I'd scribbled down my plan: to train with the most renowned trainer and to ride the most athletic horses in the world for twelve months. But here I was, still on the road, still learning. Still not ready to go home. I had told my dad that I wanted to get away, that I wanted to do something "different."

Well, Dad, I thought now as I rode after that chocolate-brown calf, I am! But not in any way that I might have foreseen. The measure of this adventure was not going to be reflected in the success that came of it, nor in the amount I eventually learned. The measure of this adventure was that *it was still going.*

I would rather be right here, messing up, than anywhere else in the world right now, I thought.

The next calf Bruce cut looked right at me. It was a light dun with a mottled face. I grinned and stared back at it, spurring Three-Sixty forward. I was ready this time! The calf galloped a semicircle around the herd, and Bruce had to take Joker all the way to the fence to keep it clear. I could feel, more than hear, the drumming of Joker's hooves, his feet beating out a crisp, clear rhythm that carried, the way thunder carries, through the air and into my bones.

The calf escaped past me again, of course. I cantered after it, one hand holding the reins, the other relaxed at my side. As I drove it back, Bruce gave me a pained look.

"I know," I said ruefully, "sorry."

I looked over at Rhiannon. Her face was stern but her eyes were smiling. I shrugged and mouthed the words: *That's a good calf.*

She laughed. We looked back toward the herd. Bruce was preparing to make a deep cut this time, his stallion stepped lightly in anticipation, and I picked up my reins.

Ready.

CHAPTER 22

A Different Kind of Education

Most days in Loving nothing much happened. Little things, though…little things happened all the time.

Mouse darted through the middle. He threw his head and the wind grabbed his mane. He raised his upper lip. Then Chrome, all knees and hocks, bucked once, twice, and snaked after him.

The two chestnut foals galloped toward Doc, a tall bay gelding, who raised his head, flattened his ears, and let fly with his hooves. Then Doc's head went down, back to the tough winter grass—long stalks that wilt at the top and turn brittle near the roots. It was the season's last available forage.

Nemo, a yearling with big eyes and a soft brown-bear nose, left the safety of his mother and ran briefly after the other two. The mare, Elle, a gentle sorrel, watched him as he began to trot back to her, then wheeled out of the way as Ruthie, an old piebald, headed right for the colts. The other horses scattered and then paused, heads high, nostrils flaring in the wind. Something had caught Ruthie's attention, and curiosity got the better of her—she took a few steps toward the barn and whinnied as we rode out.

Rhiannon and I were on two green horses, so we let them stop and eye the others. Bruce led on a calm, older mare. Our ride that day would be simply a long walk to let these youngsters take in their surroundings and find their balance under our weight.

The herd congregated near the barn every day around this time. They hoped the wind would scatter the breakfast hay that we carried to the stabled horses. Sometimes the babies were quiet and stayed close to their moms—but not today! The two-year-olds were skittish. And Pistol, a new arrival, stood on the outside looking in. He hadn't made any friends yet.

Pistol, and Mouse, too, left the herd and followed us into the woods. Pistol's coat was thick and dark, but when the sun slipped through the branches, it appeared fuzzier and lighter. He seemed to sense the sun's warmth, and he took a long breath. He followed Bruce's mare, but lazily, each step short and quiet. We were happy to let him plod along in our company. Mouse, on the other hand, seemed to relish the feel of the hard earth beneath him, solid and dependable, and he trotted ahead, wanting to take over the lead. But we had no set path, so Mouse was forced to abandon his position as scout and instead skirt along the side of us, sometimes trotting, sometimes cutting in and out of the line.

Rhiannon was relaxed and smiling.

"These colts are being so good!" she said. "Already carrying us through the woods."

"They do look good," I agreed. Bruce patted his horse and nodded along with our praise.

We had started the youngsters in the round pen. Our third ride was in the larger high-fenced arena where we had turned back the calves for Bruce. On our fifth ride we went out onto the ranchland. And then there was today. We still hadn't put a bit in their mouths— we just rode in hackamores, using opening reins and pressure on their noses and sides to direct them. They still didn't have names as they had been born and bred on the ranch, and there had been no need. We called them, for today, Blaze and Snip, to differentiate the two. They were both chestnut, almost twins.

The horses quickly learned that the mesquite branches bent before and around them, but the thicker oak branches, still covered in brown leaves, were stiff and scraped their sides if they forced their way through. We came to a gully about three feet deep. Most of the gully had steep sides, but in this place it was worn down to a smooth slope by many horses that had crossed at this same point. Still, Rhiannon's mount refused to go on.

Rhiannon got off and led him down the slope, into the gully. Blaze's ears were back. He jigged in, but in the end, allowed her to persuade him. Rhiannon and Blaze left the gully the way they came and entered again. They repeated this four times, until the horse was confident with the exercise. Then Rhiannon mounted, rode through the gully without trouble, and we all continued on.

"Back home, when we started colts, it was always, *SSHHHHH!*" And a finger, like a gun, went to Rhiannon's lips. "We would tip-toe around the horses."

But in Loving, if the horses were scared of a saddle, a cow, or a rope, they were exposed to it again and again, and they learned to not be nervous. Horses are learning all the time, and two of the things they're learning are what to be afraid of and what to safely ignore. A horse in the wild will run when he's scared, but if he is scared of everything he never gets time to eat, or drink, or play. And of course, horse trainers want to influence that—to *change* what the horse reacts to and what he doesn't. We want the horse to listen to our seat, our weight, our hands; to not shy away from playing dogs, swinging ropes, and bison. The key is the progression, every-thing in steps, everything calm and measured and without anger or frustration. The most difficult skill to learn with horses must be this: to not take anything personally.

Bruce and Rhiannon and I talked about the herd—the nature of a group of horses—which is a tough thing and a beautiful thing and something often misunderstood. When one of us walked through Bruce's herd, Pistol nuzzled our arms. Mouse would linger but not allow himself to be touched. Another horse, if cornered, might kick out. I watched. I wondered how a wild herd, with stallions and open land, was different than a domestic herd, with fences, people, and the often constant change of new horses added to the group, and others sold and shipped off.

For a human to enter the herd—even if it was just to become a herd of two, human and horse—he or she must find a niche, form a bond, or take charge. The human who wishes to communicate has two choices: to earn respect or to dictate through fear.

Snip and I wandered to the side, passed through a stand of oaks, and suddenly catapulted ahead. I ducked under a branch and leaned far forward onto the colt's neck. And then he bucked! And again! And again! The others, human and horse, watched, amazed and startled. All the horses' energy was up…up like steam in a kettle.

I loosened the reins and tightened my legs to calm him and urge him forward. Finally, he trotted off, back hunched and stiff-legged. After a minute or so, he swung his legs more easily and lowered his head. He was happier.

The trees thinned out, and we made our way into a large field. Mouse knew the ground well and ran ahead. He had tasted the freedom of wide open space, and he moved faster and faster until he realized he had left us behind. Then he turned. Our young horses were learning to listen to us: We were relieved that they only tensed but didn't move as Mouse galloped past, hoping to incite more play. Pistol, meanwhile, had trotted ahead of us a few steps and now looked back.

"I'm waiting," his eyes said.

To have been around horses for two-and-a-half decades, a big chunk of a lifetime, and to have never been part of a herd before that moment was a shame. Imagine if an alien traveler, capable of reasoning, were to enter a tall, gray office building. It would wander (if it *could* wander) through the long, gray aisles, peering into the cubicles where it would see people with blank eyes staring at blank screens. It might visit the break room and hear voices speaking of sales numbers and office politics. It might go to the loo and see still more walls and dividers and hear people speaking about reality television. Then it would watch the people leave the office and step into another box—this one on wheels—to go home. That reasoning being might then fly to its own home and declare (if it could talk): "I have seen humans. I have met them. I spent time with them. And now I *know* humans."

Last year I thought I knew horses, but I had learned so much at the O'Connors' I had been tempted to say upon leaving, "I did not know much before, but now I *truly* understand horses." Then I had come to this place, seen this herd, observed these horses. And now, I caught myself again thinking, "I must *surely* know horses *now*."

I laughed at myself.

The sun was high in the sky as we arrived back at the barn, each of us not quite ready to call it a day, and so we stood by the gate and talked on.

"Weather's changing," one of us said absently, resting a hand on a saddle horn.

We watched the herd, the foal following its mother, the two-year-olds playing. We observed the fillies, the colts, the innocents, and the jokers.

"Sure is. Wind's coming from the north now."

Finally, our hunger got the best of us. We entered the yard, latched the gate behind us, took the reins over the horses' heads and led them to be unsaddled. We looked back: Pistol waited at the fence, reluctant to leave, but Mouse was already gone.

I could have called that day many things, but truly special times, when spoken of with a friend, sometimes call for understatement.

"Rhiannon, that was a *good* day," I told her.

She smiled and nodded. "A good day," she agreed.

The next week I flew back to Vancouver. To change clothes. It was time to work for a show jumper.

As I left Loving, I wondered if I would ever be back.

CHAPTER 23

It's Easy to Teach Someone to Ride

There is camaraderie amongst travelers. They share stories, meals, secrets, sometimes beds. People met are nostalgically remembered months, years, decades later. On the road, conversations are more interesting; silences are understood and appreciated.

From the window of a train, countries seem more scenic; events are remembered more clearly. The senses, when so sharpened, fill us with wonder of the world we travel. The traveler absorbs, unwittingly, the best and the worst of all he experiences.

One night soon after I had arrived home from Germany, I met an old friend for a drink.

"I need to talk to you," Hilary, a fellow traveler (she was born in England, raised in Singapore, and now lived in Vancouver), had told me earlier that day.

"Well?" I asked her as we slipped onto stools at the bar. Sitting next to her felt safe, like burrowing into a comfy sweater. I leaned back and watched the bartender place our drinks before us.

"Where does 'Tik' come from again?" she asked. Which meant she wasn't ready to talk...yet.

"Thomas Ian Kevin," I reminded her. It was Telf, my older brother, who had dubbed me "Tik." The bar was dark, like a cave, but not too loud to chat. Which we did, until finally she got around to saying what was on her mind.

"I heard about the lessons you gave today," Hilary blurted as I ordered our second round.

"Yeah?" I watched her run her fingers through her tangled hair. I took a long pull of my beer. Sleeman Honey Brown. Her hair and the beer were the same pleasant, unusual hue.

Hilary looked back at me, full in the face, for the first time since I'd picked her up in my parents' car earlier. "You made Miya cry, you know."

I moved my beer around the bar top in front of me. I could feel the condensation from the glass moistening my hands.

"What do you mean?" I asked. "I was *helping* her."

"My God, Tik, she was in tears after! I'm glad you don't 'help' me. What did you do to her?"

How to explain? How to say that I only pushed her because she was so talented, because I saw so much potential?

"I was working on her position. Asking her to keep her hands still, mainly. Shoulders back. Working on transitions."

Hilary took a sip of her drink and looked at me intensely.

"You have to be careful. Miya really looks up to you. You don't want to turn into *that* person."

"*What* person?" I asked, still holding my full beer.

Hilary laughed. "She's sixteen, you know. Riding horses is supposed to be *fun*."

"Riding is dedication and perseverance. Hard work."

"Sure it is." Hilary pushed her almost-empty pint glass to the back of the bar. "Everybody knows it is." She stood up. "I have to visit the loo," she said crisply, and walked away.

When she came back from the restroom, the conversation changed course; we talked about her horse and her plans for the next year. We didn't talk about my lessons again. We didn't need to.

When, a year later, I arrived home again—this time from Texas—I saw the same people, and I taught the same students. Some of them, I hoped, were glad to see me.

"When are you going away again?" Miya asked after her lesson. A lesson I was more confident and patient in giving than the year before. A lesson I tried to make *fun* for her. After working for a professional it was easy to end up riding the way he or she rode, and teaching the way he or she taught. It took much more thought to take the good and leave the bad. I told her I wasn't sure; it depended on where I could find a job.

"*Why* are you going away?" Miya looked down at me from under her helmet, as her horse walked in a small circle.

I paused before answering. All the reasons flashed through my head like pages in a child's flip book. What if I told her I was on a personal journey? What if I explained that I was on a transcendental bus ride that might lead to understanding the "why" of it all? What if I claimed it was not about medals at all? What if I said I was leaving *just because?*

Just because I wanted to.

Marcel Proust once wrote: "We cannot be taught wisdom, we have to discover it for ourselves by a journey which no one can undertake for us, an effort which no one can spare us."

Richard Spooner, the American show jumper, once said: "It is easy to teach someone to ride; it is much harder to teach someone to think."

But I said lamely to Miya: "It's kind of like more school...for riding."

"More school?" She frowned as she fidgeted with the reins.

With jobs, with careers, with school, they sympathize, and they understand right away. But with adventures, people ask *why*.

"This kind of thing is good for your riding résumé," I tried.

She nodded. Her nose twitched as she thought.

"Do you get paid?"

"Not with money."

She looked confused again, and so I added, "No, I don't get paid. But it has other rewards."

A feeling of incompleteness itched my brain, the way my beard itches my throat after a week without shaving. I felt like I was in a temporary state: at home and teaching but wishing I was instead traveling and learning.

I had one final chapter in mind before I would come home for good: to work with a show jumper. I wrote to Brazil's Rodrigo Pessoa, American phenom Beezie Madden, and Canada's Eric Lamaze. No luck. So I looked at other opportunities, too. Maybe Ingrid Klimke needed somebody since she was pregnant? No dice. I emailed eventing super coach Christopher Bartle in England. His secretary wrote back: "Could we have your height, weight, and specific dates that you would be available?"

These were all reasonable questions. When I applied for these working student roles I was often asked for height and weight. Most places wanted to see a video. Surprisingly, I was never asked for references. "Do you want to bring a horse?" was a common query. A couple stables asked if I was single.

"Six feet, 180 pounds, I want to come for three months, and I am flexible with dates," I wrote back. But then the trail went cold. A month later and I still hadn't heard back. What was I left to assume? I needed to move on.

So I decided to reach out to Anne Kursinski. She was a student of the revered "godfather" of American hunter-seat equitation George

Morris. She'd won a few Olympic show jumping medals, too. People told me: "Her riding is impeccable, but she can be tough." I sent her a résumé anyway. She wrote back the very next day.

"Thank you for your email. You sound interesting."

Interesting. That was good.

"Could you send me a video of you riding?" she continued. "At the moment I have enough grooms but could use an extra rider."

I sent her a video.

I waited for her response. I taught lessons. I tried not to make anybody cry.

And I thought about something else Hilary had told me that night, over a year before. As we left the bar her fingers brushed my arm, and I looked down at her.

"Think about what kind of rider you want to be, but also think about what kind of *person* you want to become," she implored.

"Okay," I replied.

What else could I say? She was right.

CHAPTER 24

On Eventing (II)

My hands were in fists, and they were still, steady against my mare's withers. Twelve strides out and I stood up a fraction in my stirrups. My hands came up and the reins went tight. She pulled against the pressure. *Damn it! Pay attention!* Her mouth, her weight, her energy, all pulled firmly forward like a train. Seven strides out and I leaned back against the reins. Her head came up, but she didn't slow down. My knuckles went white. Four strides out and I changed my mind. I let her reach forward again. I urged her on. *Come! On!* Her mouth closed around the bit. I hit her with my stick. *Damn!* My arm swung high, I smacked her again. Two strides left.

Maybe, I thought.

And then we hit the jump.

Her legs collapsed above the knees and whipped back toward her ribs. The impact threw her chest forward and her head down. Her body slid over the brush and the log. Bark and branches grabbed at her stifle. Together, we hit the ground face first.

I had no idea where she was. I stood up as a soldier stands after battle; the happiness of being alive quickly overcome by the shame of not being dead.

I looked around. Was she okay? Oh my God, I hoped she was okay. *Was she okay?*

Sapphire was being led off the course. Someone took my arm and steered me after her. The two-way radios burst with noise. Back and forth they talked. *Are they okay?* they asked. *Are they okay?*

The first time I evented had not been like this. The first time was easy. It was sensual and tactile. I had smelled the wind as it carried the scents of the Pacific Ocean over Vancouver Island. I saw the light shining through bowed maple leaves and dappling the mossy earth into a thousand hues of green and brown. My mare's stride had been rhythmic and perfect, like a long-distance runner's.

I'd seen a rainbow in our wake through the water. I'd sensed a gull at our wings on the hills.

Of course there had been no rainbow! And there was no Jonathan Livingston Seagull escorting us either! There was only my beatific memory of them. Why was this time so different? Why couldn't every time be like that first time? I remembered that first event the way a middle-aged parent daydreams of the summers of his school years.

But this time was no easy gallop in the clouds. This time, coming down to that last jump, it was RAT-TAT-TAT-TAT. Sapphire's legs moved in the uneven staccato of a Gatling gun. RAT-TAT. There was no dance that day—we were trying too hard! RAT-TAT-TAT. No ocean breezes filled my senses. No spotlight lit our path. There was only courage and shame and love and guilt spilled at that last fence.

After slipping under the ropes of the cross-country course, we were led to a trailer and a truck. As one my mare and I kept our eyes down and followed instructions. She was loaded in back; I was loaded into the cab. The door shut limply after me. The loudspeakers marked the continuation of the day; our fall meant only a pause in the competition's schedule.

The driver of the truck didn't try to talk to me. My head felt heavy against the seat. My wrist hurt. I shut my eyes and remembered the first time I had gone to a big event as a spectator, how I had over-heard a woman say how ridiculous she found the whole sport.

"But it hasn't even started yet," I said to her.

She lifted her hands, gesturing a question.

"I've seen too many accidents. It gets harder and harder to come to these. I've seen horses die," she replied.

"You're exaggerating," I told her.

The woman blinked. I noticed her eyes suddenly: pale and lucid.

"At least these horses are doing something they love," she went on. "Any horse that makes it this far believes in what he is doing. Really there is nothing like it! His ears go up, they're glued to the jump, and the horse never lets go. I don't know how they do it. Gives me goosebumps just talking about it."

"I still think you are exaggerating."

The woman wore ripped jeans, and she put her hands in her back pockets. She answered me finally: "I hope I'm exaggerating. And I hope we are improving this industry and not just condoning it. Because this sport is worth it."

I nodded. I got that she both loved and feared the sport.

Months later at the Kentucky Three-Day I watched thirty or forty horses gallop around that great American course. My Boy Bobby, Buck Davidson's Irish Sport Horse, was the first I saw at the famous Head of the Lake—which combines drops, jumps, and water. The skies parted and Bobby flowed into our lives from above. He galloped between the clouds, then the crowds, then through the water.

The crowd, sometimes five deep, pushed against the ropes that kept us off the course. We wanted more.

And then, in the afternoon of that day, King Pin, a horse from the Canadian Eventing Team, took a fall and never got up. The authorities declared a death of natural causes:

It appears that it was not associated with the fence itself. It's possible that it may be determined as a rupture of a large blood vessel, which isn't unheard of in human and equine athletes.

There was a pause in the scheduling that day in Kentucky while we sorted our souls. We all knew that not every round is sunny skies at the lake. It was sometimes gray clouds and thunder.

As we drove back to the stables after our fall at the last fence, the vet and I worried. I knew back in the trailer my mare was standing square, every brake of the vehicle a jerk she absorbed in her legs. Every bump rattled the trailer. I could feel it through my body. I wished I had stayed back there with her.

Sapphire came off the trailer easily and the veterinarian took her time going over her. She looked at the mare's legs and stifles. She checked her lungs and heart.

"The cuts are pretty superficial," the vet told me. "You're lucky."

"Thanks," I said. But I didn't feel lucky at all.

Back in her stall Sapphire lowered her head and took a deep breath. I gave her some hay. By myself with her, finally, I put my hand on her shoulder.

"I'm sorry," I told her. "I'm sorry."

I laid my forehead against her withers.

"I'm so sorry."

My mare sniffed at the hay. She was hungry. I watched her start to eat.

CHAPTER 25

"She's Tough"

There is an old saying: "There are two secrets to be successful in this business. The first: Don't give away all your secrets." Some masters guard their methods like a bag of cash.

Anne Kursinski was not one of those people. *Anne Kursinski's Riding and Jumping Clinic: A Step-by-Step Course for Winning in the Hunter and Jumper Rings* details, in sometimes beautiful prose, every aspect of riding a jumping horse that one could reasonably expect to be included in a book. She had studied widely, and her writing reflected that.

She instructed on the basics. On mounting:

As you swing your right leg down, feel for the right stirrup and lower your seat gently into the saddle—don't just flop onto his back like a sack of potatoes.

She commented on flatwork. On the feeling she gets when riding on the bit:

I like to think of it as a little like plumping feathers in a pillow: your legs are almost tickling your horse, making him straight and forward and more animated; your seat is pushing a little, accentuating the natural motion of his back in the stride, telling him he's got to be more active from behind; but your hand is saying, "I don't want you to go faster, even though I'm asking for impulsion. I want you to let my hands package that impulsion, contain it, while you stay light and lively."

And finally, on jumping theory:

Your goal is to accompany him, not interfere with him. The great hunter and jumper riders appear to be at one with their horses—almost centaur-like—because they've mastered the art of noninterference. You want to master it, too.

I do! I thought, as I read through her book. I do!

I got a phone call from Anne Kursinski late in the afternoon. My riding was done for the day, and I was helping my mother prune blueberry bushes—"It will just take five minutes," Mother had told me.

"Sure it will," I had replied with a knowing laugh.

"Thanks for sending the video," Anne said. "Why don't you come down right away?"

She seemed nice and talkative, and strangely interested in my desire to be a working student.

"We could use you," she explained. "I'll need some help with the horses in Florida, and I think you could learn a lot, too."

She asked me what I had done with horses, what I wanted to do in the future, how long I could come for. And she answered all my questions as well.

How was this approachable woman an elite professional, a busy horsewoman, an author, a trainer? Where were the secretaries? The assistants? Where were the airs?

There were, of course, rumors about Anne.

"She's tough," people said, "*reeeeaal* tough," with a nod of the head and raised eyebrows, as if to then say, "I'm glad it's you going and not me."

But when I asked these people what they meant by "tough," they had no answer. "Long hours," they said, or "She's detail-oriented," or "High standards."

"Great!" was my grinning response.

No one faulted her riding, which was seemingly above reproach.

While looking for a good show jumping barn to be my next destination, my dad and I had a long conversation about what it means to be a "great jumper rider."

"It seems like there are only two ingredients necessary to compete at the highest level," I stated.

"What's that?" he asked.

"An eye for a distance. And money."

He laughed.

"I guess so. And maybe a bit of training and athleticism thrown in. But what separates the competitors from the winners?"

"That is a good question." I pondered it. "What was it George Morris said? Ambition. Emotional control. Management. Selection. Talent."

"What about training? Having a good coach?" Dad pressed.

Most people can write a sentence. Does that mean we are all writers? Lots of people can sit on top of a horse. Does that mean we are all riders? What separated the flash-in-the-pan authors from the Orwells and the Atwoods? In what way did Anne Kursinski rise above the rest?

My guess was what other people told me: She was detail-oriented and had high standards. Her horsemanship and flatwork were great.

And then there was toughness. *Real* toughness. No question about that.

But was there something more? Was there some secret, some alchemy that the masters of equestrianism practiced behind closed doors and curtains of smoke, like the sorcerers of old?

Before I committed to going, I asked Anne one more question: "Is it okay if I write about my time with you?"

When *Gaitpost* stopped publishing my articles, I'd approached *The Chronicle of the Horse* with a query. The *Chronicle* was based in Middleburg, Virginia, and was one of the oldest, most prestigious equestrian magazines in the world. A classy horsey magazine, in a classy horsey town. The reply from the editor had been favorable:

We're launching a new website at the beginning of November, and I'm working on gathering up bloggers and columnists. I ended up reading all of the articles you'd written on your experience of being a working student, and I really enjoyed them.

Anne did not hesitate before saying, "That's a great idea."

I smiled on the other end of the phone.

"I'd like to take a look first," she continued, "but horses, and the horse community, have given me so much, and I love giving back."

What more could I ask for?

"I'll book a flight today," I told her. I held the phone next to my ear while the connection clicked off.

Florida again, I thought. One last trip.

And then I'll be done.

CHAPTER 26

Wellington, Florida

A few days after arriving in Florida, Anne let me have a day off to watch a George Morris clinic. I couldn't get the grin off my face as I put my broom down and practically bolted over to the show grounds where I found a place in the stands to watch.

As a younger man George Morris was a winning show jumper, and he was competitive, but his greater legacy was as a trainer of riders. He was so successful and so unique as a coach that he was as recognizable and awe-inspiring to me as Robert Redford would be to an aspiring actor.

The man was still as he sat in his golf cart. His body looked sinewy, but also old, like an elastic band that was drying up. His very distinct voice, however, as it came over the loudspeakers, was strong.

"WHERE DID THEY GO?" he demanded.

The crowd looked around. The teenagers George Morris was seeking had been absorbed into the grandstand. They were acting as jump crew, and they had obviously, mistakenly, believed the session over.

"WHERE ARE THEY?" His voice was louder now, not angry, but accusatory and demanding. "I TOLD THEM NOT TO LEAVE."

Everybody was still and silent.

I watched as the kids separated themselves from the crowd, urged forward by their parents, but not eager to be the center of this man's attention. They left their families reluctantly, walking slowly down the steps to the ring.

"Hurry!" George's voice bellowed over the loudspeakers and settled slowly over the stands. "HURRY!"

We all watched as one by one the kids broke into a run. As the first kid, a boy, got to the golf cart, he slowed down and paused beside George. It looked like he was trying to explain himself, but the other kids ran right on by, heading out to the jumps.

Then, we could hear over the loudspeakers: "*Don't* think. *Don't* THINK!"

The boy who had stopped turned red, a crimson I could see from 300 feet away.

"*I'm* here to think!" the man declared, looking out at the crowd and seeing that he really had its attention now.

"In a few years, you can think," he finished, motioning the boy away with a small wave of his hand. "IN A FEW YEARS, you can think!"

George Morris is known for saying exactly what's on his mind.

They were schooling the water jump, and he had the riders all in a light seat.

When one boy couldn't quite get it right, George—seventy if he was a day—got on his horse.

"The *modern* way of riding," George said as he cantered down to a jump and over it. "It's simple. See?" His breathing came clearly over the loudspeakers as he cantered around to jump it again. "Simple." More heavy breathing. "SIMPLE. You can't knock it down!" And then as he approached the jump he let the reins loosen a little, lowered his hands, but maintained his pace. "See?"

There were three components to a water jump, I learned: "Pace, distance, and tape." A horse needs a good pace coming in; the rider needs to see a good distance and then ride past it, getting in close to the base; and finally, the pair need to jump the tape. Keep riding! Like a sprinter hurling his chest forward, there should be no letting up until the finish line.

The next horse to try didn't quite clear the obstacle. There was a small splash as his hind legs dipped into the water.

George called out into the stands: "Com'ere, Frank. Give me a hand."

Frank Madden, an established trainer in his own right, stood up. He had been sitting in the front row. I recognized him from Animal Planet's reality television show about a group of teenage riders, *Horse Power: The Road to the Maclay*. As a younger man, he had also learned from George. I'd read a *Horse Connection Magazine* interview where Frank explained:

> *George Morris was a huge influence. I rode for him for eight or nine years. I'll never forget the time I heard George say to a kid, "I'll forget more than you'll ever know." I was an impressionable twenty-one-year-old and when I heard that it just rocked me back on my heels. I couldn't imagine anyone saying that to me and I would never say that to someone, but now that I'm older, I sure understand what he meant. It's not an egotistical statement—it's reality.*

George and Frank stood on either side of the water jump, about two-thirds of the way down. A water jump is wide, maybe ten feet, so horses need to learn to jump *across* them, like a long jump, not *up* and over like most jumps. Both men were bent at the waist, arms straight. Each one held one end of a blue-and-white rail. The same horse cantered down to the water, his last few strides longer and faster. The horse jumped, then stretched. He seemed suspended for a second as the pole was lifted by the men holding it. The horse hit it, and the two men immediately dropped the pole. It fell and splashed.

George looked out at the crowd. He knew full well what he had just done was not allowed at horse shows and that few professionals would speak in public about it.

"Rapping..."

I couldn't wait to hear what he would say.

"...done carefully..."

This could be a very touchy topic.

"...makes a safer jumper."

And with that, the lesson was over, the subject closed for discussion. The kids manning the jumps were dismissed, and the crowd in the stands dispersed.

"That was sort of anti-climactic," a skinny girl a row ahead of me whispered to her friend.

"Yeah," her friend agreed.

In order to understand Anne Kursinski, in order to understand her style, it helped to first see George Morris in action. The two biggest equestrian influences in Anne's life were Jimmy Williams and George Morris. Jimmy Williams was a California horseman I wished I'd had the chance to meet. He was known as an innovator, especially difficult in a world of tradition. And George was Anne's mentor at the famed Hunterdon Farm for seventeen years (and in many ways he still was). Whenever Anne had competed for her country, he had been there, ready to help. He was the one on the ground, or in the golf cart, shouting directions, or offering advice. (Anne had also competed up to Grand Prix in dressage under Olympic-medal-winner Hilda Gurney. Although Anne was a show jumper, she had seen, and done, a lot.)

Over time Anne developed her own style, but she stayed true to many of George's philosophies. Like George, she was a perfectionist and a hard worker, and she expected the same out of everybody she worked with. And, like George, she was honest and outspoken, *but* nothing she said was personal. She was quick to forgive and forget. She didn't like whining. She didn't like excuses.

The next day I again walked from Anne's farm, along the canal, over to the show grounds, to watch the clinic. It was equitation day: Flatwork with no stirrups. Lower leg position. Leg yielding. Upper body position. Soft hands. It was a tough lesson; they were going to learn whether they liked it or not. And it was raining, almost pelting down. The crowd was only half as strong as the day before. Those who were there were huddled up under horse blankets or umbrellas.

The riders used most of the ring—a large oval. As they did walk-trot transitions, George warmed up his voice: "Jumping is not dressage," he declared. "It's more like racing."

And then he corrected himself: "Actually, it's fifty-fifty."

George watched the transitions before him. "The great masters of old called impulsion the 'mother of equitation.'"

He wanted to see more engagement, more from the horse's hindquarters. A horse had to be worked from the hind legs. "Everything comes from the hind legs!"

"A horse is built like a bridge," George said. "Just like the Brooklyn Bridge, which my great-great grandfather helped build."

The point he was making was that the foundation of movement in the horse was key. And the hindquarters were the foundation. "Most horses," he said, "have back problems, and it's not their fault. Most riders don't know how to work a horse. They *think* they know how to work a horse."

The clinic was almost non-stop talking. He lectured like a fine university professor: without notes and on a variety of subjects, sometimes flowing, sometimes flying, from one topic to the next.

And all the time he eyed his students. He didn't miss a thing.

Not a *thing!*

"Don't *ever* let me see you saw your horse's mouth!" he shouted, but this time the rain dampened the effect of his words, beating them into the ground. The crowd was subdued, and a few people left early. But I was happy to stay and watch. I hoped to see George ride again.

Great riders like Anne and George make the sport look easy. But they also know how much work goes into getting there. Anne has had George yell at her. And Anne has yelled at me.

If we are never taken out of our comfort zone, we never learn.

After yelling for the fourth time (or maybe fifth) at the same rider, George admitted, "I recognize these things cause I did 'em. Those faults...I had 'em."

No one is born a rider. It comes easier to some, through money, coaching, or raw talent, but no one is born a rider.

Next George had the riders practice flying changes. They flew across the arena, some slowing, others speeding up, as they tried to switch canter leads smoothly, in stride.

"It's disgraceful how horses make flying changes at these shows: bucking, tail swishing, pulling!" George ranted. He paused, and his breathing could be heard, even above the rain. "That's *not* permitted in my horse!"

Each horse tried one more change, and each one was better, and then George asked the riders to walk. Before they were even out of the trot he was yelling again: "It's legs!" His students were walking now, but George was still going strong: "It's legs. LEGS! It is not about *hands* so much as *legs!*" He wanted the horses to slow down *and* stay in front of the leg, not an easy concept for those new to riding.

Finally, he dismissed the riders, and as they filed out, tired and wet, the jump crew handed each student a cooler for his or her horse.

George looked out at the crowd. He had a few final thoughts to share, and he delivered them eloquently, like the patriarch of the sport that he was.

"It's not about the social accessories, the money, the ribbons. It's not about the winning. That comes easy." He got out of his golf cart and picked up his helmet from the back. "No, that comes easy." He walked a step toward the crowd. "It's about the horse: how to care for the horse, how to ride the horse, and how to look after this great animal—the horse."

He stood there in the rain, which puddled and splashed around him. If somebody had not known his greatness they would have simply seen a man, by himself, wet, and old, in a big ring on a gray day. The crowd seemed anxious around me, ready to leave, but I sat there for a minute, absorbing all that I'd heard. And in that minute, I got to hear this man's *actual* final words. An organizer approached him, motioning to take his headset, and I could hear her thank him for his time. I only caught a few words, quiet as the microphone was transferred from one to the other: "...were great...always a good..."

And then George's last words, as he fumbled with his headset, drifted through the rain to where I sat, almost alone in the grandstand: "My typical obnoxious self, you mean? Which I enjoy being. Difficult." And he laughed a small laugh. "If I'm not being difficult, I'm not breathing."

In that laugh and in those last words it was possible I glimpsed more of that great man than most people ever did. I saw the awareness he had of his own powerful, fastidious, and often rude character. And beneath all that I saw an unpretentious, kind visionary. A private man. Someone I would consider a Great Horseman (capitals, I think, needed).

And then, I thought, since I had seen George teach and heard him speak, maybe I was a little closer to understanding Anne, the woman who became one of his greatest students, and the woman from whom I would spend the next three months learning.

Back at Anne's barn I picked up a broom. It felt familiar and strong in my hands. Here, too, it was about the care, the thought that went into the horse-and-rider partnership. It was about the details. When Anne traveled to shows, she took two boxes of spare bits, probably 200 bits in total. Like some women and shoes, she had one for every occasion; some had been used once, and some would never get their chance. She had a box of spare tack that traveled with her, as well. It was full of nosebands, browbands, reins, cheekpieces and bitless bridles. (But like Ingrid, not a single pair of draw-reins.)

There were no shortcuts. Everything was in the details.

I was on the board to ride two horses that day, but for a while I just continued sweeping the aisle.

CHAPTER 27

Anne Kursinski's Secrets

There were days when, like a butler, I just followed Anne around. I faded into the background. I was quiet, but ready to leap forward and hold a horse or raise a jump at a moment's notice. I knew how Anne wanted her saddle set, how tight her horse's noseband should be, and how she expected to be given a leg up. (Not on "1, 2, 3," but *now!*)

I also saw how she rode and how she coached. I observed her making deals, and I saw who the players were. It's a small circle at the top of the sport. Everybody knows everybody. Everybody has something to say about somebody. Horses worth hundreds of thousands of dollars are bought and sold every day. (Sometimes, I got to ride those horses!)

On my twelfth day working for Anne I stood a canter stride away from her as she ran into an old friend at a horse show. We were at the in-gate, ready to walk her course (sometimes, I got to walk her courses with her!), when a curly-haired woman touched Anne's arm.

"Anne? Is that you?"

It took Anne a second, then: "Milly?" followed by, "*Milly!* How are you?"

I don't remember what they talked about. Vacations, I think. I was watching show jumping superstar McLain Ward walk the course. He was much smaller than I expected, the way celebrities always look when stripped of their catwalks and upward angled cameras. I watched him walk a line away from me, a short four strides. Fifty-seven feet. He had a confident walk, his shoulder blades pushed together. Was he the same man on the ground that he was on a horse?

"...and how's your horse?" I heard Anne ask Milly.

"*Ooh,* Anne," the woman declared, drawing the *oh* out, but speaking quickly as well, each word tripping over the next, "he is doing *soooo* well."

Anne put her hand on the back of Milly's arm, inviting her to say more.

"It's been so great since we talked to our animal communicator. You have one, don't you? They're the best! Mine told me my gelding is Hawaiian. Can you believe it? And she said I must change his name. So, I did. And now he's called Ki-Ki."

Anne nodded from beneath her helmet. "A sweet name."

"And now he is *soooo* well behaved," she said as she took Anne's hand in hers. "I just *can't* believe it."

"I know, Milly. Marlene has helped us so much with our horses."

I looked at the two of them, both wearing fitted navy jackets, discussing with all seriousness how some woman, whom they'd talked to on the phone, and who hadn't ever even seen their horses, knew what their horses were thinking or feeling.

Wow! I thought. I'm working for a crazy person.

Sometimes a groom was invited to join such ring-side conversations. When that happened, I would step forward and introduce myself. I would shake hands, look the guest in the eye (best if it was a quick look), then step back again. Sometimes I would be asked to answer a question or to give my opinion on something. It was preferable to be brief and neutral.

When Anne jumped, or taught a lesson, she always tried to have at least one person on hand to act as jump crew. Two was better and sped up the process quite a bit. But later that day Anne was helping an older rider with his young Warmblood, and I was the only one there to help. Three times in a row he held the horse back and then rushed the fence, squeezing and kicking, trying to "throw" the horse over.

"Relax," Anne kept saying. "Don't rush at it!"

Finally, Anne stopped him, calling him over. She looked at me.

"Tik," she said, "when you saw me ride this morning, how did I ride this course?"

Well, she sure didn't ride like that.

"Relaxed," I guessed.

"I rode it loose," she told me, nodding. Then she looked at her student. "Loosen up! Ride it with a little feeling!"

Anne believed she could teach "feeling." Feeling, like art, is with our soul, while skill is with our head. It is not just the mechanics of what we do in the saddle, it is our intention, as well. Sometimes it had to seem like she was teaching the unteachable. And sometimes she did get frustrated, but she never gave up.

In her book, there were thirty-eight pages that were referenced for feeling. Bending and feeling. Hands and feeling. Life and feeling.

Some people claim you cannot teach feeling, saying: "How can you tell somebody what a strawberry tastes like?"

"Do I have feeling?" you might ask.

Try this exercise: Go down the centerline and alternate between shoulder-in and half-pass.

The aids (inside leg on the girth, outside leg back, riding into the outside rein) are the same for both movements. The only thing that changes is the *relative pressure* of the aids. It is only the *feeling* that changes.

I actually disagreed with Anne. I believed one could learn feeling but that it could not be taught. An instructor could teach *craft* but could only hope to inspire *art*. Make no mistake, great riders transform riding into an art. A great rider shows off her horses in much the same way a sculptor mounts an exhibition. The artist creates, molds, and coaches the piece into being, but in the final analysis, the final test, it is the horse that matters. It is the horse that draws the eye.

Watching a great ride, in dressage, or jumping, or cutting, or whatever discipline, the viewer is left full and sated but unable to judge or criticize. The viewer finds she has been brought *into* the performance, and instead of a critique or comment coming to her lips, she is left with only the welling up of an emotion—of delight, or contentment, or glee, or excitement. She is left with feeling.

Anne would sometimes ask her students, "Do you feel that?" when they did something right.

And Anne would also talk to her horses and ask them how they felt. The more she liked a horse, the more she talked to him.

It was a certain kind of horse that Anne appreciated.

When Spitfire arrived at the barn we were excited; we watched, unseen, from the dark windows of the barn as Anne rode. Afterward Anne slipped off the gelding and bounced back into the stable.

"A nice horse," she said to me as she went by, smiling to herself.

The horse that Anne liked was a confident, cooperative, forward-going horse. Light, relaxed, and athletic in mind and body. "The modern horse," she called it.

It used to be that rails were wide and heavy, cups were deep, turns were wide, and jump-offs were decided by analog stopwatches rather than thousandths of a second. Today's show jumper needed to be light on his feet and supple in the back. Anne jumped her horses in an almost perpetual half-seat, always allowing the horses the freedom to use their bodies and go forward.

"Sitting down in the saddle shouldn't be needed to collect a horse. Instead, sitting down should be a driving aid and used rarely," she proclaimed.

The modern horse went with the modern way of riding and the modern athlete: forward and fast and confident. No heavy horses and no heavy hands.

"I like his type," Anne would often say, nodding at a light Warmblood or Thoroughbred. "A nice type."

One sunny day while riding with Anne I asked if she still felt, at the start of every season, as though she knew a lot more than she had the previous year. I told her: "I'm embarrassed to think of how I rode a year ago. The amount I've learned is incredible. When I left for Germany I thought I knew how to ride…but I didn't."

She looked at me. She waited.

"Probably still don't," I admitted.

She gave her horse a rub on the neck. "It will always be like that," she said.

We walked on in silence. I saw a snowy egret land in the canal. Wellington Village was once all swampland, and the displaced birds made do with a series of heavily managed canals.

"You know," Anne said finally, looking at me, "these eyes I have. They are the same eyes I had when I was twenty, but they sure see things differently now."

She gathered her reins and made to trot off, but then changed her mind, settled back in the saddle, and turned to me.

"There are so many things I learn every year. And you'll see some of these things for yourself if you stay with us. Like Marlene, our animal communicator. It's taken my relationship with my horses to another level."

I looked at her, trying to keep a poker face.

"Maybe you think I'm crazy," she said.

Suddenly, from the canal, a grumpy looking wood stork surprised us. The horses startled but then settled quickly. I watched the big bird fly off, its feet outstretched and trailing behind, then looked back at Anne. Anne, with her firm, but relaxed, lower leg; her seat that moved as one with the horses back; her hands that moved often, but always with the horse, smoothly, even on a loose rein, never against the horse; Anne who looked good on a horse, even just walking.

"No!" I declared. "No. Of course not."

When I set off to work for Anne I wondered what secrets she might share, what alchemy she might reveal. What I actually found could be broken into two categories.

First: She did what everybody else did—except she did it better. She worked with the best vets, the best farriers, the best animal communicators. She had no secrets in her tack trunk or in her feed room.

All her methods could be bought for twenty-six dollars at the bookstore. But you still had to wake up pretty early to do it better than Anne.

Second: She consciously developed feeling in herself, and with her horse, to an almost unbelievable extent. If a horse had a sore back, she would have a sore back. If her stomach hurt, one of her horses probably had ulcers. She wanted to know how each horse felt, and she wanted to feel it in her own body. She also wanted *them* to know what *they* felt in their bodies. One idea that Anne used, made popular by animal behaviorist Linda Tellington-Jones, was to tie two tensor bandages in a figure eight around a horse's body. The theory was the bandages made the horse more aware of where his body was in space and how he moved. Imagine you were walking down the street and someone tied a string around your thigh. Suddenly you would be aware of your leg. You would feel the string tighten against the muscles as you lifted and extended your foot. Then, as you put your foot down, the string would go loose and flap against your knee. You would now be aware of how your leg was moving.

Anne also wanted to know what her horse was feeling in his mind. Was he nervous? Maybe he was excited or scared? She wanted to know how she could fix it or in some cases use it to her advantage.

In her book, Anne wrote:

I have learned that your horse will teach you almost all you need to know, if you will only listen to him and allow him to educate you.

Anne picked up the reins smoothly, like a dancer, preparing to trot off again.

"You are definitely not insane," I said, watching her.

"Thanks," she replied, looking back at me with a bit of a glint in her eye…not unlike that of a crazy person.

CHAPTER 28

Asa Bird

Almost every barn I've visited claims they don't have a hierarchy amongst the workers. "We *all* do stalls together in the morning," so many managers have told me, magnanimously.

The managers, I've found, are always wrong.

In every stable a pecking order emerges after only a couple days of study. At Market Street, Anne Kursinski's stable, Anne and her partner Carol Hoffman ("Hoffy") were the bosses, but Asa Bird—it was more fun to call him by his full name, *Asa Bird,* the three syllables somersaulting off the tongue—was the first mate.

Asa Bird was the son of a Pennsylvanian mushroom farmer. He was a high-school wrestler: six feet, 220 pounds. He had lost forty pounds since then, but he still walked with the swagger of the bigger man he once was. At Market Street it didn't matter if someone else had the title of manager or rider or assistant trainer, Asa was the go-to guy.

My theory was that this happened for one simple reason: Asa Bird was a hard worker.

Make that two reasons: He was a *smart,* hard worker.

And because he was such a good worker, and because he had been with Anne for a number of years, he had earned and inherited many responsibilities.

Asa administered the medicines. He packed for shows and looked after the top horses. (Somewhere along the way, when working at stables like Anne's, you could forget that one, just *one* of the horses there, might be worth more than most people made in their entire lives.) Asa did the ultrasound and infrared and made decisions about when horses should be turned out or have blankets put on. Asa was in charge when Anne and Hoffy weren't around, and that was a lot of responsibility.

I only saw Asa crack once; only saw him really well up, about to stomp and shout and yell and swear, *just once*.

It probably wouldn't have happened if we hadn't gone out to Players the night before.

In Wellington, everything that didn't happen at the show grounds happened at the Players Club. A night out always started with a nap after work. It hardly seemed like I had fallen asleep when Liz, a new groom, whom we affectionately called "Skinny Jeans," came and woke me up.

"What?" I asked groggily. "A bit more…it's still early."

"You're not really tired. You're just tired 'cause you just went to sleep."

Her reasoning was often like that: logical in a way. And then she stood in my doorway and started to rap my name:

"*Tik*-tock on the clock! DJ, blow my speakers up!" Liz went on with the song. She knew all the lyrics. She snapped her fingers in rhythm, and grinned. Then she stopped and pouted, "*Tik*-tock. Plee-aaase. Let's go!"

At Players it was all about who you knew. Liz looked around while we waited in line. She occasionally pointed people out: "That's so-and-so, who is riding for such-and-such."

And, "Look at *her*. I can't believe she's here, she's grooming for whatshisIrishface."

And, "Look at her skirt. My *God.*"

The night started off slowly, with sangria, but finished full of thunder, full of sweat and Red Bull and vodka. At three in the morning, we fell into our separate beds. I wasn't sure I would sleep with the ringing in my ears, but the linen felt clean and fresh, although I knew it wasn't. The next sound I heard was my alarm. It was 5:30 a.m. Still dark outside.

Our work week averaged more than seventy hours, so most nights we were in bed by nine. Even so, mornings could be tough. Tiredness had a way of creeping up on me, and I wouldn't even realize it until I found I couldn't remember what I had been doing for the past hour. Going out to Players was a risky move. One that I instantly regretted the next morning as I was cleaning stalls. I had my head down, and I was mucking quickly and efficiently, trying to find a rhythm.

Working in a horse barn is not often physically tiring, nor does it require constant intellectual gymnastics. Rather it is about stamina. It is an exercise in patience and vigilance. I relate to the outfielder that has to be ready every pitch but seldom has the ball come his way.

With enough sleep that thoughtfulness is not a problem. But tiredness and negligence are like father and daughter: one begets the other. It is the overworked, under-slept working student who makes mistakes.

I didn't notice when two horses were taken out to the paddock by two new grooms. If I *had* been paying attention, I would have seen that those two horses should not go out together. They were two very expensive horses that would canter and kick and most likely injure themselves when out together. I should have seen the ball soaring out to right field.

It was Asa who realized the mistake. Asa, who already had two horses he was preparing for a show, and another horse to ultrasound.

And I was just doing stalls. It was Asa who dropped everything and was suddenly running to stop the grooms from making an imminent and most definitely costly mistake. Then he was leading one horse back into the barn, a stomp already appearing in his step. Seeing me, he shouted.

"You gotta help me out, man!"

He stood there in the middle of the aisle, the big horse a step behind him, and informed me I had to think more. He told me that he couldn't do everything. He said that Anne needed the two of us to take leadership roles. That I had to start taking on more responsibility.

"Man up!" he shouted. "Man the fuck up. You're tired? We're *all* tired. I know how it is, twelve weeks of showing. But I need you *here. Now!*"

And when I stood there and didn't say a thing, he turned his back on me and led the horse to his stall.

I went back to mucking. I worried. Was I really meant to do this job? In the last several weeks, two grooms had already quit or been fired. They left without much worry; there were other jobs out there, and lots easier than here.

The horses, of course, didn't have a choice; through fate or chance they were there to work for us. But us? We had a choice. I could decide where I wanted to work. I could leave if I wanted to. I had to decide if it was worth it. And I would have to tell Asa, I thought, watching him slip the halter off the horse and walk by me, not meeting my eye.

CHAPTER 29

A Horseman's Pledge

I walked into the kitchen that evening prepared to apologize, but it was not the right time. Besides Asa Bird, Skinny Jeans, and myself, there were two other grooms, and we all lived in a rented house together. A typical Wellington house: one story, neighboring a canal, built in the last twenty years. Off-white walls inside. Green palms and green grass outside, even in February. It wasn't until a few days later that Asa and I got a chance to talk. It was not a good feeling that I carried in my stomach.

Asa and Liz had the television on in the living room, which was connected to the kitchen by an open doorway. They were watching some reality show, which took place in Mexico, and I could hear the program being narrated in Spanish. Neither Asa nor Liz spoke Spanish. Nor did I.

Asa didn't look up as I came in.

"Hey, what's on?" I asked.

"Nothing, man. Nothing. But check this out!" He didn't take his eyes off the screen.

He was slouched on the couch, with a dented beer can on the floor between his feet. His right sleeve was wrinkled upward, and I could see the start of his tattoo, which I knew was a colorful jester, but he didn't show it off much.

"Asa, man, the other day..." I started. I wondered what I could say to make it all right again.

"Yeah. Don't worry about it. Things have been pretty intense lately."

I knew Anne and Hoffy thought things were going smoothly, which in a way was unjust, considering all the hard work Asa put in. But the simple truth was that the less stress *they* felt in their jobs, the better Asa was doing his. And he took pride in a job well done in the same unassuming way Boxer the Horse was proud of his work in Orwell's *Animal Farm*. I knew he was doing a good job. So I told him that.

"Thanks, man."

And that was it. Things were okay between us. No hard feelings. Just like that. Thanks, Asa Bird, I thought. I looked at the TV. A girl with large hoop earrings was crying. There would always be plenty more drama.

The drama in the Village of Wellington could seep into a person, eroding all peace and common sense if you were not careful. Village life was straight out of a Jilly Cooper novel: drugs, sex, money, high stakes, competition, rivalry, and gossip that spread faster than panic in a herd. Wellington was not actually a village under any normal definition, but it was still known officially as "The Village of Wellington." In the fifties it was developed from swampland into the world's largest strawberry patch by Charles Wellington, then it became a sprawling bedroom community in the seventies, and was now, from January to March, the premiere destination for show jumpers, and their owners and sponsors, from around the world.

In the face of massive consumption, expensive horses, long hours, and parties that didn't end 'til Tuesday, I was not surprised that everyone there was desperate to be somewhere, to know someone, to *be* someone. I looked at Asa Bird, already asleep with the TV still on, and Liz in a new little black dress, ready to meet a friend for dinner. Liz, who wished every day she was riding instead of grooming. She knew it was hard not to *want* in Wellington. It was hard to see the million-dollar horses and elite riders and be happy with what you had.

Liz stood up.

"How's my dress look?"

"It's pretty short, isn't it?" I answered.

"Yeah."

"I like it."

"Really?" she said, smoothing the fabric against her thigh. She stood straight up, her cheeks were rosy, and her dark hair fell just past her shoulders. "Really?" she asked again, looking at me with big fawn-like eyes.

"Really." She wasn't sure, I knew, so I told her again, "It's great, it suits you. You look hot."

She smiled and twirled. "Thanks, Tik."

Liz was not staying beyond the end of the Florida circuit. She had decided she was needed at home. More to the point, she argued, she would get to ride.

"And I'll come back," she promised.

Employers claimed it was hard to keep their staff, that no one was willing to work hard anymore. On Anne's bulletin board there was a sign with a quote that bore some resemblance to words once uttered by William Makepeace Thackeray: "Whatever you do, do it well." It doesn't matter if you are a groom, or a Grand Prix show jumper, or a president, Anne told me, *do it well!*

Grooms whined that there weren't any good jobs. That there were no benefits, only long hours with little reward in being behind the scenes. I recognized that it takes a special kind of person to become a lifelong groom. And it was rarer still to see a groom work his or her way up to become a rider, trainer, or all-around horseman.

On more than one occasion I'd been told that the horseman was a dying breed. And that was when I looked around and saw more people and more horses and more money changing hands than I'd ever seen in my life. Maybe Liz would be better off riding at home. It was not an easy road in Wellington. But then again, it wasn't easy anywhere.

I watched Skinny Jeans pack up her purse, quickly apply lipstick, wink at me, and head out the door. "…when I leave for the night, I ain't comin' back," she sang.

I looked at Asa Bird after she left.

"You awake, man?"

"Yeah," he said, without opening his eyes.

"Did I tell you who I talked to today?" And I named a very famous trainer, one who sells a lot of horses, and whose horses win a lot of classes.

"You don't need to listen to him," Asa said, opening one eye.

"Yeah," I agreed, staring at people on the television in front of me. I went on, "It was by the Mogavero Ring this morning. Before the first class. I asked him what he liked about his sport."

Asa Bird didn't say anything, so I stopped talking and just stood there, remembering. It had been a quiet morning. And the trainer, who had the seed of a paunch appearing above his freshly creased jeans, took me aside with a hand on my shoulder.

"Tik," he started, "let me tell you how it is."

"Tell me," Asa Bird said now, interrupting my thoughts.

I sat in a chair next to the couch and tried my best to remember.

"He said: 'I've been in this business for thirty-three years. I've seen a lot. But it's only hunters for me now. And I'll tell you why.'" I paused to see if Asa was actually listening. Both his eyes were open and on me, so I went on. "'First, you have to know something about jumpers, and this is something I learned the hard way. I can go and spend $300,000...' And Asa Bird, he said that like how I might say I'm going to spend ten bucks on a sandwich. Like it was maybe a bit much, but then, why not splurge once-in-a-while if it's important."

"I told you, Tik, there's no use listening to that guy," Asa Bird repeated, rubbing a hand across his forehead.

"Then he squeezed my arm like this," and I reached over and squeezed Asa's bicep quickly, just where the tattoo was hiding under his shirt sleeve, "and said: 'And then my rival might spend $50,000 on a horse. And you know what? He'll win! I don't think my rival ever paid more than $150,000 for one of his Grand Prix horses. Not bad, I guess. Good for him, I guess. But where does that put me?'" I paused for effect.

"So, Asa Bird, where does that put him?" I demanded.

Asa Bird looked at my hand still on his arm. "I dunno, boss."

I didn't know either, I thought. Maybe it put the guy in the camp of those that want immediate value for their money, or in the generation-of-now, or with the super rich and lazy. I didn't know. I didn't know where show jumping was going as a sport.

"You know what else I saw at the show?" I asked.

He looked at me with raised eyebrows, and I told him about the horse in draw reins, his tongue lolling to the side, the whites of his eyes pleading, trotting and trotting in endless ovals, his rider with the reins in one hand. Why? Because she was using the other hand to hold her cell phone to her ear.

"I'll tell you what, Asa Bird," I said. "I think we are lucky to work for what we get. Sure, you won't make as much in your whole life as one of these top horses are worth, but at least you're a good worker. At least you are honest and dependable and care about horses."

"I guess you've thought about this a bit."

"A bit."

Asa Bird lay on the couch, feet close to me, his head at the other end. His eyes were closed as much as they were open.

"I like what Anne says," he said after a pause. "The sign of a good rider is a happy horse."

"A happy horse. Exactly. I just don't get why *they* don't get it," I replied, motioning with my hands as if to mean everyone *out there*. I suddenly realized I'd been talking too much. "I'm going to get a drink," I told Asa, and left him on his own with the television.

Later, I sat with a beer and wrote down my second promise:

I pledge, now, on paper, that I want to help fend off the extinction of that endangered species, the "horseman." I'm not going to take the easy way. I'm not going to do it for the money or the fame. I'm not going to trade my passion for prominence or popularity. Asa Bird, here is my promise: I'm gonna help you out, dude. I'm gonna man-the-fuck-up.

A few weeks later Anne offered me a job as Assistant Trainer. I did not know if my personal pledge and her offer were cosmically related, but it was a big deal to me. As part of the offer, I could bring two horses to Market Street. One was for me to keep long-term, Sapphire, and the other, TJ, was a horse my family wanted to sell.

When it was time to leave Wellington and head to Anne's summer facility in New Jersey, I made the drive north with the crew, then promptly caught a flight back to Vancouver. I had to pack up Sapphire and TJ, and make the long drive back across North America with my father.

Things were finally falling into place.

CHAPTER 30

On the Importance of Correct Paperwork

I looked around the room and crossed my hands on my stomach. Then I moved them to my lap. I started to sweat.

The room was a small warehouse divided into a lobby on one side and a series of cubicles on the other. The two areas were separated by a long counter.

I had already seen many people enter and leave the lobby as I waited, detained. Mostly the passers-through seemed to be Canadians making routine trips. A lady in a white hat and her daughter were going shopping in Bellingham. A Japanese man in a dark suit was heading to Seattle to open a sushi bar with his sister. The sister was a slight young woman in a skirt, who had just left a troublesome marriage (or so I imagined). There had also been a flock of Dutch tourists, heading farther south to San Francisco. Some of them looked at me curiously, but I wouldn't meet their eyes.

On my right were the cubicles where the US Customs and Border Protection had its center of operations, and on my left was a wall made of frosted glass. Embedded in the wall was a phrase written in clear glass: *The Grass Is Always Greener.*

A bold statement. I looked through the letters and saw a long line of cars outside. But I couldn't see the horse trailer that I knew was out there, or my two horses inside it. They were just out of view.

"Could I check on the horses?" I had asked after my first interview.

"Not until you're cleared."

"Can my dad go check on them?"

"Not until he is cleared."

"Can I go to the washroom?"

The officer frowned. His uniform was crisp. He didn't look up from his desk. "No."

I walked over to the water fountain and had a drink, and then I tried the washroom door. Locked. I could wait.

I wondered if all my paperwork was in order. I should have spent more time on it. And as my second interview started I wished I had confirmed my story with my dad before we had entered the building. I hadn't looked at him more than once in the past two hours, but I could hear him breathing, and every half hour he would clear his throat. He was as uncomfortable as a foal without his mom. I wasn't much better.

"Mr. Maynard?" a CBP officer called out. It was my turn again.

"Yes?" I heard my dad say innocently beside me. I was surprised because we both knew who the officer meant.

The man glanced down at the passport in his hand. He may have forgotten my first name, but he certainly knew who I was.

"Thomas Maynard," he said, then looked at me. I nodded. "Follow me," he said.

I stood at the desk and looked across at Officer 952. He wasn't much older than I was, thirty-two, maybe thirty-three. He sported frizzy sideburns but was otherwise clean-shaven. This would be my third time talking to him, and we already had a routine. He would try and get me flustered, and I would stick to my story. His boss might come over and threaten me when he thought things needed moving along. Officer 952 was learning to frown when appropriate and to squint when needed. He was learning when to play tough and when to cajole. His baby face prevented him from being as grave as his boss…which I appreciated.

"Where are you going?" demanded 952 again.

"To Frenchtown, New Jersey." I tried to keep my voice steady, cool.

"What will you be doing?"

"Riding horses."

"Will you be working?"

"No."

"Will you be paid?"

"No."

"Do you understand that *any* form of payment, even payment in kind, means that you are working?"

"I do now."

"And are you?"

"Am I what?"

Officer 952 raised his voice, ready to play Bad Cop: "Will you be working in New Jersey?"

And that was where I was stuck. I had heard of people being working students in many different countries. They traveled to learn. It was not a career move or a paid position. It was more like school. The last time I had entered the United States, I had just told them I was visiting and learning to ride, and I was welcomed. No problem. But I knew what he was getting at. How do you define "work" anyway? Is being a "working student" the same as being paid in kind? And if my title was changed to "Assistant Trainer," surely that would be taken more seriously?

"I will not be working there," I said decisively. Officer 952's boss frowned at me. His mustache quivered like a cat's whiskers. Officer 952 put his hands on the table, palms down.

"I may or may not help out from time to time to help pay for lessons," I ventured. This was going badly. I frowned as well.

The boss stepped in: "We know about this industry. Canadian boys come down and work illegally in the US all the time. We're on to you!" He raised his voice: "Tell us the truth!"

I insisted that I *was* telling the truth.

"Why do you have to come to America to ride?" he demanded. "Why do you have to go to New Jersey?"

I repeated myself again: "I'm going to learn to become a better rider and horseman."

But why did I really want to go? Surely there were good instructors, good horses at home in British Columbia? Maybe he had a point.

"Go sit down, Thomas," the boss told me. "We've heard enough. We're going to talk to your father again."

"Thanks," I said. But I don't know why I thanked him.

I went and sat next to my dad. We didn't say anything, and five minutes later they called him up. What would my dad tell them? We hadn't thought to practice our stories. I leaned back, crossed my legs, and studied the wall opposite me, which was somewhat interesting because of the taxidermy on display. A sign said they were CITES animals. CITES stood for Convention on International Trade in Endangered Species—the poor creatures that were poached and smuggled, I gathered. One was a polar bear. He stood eight feet high, the sign said. I wondered if standing was an action—a dead animal was upright, but was he *standing*? I looked up at his head. His eyes were black and unyielding, but he lacked the menace of his former life.

I again asked if I could use the men's room. The officer on duty thought about it, then reached under the counter and pressed a button. He nodded at me, and I rose from my seat and entered the restroom. Maybe he would let me check on the horses now, too?

In the washroom, signs warned that cell phones weren't allowed in the building. I didn't see any security cameras, but I wouldn't have been surprised if they were hidden. When I came out I could see my dad, still talking to the CBP officer. My father had built a quiet life that consciously avoided dealing with people in uniforms. I sat down again across from the polar bear. There was nothing I could do.

I thought about my horses in the trailer outside and felt a stab of guilt: three hours so far without water, in the heat of the trailer. I thought about the job that was waiting for me. Why did I want to work with horses, anyway? On paper they really aren't that appealing. I usually enjoyed sports that didn't require a lot of equipment or money. Running, say, was a sport I could practice anywhere, anytime, with a friend or by myself. There were few expensive accoutrements in the world of running. And no vet bills.

My dad came back finally. He looked like he wanted to tell me something of significance, but all he said was, "I'm allowed to check on the horses now." And so I sat there, the polar bear eyeing me, while he went outside to water Sapphire and TJ; maybe hay them, too.

I was called into the office for a fourth time, and Officer 952 and the boss kept at it. They asked questions the way a Border Collie herds sheep. At one point the boss asked me about working for the O'Connors, and I knew then that they'd Googled me.

"Yes," I admitted, "I was a working student in Florida last year."

Officer 952 raised one side of his thin pink lips.

"Finally, a bit of truth out of you. Why didn't you tell me this before?"

"You didn't ask," I answered.

We were held at the border for five hours. I heard a CBP officer yell at another suspect, "I can see liar written all over your forehead!" It took three hours for that guy to crack, and he left in tears. He was twenty-three, and his family was waiting for him across the lobby. They left together, returning north.

I found out later that my dad never told them anything that would have incriminated me in any way, but with only suspicions to go on, they still gave it one last try. Before being released, I was taken into a small white room, fingerprinted, photographed, and then asked to give a final declaration, which would determine my fate. Even if they got nothing, they could still stop my entry. Like wolves in the forest, they could bare their teeth and had no one to answer to.

"I am going to type everything you say," Officer 952 told me. "This will go on your record."

I remained silent, so he went on, "Any statement you make must be given freely and voluntarily. Are you willing to answer my questions at this time?"

I wasn't ready to lie down, so I asked, "What if I say no?"

He eyed me from across the desk. His fingers danced on his chair, next to where his gun might have been. Then he leaned back. But I could see his arm was still tense. I imagined us pacing off from each other, acting cool, counting to ten, and seeing who had the quicker draw.

Finally, he said, "In that case we would send you to prison in Los Angeles where you would await a trial and deportation."

Hmmm. "I guess I should say yes then?"

"Yes."

"Then yes."

"Is it all right with you if I just put down 'Yes'?" he asked impatiently, fingers over the keyboard.

"Sure."

That was how the declaration started—I still have my typed copy—and the rest of the interview went by mechanically as I repeated the answers I'd already given. I found myself thinking about New Jersey. I hoped Anne wouldn't be mad. I wanted her to keep my place. The real reason I was going away was about more than just the riding and the horsemanship—it was also about the culture. For equestrians the East Coast had more competitions, more talent, more history. Nobody ever jumped higher by lowering the bar, they say, and for me, Frenchtown was raising the bar.

And still, there was even more to it than that: I wanted my adventure to continue! And I wanted to find my own way!

Vancouver had a lot to offer, but now whenever I returned I moved around the city like a Mustang pacing the fence line, eyes on the horizon. I wanted to travel my own path, and I still saw it stretching and winding in front of me. I would not turn my back on that road now. I could not back down while it was still calling me. I refused!

Suddenly I was conscious of my interrogator looking at me.

"Do you understand that you are not admissible into the United States at this time? In the future you will need to provide strong ties and equities to Canada before attempting to make entry, and if you attempt to make entry without this documentation you may be banned from entering the United States for a period of five years or more. And if you attempt to cross at another port of entry you are subject to the same proceedings?"

"I do."

So I would have to prove that I'd be returning to Canada after my stay in New Jersey. They wanted to see that I owned a house, had kids, or a job, or a wife.

I left the office and nodded to my dad, signaling we were free to go. I met TJ with a rub at the withers, and Sapphire with a scratch by the ears. They were calmer than we were, which lifted my heart a little. They still had hay, but we offered them water again. We were silent until we got in the truck and started driving back across the border; back the way we'd come almost six hours before.

My dad told me how he stuck to his story: *He knew nothing.* He just kept repeating that to himself: *I know nothing.* The arrangements between Anne and me were just that—between Anne and me—as far as he was concerned.

They had threatened him with being an accessory. They told him he could go to jail.

"Accessory to what?" I asked.

"I forget," he said. "Murder in the first, maybe." He tried to laugh, but it was weak and strained. I felt bad for him, for the horses, and for Anne. For myself, I felt anger and frustration.

You're an *idiot,* I said to myself. You should have been better prepared.

"Mum will never believe this," I said out loud, looking out the window. The big farms were giving way to stores, and gas stations, as we approached Vancouver again. "And now, in order to leave the country, I will have to prove that I'm going to come home again."

My dad didn't say anything for a while, then, "You'll probably have to get a lawyer."

Once home again, we unloaded Sapphire and TJ. They trotted out into their familiar paddocks and greeted their friends, who nickered to them. Horses are soulful animals, I thought. Why am I taking them away? For my own ends? For my own pleasure? Humans are always organizing other animals, moving them about, or stopping them from moving. It's all about control. Are horses different than cattle, or dogs, or polar bears? Why do we eat some animals and not others? We call horses our friends. Yet we buy and sell our friends.

To be a professional horse trainer or rider, I had to learn to distance myself from my horses. And from my family too, I realized, if I kept leaving like this. For the moment though, the decision had been taken out of my hands. I was back home again, and I would have to make the most of it.

I found some carrots in the barn and took them out to Sapphire and TJ.

"Happy to be home?" I whispered.

CHAPTER 31

The Almost End

It would make sense to end here. To begin with, in my original plan, I was only supposed to be gone for a year. Now here I was, almost two years in. My goal had been to be a working student. I had done that. I wanted to travel. I had done that, too.

Second, it made a lot of sense to stay in Canada. I could be an assistant trainer in British Columbia or Alberta, or help my dad.

Third, discouragingly, *The Chronicle of the Horse* had stopped publishing my articles.

I had really started writing at the same time I started being a working student. There have been many riders throughout history who were also writers: Alois Podhajsky, Bill Steinkraus, George Morris, Jimmy Wofford. Monty Roberts inspired millions with *The Man Who Listens to Horses*. And Dick Francis, that storyteller, would be forever entertaining on a bus, a plane, or a rainy evening. Reiner Klimke's *Ahlerich* was the first book I read where I realized how much *thought* goes into training horses; that it's not just a matter of riding them around like skateboards. Klimke was thinking all the time, pitting himself and his horse against fate, like an endless chess match. Later, American horseman Mark Rashid's books made me start to see horse training as a series of puzzles. Whenever something was not going well he would step back and study it the way Hercule Poirot studied a murder. Like it was an interesting and fascinating riddle. Or a fantastic brainteaser. Not something to shy away from!

When I told Ian Millar that I wouldn't write if he let me stay with him, I had meant it. But as time went on, I became more invested in the writing part of my working student process. It gave me a chance to gather and process my thoughts about different training ideas. Writing and publishing the articles became almost as important to me as working with the horses.

When I had first gone to Germany and was being published in *Gaitpost*, I was getting a few dollars for each article they accepted. But I was also paying by the hour for a writing coach. It became clear, almost from the beginning, that writing was a skill that I wanted to improve, just as I wanted to improve my riding and horsemanship. So far, I had spent more on each article than I had been paid, but I chalked it up to an education.

I also read books on writing: *On Writing* by Stephen King and *Stein On Writing* by Sol Stein. What impressed me was their sincerity. How truth, although uncomfortable to muster, was in even the strangest fiction.

American gossip columnist Walter Winchell wrote:

[Sportswriter] Red Smith was asked if turning out a daily column wasn't quite a chore. "Why, no," dead-panned Red. "You simply sit down at the typewriter, open your veins, and bleed."

I was proud to be published by *The Chronicle of the Horse*, a magazine that included commentary by the leaders, movers, and shakers of the horse industry. But after I submitted a piece describing my ill-fated border crossing, they chose not to continue my articles. And their decision was entirely justified.

One of the things I wrote in my original article was this:

The building served two purposes. First, it was to welcome visitors to the United States, and in that sense, it was fitting: The lobby, like the country, was bigger than it deserved to be, and the welcome underwhelming. The people that worked there— uniformed, mustached men for the most part—took its size and strength for granted.

Another sentence I wrote was this:

Americans, I find, lack the efficiency and kindness that smaller countries like Luxembourg or New Zealand have perfected out of necessity.

These were foolish statements for me to make. Kind people and unkind people, efficient people and lazy people, live in every country. Megalomaniacs can sprout, like weeds, in an African desert, in a South American jungle, or in a New York borough. Furthermore, those who work border control, well, it's not their *job* to be nice. I knew that.

There are many ways we try to communicate with horses: We talk, in English or French or Spanish; we whisper; we cluck; we yell; we use body language; we move our seat, legs, and hands. But it seems horses have two main ways they let us know what they are feeling: They either show more tension, or they show more relaxation.

When we see a horse get scared and bolt through a fence, somebody might say, "That horse has no self-preservation instinct." Instead, the opposite is true. Horses are born to move first and think second. That's their nature. They are emotional, but they do not lie. If they are nervous, they raise their head and look around. If they feel scared, they run. Where equids evolved, there were no fences.

It is up to us to teach them how to survive in our world; how to think under pressure, to relax, to focus, to become problem-solvers. In other words, we are trying to teach them to be more like us.

To live with horses we learn to be aware of every little nuance, like the way we touch them for the first time each day. We learn to have a soft vision. We learn to hear that bicycle coming up behind us. We learn to not be so focused on words like "I love you," or "You're so handsome," or "You won!" Instead we learn to focus on how we feel. In other words, we learn to be more like horses.

If we succeed we meet our horses in the middle.

In that piece for the *Chronicle*, I wrote insincerely because I was emotional. To be sincere can be difficult. To admit vulnerability can be hard. After the botched border crossing, and the disapproval from the magazine I so admired and respected, I recognized that I needed to do better. Even so, it would be years before I wrote for *The Chronicle of the Horse* again.

Around this time I got serious about another idea: to take my articles and journal entries from my working student experiences and make them into a book. I asked my editors at the *Chronicle* if it was something they might be interested in. They were not.

"But try Trafalgar Square Books," they said.

Trafalgar had bought Half Halt Press previously, which was the company that published my parents' book, *Horses in Focus*, in 1988, so I had heard of them. I spent weeks writing, editing, and re-editing my query letter to them. I finally took a deep breath, and hit send.

Opened a vein.

I did not hear back from them.

Not for four-and-a-half years.

In the meantime, it made sense to stay in Canada...but I was determined to go back to Anne's. So, I sat at the computer and typed "immigration lawyer" in the search bar. Many sites appeared and I began to make notes. It was tedious, like a long straight run uphill with no trees for shade or turns for inspiration. The kind of run where the horizon was always in front of me but got farther and farther away. I just had to keep going. One foot in front of the other.

CHAPTER 32

"Nope, No Cattle"

"I've done *dozens* of these. Hundreds. Let me tell you something," Matthew said, "You have a *really good* shot."

And I believed him. I felt like Sandra Bullock in *The Proposal*. I mean, it would be kind of harsh if the United States didn't want me, wouldn't it?

"There are just a few problems…" he then admitted.

Matthew Martinez, Esquire, of Fennemore Craig, PC, in Phoenix, Arizona, spoke with a soothing voice, as if he was explaining the situation to a particularly bright Golden Retriever. He gave a good first impression, partly for what he said, but more for how he said it. Although I never met him in person, I paid him in advance and committed myself to his plan.

It was a tolerable plan, I thought, for my second run at the American border. Fennemore Craig oversaw everything, collecting letters of reference, letters of introduction, and letters of intent. The P-1 petition was prepared, couriered to me, and submitted. They knew the difference between the P-1, P-2, and O-1; they knew that I needed an I-797B, and that getting around the I-831 might be a problem, but a workable problem. I understood, well…over fifty percent of what he said.

"Remember," was Matthew's last advice, "remember one thing: The people who give out work visas and the guards at the border work for different organizations. Just because you have a visa approved does not guarantee your entry."

"It doesn't guarantee my entry?" I repeated.

"It does not guarantee your entry," he parroted. "But then, nothing is guaranteed, is it?"

"And does it matter that I was turned away the first time?" I stood in my parents' kitchen, phone against my ear. Pen and paper on the yellow table. I held my breath.

"Look, I prepared a good application. The petition was approved. We dotted all the 'i's.' I think you have a good chance. Either they like you this time. Or they don't."

"Okay," I told him. "Sure."

But I wasn't sure at all.

As before, I was driving with my dad, and taking TJ and Sapphire in the trailer. TJ always knew when a trip was planned, and his kicks against the stall walls woke me earlier than I wanted. I threw hay in his stall and filled his bucket with grain, but he still kicked. Loaded for the trip he was worse, and the trailer rocked. It was only once we were on the move that he settled. Horses, like infants, are sometimes calmed by a drive.

As my dad drove I looked out the windows. I saw blueberry farms, cranberry fields, Tim Hortons, horses. The sky was overcast, and the day was dark and wet. Our mood was somber. At the border crossing we were directed to park. Dad was cleared and told he could wait in the truck. I had to go inside with my petition for an interview. As I walked toward the building I looked back and saw my father sliding the trailer windows back for the horses. TJ put his head right out, looking for a treat. Sapphire was just a dark, shy silhouette. I imagined her peering eyes, blinking and suspicious, as if seeing daylight for the first time.

I walked in, right past the polar bear. "Hey there," I said quietly.

At the desk the guard eyed me the same way as the guard had the last time. I stood my ground, hands in my pockets, trying to find the balance between deferential and casual. I didn't recognize him; I was relieved to have someone new.

This guy was of indeterminate age. Youthful, I thought, but his thick brown beard made him look older. His identification tag assigned him a number, but I knew him immediately as Officer Beard. What a beard! In this building of mustaches such a misman-aged beard was a novelty, and I liked him because of it. I could not read how he felt toward me, but I reminded myself he was trained to be hard to read, and I forgave him.

The P-1 approval notice I handed him was one page long. It had the words "United States of America" across the top, and lower down, my name. And then lower still: APPROVED in bold, capital letters.

The border guard held my approval notice in his hand like it was wet, using two fingers as pincers as he glanced at it.

"Sit down," he ordered.

I sat on the wooden bench that ran along the back wall of the lobby. The notice the guard held was the culmination of months of paperwork, legwork, legal expenses, and processing fees. The peti-tion had been as thick as a Bible, but the approval notice was just one page. The P-1 was reserved for athletes who wanted to compete or tour in the United States. Once I submitted the approval notice at the border, I hoped I would be able to exchange it for a visa—one that would let me work and live in New Jersey for five years.

The Friday before I left, some friends sat me down in a pub and demanded to know how long I was going for.

"The visa is good for five years," I replied.

I looked around The Dunbar. It had been redone since I had been there last. Now there were large glass doors that opened onto a deck that held round tables and umbrellas with logos of Granville Island Brewing. We sat in a booth and ordered a pitcher of beer.

My answer, of course, was no answer at all. And they knew it, and they knew that I knew it, too. We sat in silence a minute.

"Is it worth it?" one asked.

And another said, "It's exciting. You are going off to live in another country. To be someone."

"I thought you *were* someone?" another countered, the edges of his mouth turning up.

I sat on the hard plank in the US Border Office and wondered how long it would be until I went home again. I had started reading Steinbeck's *Travels with Charley* in anticipation of my own trip. One great American author acknowledged another when Steinbeck wrote: *You can't go home again because home has ceased to exist except in the mothballs of memory*. It scared me that home would change and I would grow. If I returned I would be a tourist, not a Vancouverite. My neighborhood of Southlands was so familiar, so dear, that as I left this time, I had said out loud to my surroundings, "Let's take a break. You know, it's not you. It's me." And that made me calm. But I also knew it might be forever, and that made me very, very sad.

The glass wall was opposite me once again, and I saw *The Grass Is Always Greener* gleaming there, the forever-welcome to foreigners who were paying, praying, and begging for a chance to live in the Great United States. I wondered if New Jersey would ever begin to feel like home. Would I ever know the trails and restaurants and cafés and birds and rivers as well as in Vancouver? Would I make new friends that would become old friends?

"Mr. Maynard." Officer Beard raised his eyebrows, inviting me forward. I stepped to the raised counter, which acted as his desk as well. I took my hands out of my pockets.

"Where are you going?" he asked. "Why are you going?" he demanded. "Really? How long are you going for? Really? What are you taking with you? How many horses? Racehorses? Thoroughbreds? Any cattle? Really? Can I have the keys to your truck and trailer and camper?"

"New Jersey. A job. Yes, sir, working with horses. Yes, sir. I'm hoping you will give me a five-year visa. That's right. That is what I applied for. Horses. Two. A mare and a gelding. No, not racing. No, not Thoroughbreds. The horses are for jumping. Show jumping. Nope, no cattle. Promise."

I slid the keys across the counter.

He looked, but not thoroughly, through all my paperwork. He took the keys from the counter, which were all on the same ring, and put them in his pocket. He didn't ask which key fit which lock. He put a hand through his hair and walked out the door.

I leaned back against the wall. How long was I going for? *How should I know?* But shouldn't I have a plan at least? *Well, maybe a plan.* But this *is* what you want to do, right? *What I want to do?* They say this is the opportunity of a lifetime. *Who says that?* Everybody says that. It's *Anne.* The next best thing to George, they say. *Then why aren't they applying for this job?*

Officer Beard finally stepped back into the lobby, disappeared through a hidden door for a moment, and then reappeared behind the laminate counter.

"Approach the desk," he said, without looking up.

I stepped toward him.

"I've just seen your camper." He shuffled some papers.

"Good."

He looked up at me. "I need to know where you bought that stove with the round door and the little chimney that bends like this." He made a squiggle in the air with his finger. "What a stove!"

I had no idea. But his eyes were smiling behind all his hair, and so I permitted myself a little grin as well.

"I'll need you to give me the name of where you bought it."

I explained that it had been installed by the previous owner. It was what had attracted me to the camper in the first place. It was then I knew Officer Beard and I would have been friends if the circumstances were different.

"Those are nice horses," he went on. "You know horses?"

"Sure I do," I replied. But it was all relative. The only knowledge that had proven itself time and again was how much I still had to learn. The only truths I knew were that all horses had similarities and that every horse is unique.

"I'd love to go on a road trip with horses one day. Maybe even in Canada." Officer Beard grinned. He handed me the petition and my passport back. "The visa is inside. You're free to go." It was a relief to accept my passport back. I left the building like a shoplifter, quickly and casually, not wanting to attract attention. I glanced back as I passed through the doorway. My guard looked like he didn't really want to stay either. He would probably rather be hunting antelope or pheasant. With an old musket, maybe. Or a fresh-stripped alder bow. I imagined he had a well-read copy of *Into the Wild* hidden in his desk.

I headed out to the trailer and put my head up to one of the open windows. The gelding nipped at my fingers looking for food, while the eyes of the mare were more wary. "Where are we going now?" she seemed to be saying.

I rubbed her between the eyes. Checked her water bucket. Closed the trailer windows. Then I got in the truck and rolled down my window. I looked over at my dad. He raised his eyebrows.

"East or west?"

"East," I said.

He shifted into drive. "East it is."

CHAPTER 33

Interstate 90

Sixty-six hours from the border to Frenchtown, New Jersey, and my dad drove probably sixty of them. The truck was a 2006 GMC Sierra 3500. She was gray and trustworthy, but without much character. The old camper on the other hand—the one the customs officer was a fan of—sat on the bed of the pickup and oozed personality as surely as Johnny Depp on a pirate ship. The inside had been redone with mismatching drapes and upholstery, clashing flooring and counters, and the fireplace stood on four iron legs only feet away from where the propane tanks were strapped in. The fireplace doubled as a wood stove, for we cooked on it as well. We'd picked the camper up for a few hundred dollars a few weeks before I left. The two-horse trailer tagged along behind us.

The plan was to drive twelve hours a day and stop each night at a "Bed-n-Bale." Horse motels are private homes and farms that offer overnight stabling for one or more horses. Some of them were down long dirt roads, others edged small towns. At lunch each day I looked at our map and decided where I thought we would end up that night. One of us would then call ahead and ask if they had stabling available. Without fail they did. A couple times Dad and I took a wrong turn and arrived in the dark, but mostly it was a pleasant way to travel.

Places were generally affordable—maybe twenty dollars per horse—and welcoming. We would park our truck next to the barn and set up for the night. My dad was comfy in the camper and I rolled a foamy mattress pad out on the ground outside, then crawled inside my sleeping bag. One night as I looked up at the stars and listened to the sleepy sounds of the horses in the paddocks nearby, I realized this wasn't just an adventure anymore. Horses were going to be my life.

I was all in.

I got up and went to the camper. I stuck my head in.

"What are you reading?" I asked my dad. The mattress he was on was at my head level when I stood. He rolled over and looked at me. I sat down next to the stove. Dad had a small light on up by his bed, but down low, I was in the dark. "I think this is my favorite author," he said, holding the book and not looking at me.

"Who?"

"Nevil Shute."

"Hmmm. He is good." I saw him continue reading, but I wasn't ready to go. "What's your favorite thing to do with horses?"

He continued reading. "He takes ordinary people and he puts them in extraordinary situations."

"What's your favorite thing about *horses*?" I asked again.

Now he had to put the book down and think. "Jumping," he said.

"Mine too. Do you think you would still have horses in your life if you couldn't compete?"

"Yep."

"What if you couldn't ride?"

"I dunno. Maybe I would get a different hobby."

I looked up at him. His hair was curly, but graying. He wore rectangular full-framed glasses. He was fit—sixty-seven and still rode horses every day.

"This isn't your hobby, Dad, this is your job. You would still teach."

But I knew he liked riding as much as teaching. That would be a hard transition.

"It's not a job if you love it," he said. "What about you?" He turned the line of questioning back on me.

"I don't know. Let me sleep on it."

He already had his book up again.

"Okay. Sleep on it. See you in the morning."

"Night," I said. I waited a moment and then stepped down out of the camper. I closed the door behind me. It had become overcast and the darkness had intensified. It took me a while to find my sleeping bag. I knew I would not have an answer by the morning. It was confusing.

If I couldn't compete anymore, would I still work with horses? I might still ride. What if I *couldn't* ride? When asked, many competitors say no, they would stop riding if they couldn't show. Horses are often a steppingstone in a person's ambition.

What was my dream? What was my goal?

If my goal was just to compete, I could choose a cheaper sport. If my goal was to have a friend, dogs were more loyal.

I chose a horse as my athletic partner, but what if, for some reason, I asked myself again, I couldn't compete? Would I send my partner away? It was easy for horses to be a part of some bigger dream, and without the dream, the passion to simply be around horses, for some people, ebbs away. But what was *my* dream? I couldn't put my finger on exactly *why* I was doing what I was doing.

Back in my sleeping bag, I looked up and there was a break in the clouds. There was part of Orion's Belt. There was Cassiopeia. I put my hands behind my head. When I tried to unravel the question it became murky and disappeared. Of course, it was impossible to overestimate the thrill of the gained agility, endurance, and sheer athleticism achieved by joining up with a good horse. The horse's legs became my legs. My thoughts became his thoughts.

There was also the joy of training. I was fascinated by the ways we could learn to nurture daily habits in ourselves and our horses. I liked the *trying* to get from point A to point B. And the challenge, the puzzle…realizing that it might take a lot longer than completing a crossword or putting together an Ikea table.

Then there was the just *being around* horses. Which was nice. But without the training, the communication, we just *happened* to be next to each other…there was no dialogue. It was like sitting next to Elizabeth Gilbert on a plane. Cool…but you are still strangers until one of you starts talking.

I could see that part of my passion was based in the thinking and planning side of horsemanship, but it was still, for me, a primarily physical enjoyment—the childish delight of running and jumping we rationalize through organized sport. At heart, when I rode, I felt more like a dolphin, leaping and diving, for no other reason than, "Why not?" But with that as my main motivation, could I really do this professionally for the rest of my life? Could being a happy dolphin be a career?

Just then, a shooting star flashed between the clouds, moving from west to east. As I drifted off to sleep I started to feel like the answer was almost appearing before me. It had something to do with riddles. There were riddles everywhere I looked. I didn't know many of the answers, but at least I was seeing the questions now.

The next morning arrived bright and early. The horses were caught and loaded easily. As we drove, Dad and I talked. I had this idea that on the drive cross-country, I would ask my father about all the things we had never talked about before: his childhood dreams; his religion; his regrets. But our conversations ended up being about one thing: horses.

And we were not upset by that at all.

The third night we stopped in Gillette, Wyoming. We pulled in to our horse motel well before dark, and my dad went to find the owner while I set up my foamy between the trailer and the paddocks. I checked on the horses; organized their dinner and ours. Twenty minutes later I heard a yell:

"Come 'ere!"

I walked around the trailer and saw a man leaning out the window of a truck older than our camper. He wore an old greasy baseball hat and overalls.

"Met tin!"

What? I walked closer. He was looking at me. Why didn't he get out?

"Get in!" he yelled again. I understood him this time. He leaned over and let the passenger door open. His eyes were bright, like a spaniel's.

I had a habit of not asking questions in situations like these. I walked over and climbed up into the seat beside him. The man rubbed his hands on his jeans and let the clutch out. He, I learned, was the property owner. Called himself Tally. He had discovered eventing in his fifties. He drove along a dirt road that bumped me out of the seat, all the time talking. He had competed at the Intermediate level on a Quarter Horse.

"Geez, that's like Hidalgo competing against the Arabians," I said.

He smiled mischievously. "But better."

Tally had built his own cross-country course on the property. When he heard from my dad that I evented, he wanted to show me the jumps he had built. He left my father to fill out the paperwork with his wife and drove down to pick me up.

Now he slowed the truck down to a walking pace as we left the road, moving through the long grass. We passed drops and banks and trakehners. There were coops and water and corners.

"We're gonna host events," he explained. "We'll have all the levels here one day." He pointed out each jump. "I'm only showing you part of the course, you understand? It's getting dark. Do you see that jump? See how I set it on the hill just so?"

It really was built in a fantastic spot—it made a gorgeous picture with the sun setting behind it.

"You should come back and ride here," Tally said, gazing with love at the fields and jumps. There were blue and white and red dots spread amongst the green grass like diamonds scattered on a beach. I squinted to make them out. Wildflowers.

"I'd love to."

When Tally dropped me back at the camper, I found that my dad had turned the horses out in two small paddocks. Sapphire and TJ were getting attached to each other by this point, and we always made sure they were stabled next to each other. He had fed them, as well. They traveled with hay, but we removed grain almost entirely out of their diets for the trip, although we still gave them a handful in the evenings, more out of habit than anything else. Social niceties are like little raindrops that grow friendships.

My dad and I made pasta on the propane stove. Other nights, if there was ready firewood, we cooked on the fireplace. We had a couple of Molson Canadians with dinner. We planned the next day's route, and I told him about Tally's cross-country course. We also talked about books—between us, we'd brought fifteen or twenty books on the trip.

I was alternating between two books: When *The Tao of Equus* had stretched my imagination close to the breaking point, and it became a chore, I would switch to the (slightly) lighter Steinbeck, as the author was traveling with his dog Charley along approximately the same route as us, although heading west instead of east. Our camper reminded me of Steinbeck's Rocinante, and I was sad we had not named it prior to setting forth on our journey. But at this point it would feel forced.

Another night we stopped in Shirly, Indiana, at a place called Cuttin' Up Stables, owned by Mike and Linda. Linda had taught her horses to sit on a large bean bag chair. She had taught them to come and to stay. Every horse had calm eyes and their ears followed her everywhere. She treated her horses with respect, and I was impressed.

We let Sapphire and TJ out together in a field. We didn't do that often on the road—we were pretty careful about them getting hurt. But there is nothing easier on the eyes than two horses that are friends turned out together. They immediately set out scratching and teething the other's withers. My father and Mike leaned up against the fence. I climbed up to the top rail and tucked my legs underneath me.

"Boy, they sure do like each other," Mike observed.

"Sure do," my dad said.

"Surely," I added, with a thought to where we were.

"Last lady that came through here," Mike went on, "she had this crazy chestnut. Didn't look like much, but she swore it was a great hunter horse. She was going up to Canada with it 'cause it had this skin problem and she thought the cold would help it."

"Yeah?" I said.

"The craziest thing, though. She thought that horse was worth twenty thousand dollars. *Twenty thousand dollars.* You ever hear of anything like that?"

"Nope," I lied.

"Crazy," my dad added.

I sat watching the horses. Sometimes I liked to sit and think, but sometimes I would just sit. After a bit I went back to the trailer where I found it clean. I was surprised; I had never had somebody muck it out for me before. The smell of fresh pine shavings was a welcome change after days on the road.

"You didn't have to..." I protested, but Mike just held his pitchfork at his side and smiled.

"This is Cuttin' Up Stables," he said, as if that explained everything.

My father had stayed back at the pasture with the horses, but now he wandered up to the trailer as Mike was heading back to his house.

"Don't you dare tell him how much these horses are worth," Dad whispered to me when Mike was out of earshot.

"I would never!" I insisted. Anyway, a horse's cost never reflected how much he was worth.

The four of us finally arrived in Frenchtown with all the windows rolled down. Warm July air rushed through the truck and trailer. It was late but still light, and I sweated as we unloaded the tack trunk from the trailer. Asa Bird was there to meet us and help with the horses. We put them in freshly made stalls across from each other. In this strange and new place, they were only content when they could see one another. The first few days one would cry and whinny and pace the stall whenever I took the other out to ride. I tried to ignore my heart. There seemed to be selfishness in everything I did, and I tried to steel myself against it, but it was no use. I kept asking myself the question: Was I doing the right thing by these horses?

Then my father flew home, and I missed him. I had never asked him any of the questions I'd intended to bring up.

Late at night I walked around the barn and past the camper. Then I checked on my horses. I gave TJ a rub on the nose and he tried to nip my fingers. I missed my dogs, my family, my friends. Sapphire watched me patiently from the back of the stall as I said hello to her. She wasn't so forward. I missed the salty air of the Pacific. I missed riding the trails in the rainforests of cedar and fir.

It wasn't that I didn't want to ask my dad those questions, or that I didn't have the nerve. It just never seemed to be the right moment.

The two horses finally settled in to Anne's Frenchtown facility. It took four days. They made new friends and found some independence. They learned to be comfortable in their new home. They learned to be vacuumed and washed every day. (Yes, there were horse vacuums!) They were on a strict schedule of training, resting, and eating. But they still watched for each other and nickered when one who'd been out returned.

As far as I knew my two horses never talked about their past or their future, but they had grown to be friends by being close to each other. They stood next to each other every day, all day, on the drive from west to east. In the stalls in New Jersey they breathed the same air every night. They ate at the same time and were watered from the same hose. When they were turned out they were next to each other. They shared time, and space, they lived in the present, and they became friends.

My dad and I never talked about a lot of things, but we had driven through mountains and across prairies, side by side, next to each other in the gray pickup. We had camped in strangers' fields and slept under the stars. And we did drink beer together in Gillette and Shirly and Atlantic.

That's something, I thought.

CHAPTER 34

Frenchtown, New Jersey

"Either you don't know anything about cars, or you're too drunk to notice."

"Oh, man, I noticed right away," I said confidently.

"Hard not to, I guess." My driver laughed. It was dark, and he was peering ahead into the narrow beam of light that illuminated the road.

"Hold on," he said as he sped through a turn. The motor whirred and spat, the window was down, and cool air rushed into the car. He had to shout over the sound of the wind and engine.

"I heard you coming up the hill. I heard you a couple minutes before I even saw the headlights," I said.

"What's that?" The guy, maybe a year older than myself, turned his head toward me, drifted over the centerline for a second, then corrected himself.

"Your engine!" I shouted back at him. "I could hear you coming from way back!"

"Yeah!" He grinned. "I could listen to her all day! Ain't she great?"

"Great!" I yelled.

"I've only had her a month. I think I'm still in the honeymoon phase," he declared loudly as he accelerated into another turn.

We had met less than an hour before. He had seen me walking home from the bar, up a long hill away from the low land of French-town-proper that sat next to the Delaware River, and had offered me a ride. He seemed nice enough, and he was going my way.

"What year is she?" I asked. He turned his head slightly, and in the shadows I saw his face change. In that one question, I became a stranger to him again.

"Sixty-eight," he told me flatly. "She's a sixty-eight Mustang."

Obviously.

"Oh, man! She's great. I mean, really great."

We did not talk for a few miles. He drove intently, and I held my hands together in my lap and stared straight ahead. In my defense, I told myself, it was dark out. And I'd had a couple drinks in French-town. But it was true, I could barely tell a Mustang from a Bronco. Or a Pinto from a Colt. Unless, by chance, you were talking horses—in which case, line 'em up. I'd take a look under the hood.

In the last eighteen months, I'd learned a few things about horses. I'd seen a few things I hadn't before. I'd been pleasantly surprised to come to the conclusion that I knew more about horses than most people. But I also discovered I knew nothing compared to a few others. It was these few I wanted to surround myself with, to learn to walk with.

"Have you lived here long?" the guy asked. He came to a stop at a red light, and we could talk normally for a minute.

"I just accepted a job here."

"What do you do, then?"

What to tell him? Should I explain that I'd be grooming, riding, teaching students, and training horses? Did I even know everything I would be doing? My new job might mean dragging the ring, mowing the field, building jumps.

As a working student, I'd never known what to expect. In

Germany, I'd swept, mucked, and moved furniture. I had a lesson from a nonagenarian. In Texas, I'd roped a horse, taught a horse to swim, helped lay a horse down, babysat a litter of wolves, herded buffalo and cattle. I'd learned to drive a tractor. In Florida I'd raked, round-penned, ridden, and groomed. In Kentucky, I'd had one drink too many, but I also walked the course with Karen O'Connor!

"I'll be working at a show jumping stable," I told him, for simplicity.

"Training horses?" He shifted into first as the light turned green.

"Sometimes I'll be training, sometimes teaching. Probably doing all sorts of stuff."

"Not a bad job," the young man said.

Not a bad job at all. Anne had offered me a chance to ride her horses and her clients' horses. She had let me show her new horse, Torino, in a schooling class in Wellington. And she'd encouraged me to bring students of my own to Market Street. These were not normal perks. I felt lucky.

Renowned or accomplished were not unimportant characteristics, and neither were medals won, but paramount to me in choosing a mentor in this business, I was learning, was his or her philosophy. To find a trainer with similar views and principles when it came to working with horses was not easy. A perfect match? Perhaps not even possible.

Every barn had different ways of doing things. Ingrid Klimke's horses were longed every week, and cavalletti were a central part of her training. I never saw an O'Connor horse longed or schooled over cavalletti, but the O'Connors' barn was the only stable I worked at that relied on a regimen of groundwork and a tool called a Carrot Stick. Somewhere, perhaps, there was a trainer who encouraged both longeing *and* groundwork with a Carrot Stick—that born of the European military and that of the American West.

I remembered once asking a German rider what the biggest difference between riding in Germany and riding in Canada was. "In Germany, we train horses. In North America, you train riders," she told me. Although there were many exceptions to this, I was sure, I also knew it might be a fair generalization. Anne Kursinski, however, seemed capable of both, as I aimed to be myself.

The Mustang cruised noisily along.

"What do you do?" I asked politely.

"I'm a pilot," the guy replied, one hand on the wheel and the other on the shifter. "I fly for a small private company. Lots of rich clients with private planes."

Outside, windows of light marked where houses stood. As we drove up the hill, away from the Delaware Valley and toward the flatter ground of the Hunterdon plateau, the houses stood farther back from the road and were more spread out.

"I grew up just over there." He gestured with his head. "I live on the other side of the river now."

"The other side is Pennsylvania, right?" And suddenly Anne's place popped into view. "There! It's there on the left!" I pointed ahead.

He pulled up in front of the farm entrance. In the daylight, the black iron gate looked shiny and professional, but now it seemed somehow solemn and uninviting. I looked in through the bars at where I would spend this night, and hopefully many more. Then I turned to my driver.

"Thanks for the ride." I shook his hand, promising to buy him a beer next time I met him in town.

"No problem, man. Name's Kendall. See you around."

"Tik," I replied. "Love your car!"

I shut the door and walked up to the gate. It was locked, and I had to climb through the fence. The gravel path crunched and skittered underfoot. What kind of car was it again? Sixty-eight Mustang?

I could hear it heading away from me now, back toward the river.

It was always nice to meet your neighbors. I wondered if I would see Kendall and his Mustang again. Would I last that long at Market Street? I pulled my hood up over my ears to keep the cold out. I hoped so.

I hoped so.

I stopped at the front of the barn before going upstairs to the apartment, looking back down the driveway, which curved to my right. The Grand Prix field, a dark swathe on the other side of the driveway, was huge, at least ten acres. A great place to gallop a horse, I thought. My bedroom was above the barn, and I started up the stairs. I was quiet because there were three other bedrooms, as well—all occupied. Once in bed I closed my eyes and let my mind wander; a warm tingle ran up my spine—not from the cold, but because, for a second, I saw the future.

CHAPTER 35

"You Just Need to Listen"

"Stop making that face!" Cruz, a groom, said to me. It was a variation of the same thing he said to me every morning.

The problem was, that *was* my face. At least it was my morning face. I tried to look professional for work: I shaved every other evening, and I hardly ever cut myself; my clothes were clean and my shirt had a collar; I did not brush my hair, but I wore a helmet, or a hat, as a matter of habit. At 5:15 a.m., however, none of that mattered; my eyes were squinty and my cheeks were bloated. There were pillow lines on my forehead. I squinted in the dark, and I kept my hands in my jacket pockets. This was my morning face, and so I said, "Morning," to Cruz and then ignored him. I did not talk until eight if I could help it, and so when he laughed at me, I mumbled, "Screw off." He laughed louder.

I was doing the stalls on the left side and Cruz was doing the stalls on the right. With only two of us working the aisle, it was easy to find a rhythm. We worked with pitchforks. *Real* pitchforks, with heavy wooden handles and four thin steel tines, not the cheaper plastic "apple pickers." I caught the edge of my pitchfork on a door, and "*PING*" echoed down the aisle, the carefully collected pile balanced on the tines flung under the manure spreader parked between the stalls. I heard the laughter from across the way. I said nothing, just struggled to find my rhythm again, relying on the soft "*WHUMP*" of manure regularly landing in the spreader, which was interrupted every so often when one of us climbed into the tractor and pulled it twelve feet forward so we could muck two more stalls.

The staff was not allowed to listen to music in this barn. I remembered being impressed my first day at Market Street when, in the middle of a conversation, Asa Bird cocked his head and paused mid-sentence, asking, "Did you hear that?" I shook my head. Then he walked to the end of the barn and added water to the two empty buckets he had heard knock together.

"The horses have a way of telling us what they need," Asa Bird said. And so every morning we listened to the sounds of the horses eating, and pitchforks pinging, and manure whumping, and I learned to pay attention.

After the stalls were done, I pulled my riding boots on, and Cruz started tacking up my first horse.

"Why the long face?" Cruz asked. Cruz was Mexican but his English was almost perfect. He liked to brag that he learned it in jail.

"I'm fine!" I put on my helmet.

"I wasn't talking to you," he retorted. I looked over at him. He was grinning. "I'm talking to her." And he tilted his head toward the big bay mare as he slipped the end of the bridle cheekpiece through its keeper.

Cruz led the horse down the aisle toward the indoor. "DOOR!" he yelled. A second later, from out of sight, we heard, "CLEAR!" After a moment, Cruz slid the big wooden door to the side, and we entered. He held the horse's head, and the far stirrup leather, as I mounted. I settled into the saddle and looked around the arena, Cruz wiping the edges and bottoms of my boots with a hand towel. Before I walked off, he looked up and caught my eye.

"Can I talk to you later?" he asked in a low voice.

"Sure," I replied, "no problem." I was not intrigued; Cruz often wanted to talk, and usually it was just gossip.

My first horse was a quiet mare, and I flatted her for forty minutes. The second came out of his stall like a hawk leaving his perch, and so I longed him for twenty. Anne's horses did not do groundwork the way the O'Connors' horses did, but she still made sure they were safe before we mounted. This horse was much calmer after being longed, but still a little anxious when I got on, so I let him relax in a long easy trot until he settled, and then put him away. Anne helped me with my third ride, an experienced dark bay mare, while she took a walk break on her own horse.

"Your hands are too stiff," she told me. "Think about your hands. *Think* about your hands. Relax! Look at my hands. *Look.*"

I looked at her hands. She picked up the trot.

"Look. Let your hands follow the reins. It's like my hands are in her mouth. Let your hands move."

I tried to ride like Anne rode, but she called over to me: "You are not a machine. Widen your hands! Relax."

I lowered my hands to follow the reins. I relaxed my fingers and wrists and elbows. I followed the mare's mouth. I worked on a circle and stayed out of Anne's way as she leg-yielded her own mount up the long side. I widened my hands and let them move. I asked the big horse to lower her head and to relax with me. I asked her to stretch. It was going well. I let her walk and watched Anne's hands as she rode.

I trotted again. I thought about my hands. I let my elbows come back, and I encouraged, with my leg, the mare's neck to go down. But I wanted the withers to stay high. I wanted the nose to go out. And then I heard Anne:

"*Keep* your hands still! Look at me."

I brought the mare back to a walk and looked at Anne again.

"You have to be able to change when the horse changes. I have a thousand hands. *Keep* your hands still! I have a thousand legs. One for every situation. Stop moving your hands!"

I trotted again. Brought my hands together. I kept them still. I slowed the trot down but my mind raced on. Were my hands doing the right thing? I looked down at them.

After my fifth horse of the day, a three-year-old chestnut, I took one of my sandwiches from my tack trunk. I made four sandwiches every morning: two cheese, and two peanut butter and banana. We took no lunch break, and I paid little attention to time, so I just ate when I was hungry. Usually I ate while I did something else. This time, with my other hand, I grabbed a bridle that Cruz needed for the next horse.

The farrier was setting up at the end of the aisle, his trailer backed up to the barn door. I waved my hand with the sandwich at him, but he didn't see me. He reached with one hand into his trailer, and music suddenly filled the aisle. Veterinarians were always greeted with a handshake and addressed with "Doctor," their proper prefix. Acupuncturists, sponsors, owners, and clients were also treated with deference. And farriers, of course, could play music if they wanted to. It got louder as I walked to the cross-ties where my next horse was waiting for me.

> *On the road I dream of home*
> *and when at home I dream of action.*
> *Our apartments are all haunted*
> *by the ghost of satisfaction.*

I remembered a girl. The song, the band, always reminded me of that girl. She had moved suddenly to Toronto with her fiancée, and I had not seen her in four years. I had not spoken to her in three. I wondered if I would ever see her again. Was it better if you didn't know when it was the last time you were seeing a friend? I pushed the thought from my mind. The music warbled down the aisle.

Cause we all want something that's bigger than fashion.
So spill out your heart brother, show me your passion.

When I reached Cruz, standing with my horse, I just held the bridle, and we all three listened to The Zolas. Like the scene in *The Shawshank Redemption* when Tim Robbins' character locked himself in the warden's office and played opera over the prison speaker system: The prisoners paused, their heads turned upward, and for a minute they forgot the concrete walls and remembered their wives and children and childhoods.

So spill out your heart sister, show me your passion.

The chunky gray gelding I was about to ride put one ear forward while the other went to the side like an antenna. Maybe he was trying to make out the words, or maybe he was just absorbing the sound because it was something different. After a few minutes we were already used to the music. It felt natural; a part of the place. A novelty is not new for very long. Cruz gave the horse a piece of candy cane as he did up the throatlatch on the bridle. He caught me looking at him and grinned. I could not imagine him in prison.

The seventh horse I rode was recovering from an injury, and was only supposed to walk, so I did loops of the arena. I held the reins at the buckle. I started to get cold and pulled my hands up into my sleeves. I watched Anne, riding a client's horse. I watched her hands; were they still? No, they moved this way and that. They moved with the reins and with the horse. They went with the horse, instead of with Anne. They went with *feeling*. Oscar Wilde once wrote: "Everything in moderation, including moderation." He was probably talking about gluttony or sodomy or booze, but still. Anne cantered by me, her body in perfect harmony with a "modern horse"—a medium-sized, slim dun. A rare color for a sport horse. I studied her.

When she eventually slowed to a walk, she looked at me. She did not say anything, so I ventured: "I think I'm getting it. I just need to change when the horse changes. I need to be able to lean forward, or sit up; I need to be able to have long reins, or short reins; I need to be able to go slow, or go fast. Sometimes I think you contradict yourself, but you don't. You're just able to react differently to every situation."

"You're right," she replied, as she kept her horse marching. She wore a fitted sweater, and of course, as always, a helmet. The horse and Anne moved together, both supple and athletic, like cats. "I want you in two-point when you jump. But not for *every* jump. I want your hands still, but not *mechanical*. Too much of anything is bad."

Anne was always ready to give advice. Often I didn't really *get* something she told me until days or weeks later. But I started to get this: Here was not like school. I couldn't get away with riding by rote. I had to *think*.

I walked next to her. We were quiet. There was just the wind on the wall of the indoor and the dull thud of the horses' hooves in the footing in the arena.

Sometimes Anne wanted me to be aggressive, sometimes passive. Sometimes I needed shorter reins, sometimes longer reins. And sometimes I got defensive and wanted to scream, *"But you just told me the opposite!"* But I kept it inside. Anne wanted me to find the balance between too much and too little, and it was a fine balance.

After my eighth horse was put away, I started to tack up my own horse. My Sapphire. She stood quietly as I picked her feet, vacuumed her, saddled her, and bridled her. I worked neither quickly, nor slowly— just properly and efficiently. In the ring, she pulled through my hands when I started to trot, and I was rough with her for a minute. Then I stopped and dropped the reins. What was I doing? She walked along quickly, her head down. She didn't sign up for this. What was causing this behavior? I wondered if she was in pain. I should ask Anne to ride her, I thought. Or maybe get the vet to look at her. I tried the trot again but with more patience and softness. That was better for a while.

The indoor had windows all down the long side and the natural light was great to ride in, but now it was getting dark. It was time to call it a day.

I led Sapphire back to her stall where I took her tack off. I pulled on a nylon halter before taking her to the wash stall (no leather allowed there!), where I soaped and rinsed her legs. Cruz was hosing down a horse in the stall next to mine and asked me how my ride went.

"You know, Cruz, that's a good question."

"Tik," he said, "you've helped me out a lot since I started here, and I gotta tell you, you could do better. I've seen a lot of riders out there, and they are making fifty dollars a horse. You gotta do something like that."

"Is this what you wanted to talk to me about?" I sprayed my mare's legs. I was not interested at all. The reason I came east was to work with Anne.

"Yeah," he said. He turned his hose off and looked at me. "The only thing that's holding you back are your horses. You could make a lot more money and have more time if you sent your horses home."

"I'll think about it," I lied.

"I'm telling you, man, those horses are what's holding your career back."

I did not even bother to answer him. Of course it was hard to balance riding my horses with my job. And I was not sure how it would work when we moved to Florida for three months for the winter season, when they would have to be at a different stable.

"Is that all?" I asked him. I turned my hose off, as well. I started on Sapphire with the sweat scraper, and then a towel around her face and ears.

"Just trying to help," he said, before leading the horse he was holding away, back to a stall somewhere down the aisle.

He thought I didn't get him at all. I thought he didn't get *me*. I took Sapphire back to her stall and then went to help Asa Bird. All the horses had their legs soaped and hosed. The ones that jumped were iced and wrapped.

The horses were usually fed at four, but we decided to wait until the farrier was done. He was working on his last horse, and hammer on anvil could be heard above the music that still echoed throughout the barn. There was smoke, as well, from hot shoes being held to hoof. The horses were used to it, and I liked the smell. Asa and I worked more slowly than usual, knowing that we could not leave until the shoeing was done anyway. We swept the aisles and feed room. We used a rag and furniture polish on the tack trunks and stall bars. We made sure the horses had the right blankets—it was going to freeze overnight.

Finally, it was time to feed. I took two buckets and went to the very end of the aisle. TJ paced until I dumped his grain. Sapphire looked out through the bars at me but didn't nicker like the others did. She waited patiently, until her grain spilled from my bucket into her feed bin. I liked having the chance to ride a dozen different horses, but there was something about having my own horse. It was not always easier. Often it was harder. But still, there was *something* about it.

I took a step back and watched the two horses eat. TJ ate quickly and spilled grain on the floor. He raised his head often. He saw me, but I had never been able to get *The Look* from him that David O'Connor wanted. That *Look* that showed he understood what was going on and asked, "What are *we* doing next?" TJ was still not a partner. I was just babysitting him.

I watched my mare take a small, careful bite, look at me, and then dunk it in her water. It was the one thing she always did. She always mixed her feed with water.

CHAPTER 36

"You Just Need To Ride Better"

One crisp Saturday morning I saw a horse slide toward the fence, spin, and take off the other way. *Damn!* I sprinted through the snow toward him—it was soft underneath with a crust on top, like freshly baked bread. As I passed the indoor arena I heard a horse spook, and a voice call out: "Hey. Hey! HEY!"

I slowed immediately to a walk. *Damn!* I again cursed quietly to myself. When I was well past the indoor, I ran again, until the horse racing around the paddock noticed me, and I slowed again. I did not want to add another reason for whirling and bolting. When horses galloped around their turnout we brought them in right away. Most of the horses seemed content to spend the majority of their time quietly in stalls, with plenty to eat and an hour of turnout a day, but some found it harder to adapt.

As I led him back to the barn I looked the big horse over. His boots were still on, but his blanket was crooked. I didn't try to straighten it. I would wait until he was calmer. He blew and pranced in the snow. He was worked up. *How* worked up? Maybe a four or a five out of ten? I had realized that people see different things in horses. A talented veterinarian might see a horse trot and say, "Right hind, a one. Maybe a half." Vets have a scale from one to five for lameness, and if a lameness is so minor as to be a half, I might not see it at all. I might just see a horse trotting. *Looks fine to me.* Other trainers could see potential in a horse, even an untried baby or an under-conditioned rescue. Some saw every phase of a horse's jump, as if in slow motion, and then would know exactly which exercises to use to improve his movement, style, and performance.

I was starting to design a rating system in my mind for anxiety. A horse is not either calm or nervous, but often somewhere in between, on a continuum. Above a three, on my scale, and the horse might be able to do what I asked, but was pretty much unable to *learn*. He would perform, but he would not improve.

A swishing tail might mean a horse was anxious. So might unblinking eyes, a high head, tense muscles. Or laid back ears, a tight mouth, grinding teeth. And, of course, an anxious horse will think less; he will want to speed up, to run, to leave the situation. Above a three on my scale and a trotting horse would break to the canter and communication will suffer. Above a six and we were likely getting close to being out of control—a buck or rear, maybe. Definitely not a horse I wanted to be riding.

A ten was a horse that would run through a fence, blind to everything except his fear.

So much of what we had to do was *preparing* the horse to learn. Once we got that far, the teaching and learning were the easier parts of the job. I was beginning to believe that all my interactions with horses should not be about how I could get the best out of them *today*, but how I could make them better for *tomorrow*.

There were not many things that caused Sapphire to accumulate tension, but there were a few. In between jumps, for example, when I tried to slow down, she had a tendency to throw her head in the air, trying to get away from the bit. She did not always understand the bit, especially at speed, or when jumping. Our fall together had been for that very reason. That fall had been my fault, and it still felt like I drank liquid lead when I thought about it. My dad had advocated for the use of a running martingale. It stopped the horse's head from elevating beyond a certain point—a common tool in the jumper world.

That afternoon, I had a jump lesson. Anne preferred to teach groups of riders—two or more—rather than private lessons. I agreed with her: This gave the horses a break between exercises, and it allowed riders to learn from watching others. Sinead, who had moved to New Jersey about the same time as I had to start her own business, was the other student that day. She and I had not seen each other since Rocking Horse in Florida, and I was looking forward to riding with her for the first time.

We started with one of Anne's favorite warm-up exercises: riding a figure eight over a small oxer, counting strides. On my first approach, I said clearly "one" when I was one stride out. Then the second time "one, two," when I was two strides out. I continued coming back to the same jump until I had counted: "one, two, three, four, five, six, seven, eight," one for each stride before the oxer. Anne raised the jump twice as I went through the exercise.

It was tough. Even as I counted "one, two, three, four…" the emphasis was on track, speed, rhythm, balance. There was no point in counting correctly if all the other elements necessary to riding to a jump accurately suffered. The easiest strides for me to count were five through seven. I was used to counting five out; the lower numbers were hard because I had to ignore where I normally "saw my distance." Seeing a distance meant finding the ideal takeoff spot, and having the quality of stride I needed to get there. Ignoring that spot five strides out was a hard habit to break. Seeing a distance to a jump eight out was also difficult for me, though it was made easier if I sped up or slowed down to fit the strides in, which defeated the purpose of the exercise.

I decided I needed to practice the exercise more on my own, even if it was just over cavalletti.

After the warm-up, we rode courses. With Sapphire, I was struggling with keeping her in a consistent contact. She was still throwing her head. I could not fix it, but I was managing it okay. Sinead was on a slim chestnut with an amazing canter—he could go from what looked like a twenty-foot stride to an eight-foot stride as smoothly as a gymnast. What a horse to watch! When Sinead rode, her laughter evaporated and she became focused. Her eyes did not invite conversation. I had noticed this determination in her the first time I met her, and it had not ebbed at all.

Afterward Sinead and I walked next to each other and let the horses cool out. As we chatted she became less serious. "Who do you think won that lesson?" she joked, with a quick smile.

"You did," I said, hoping for another smile.

Instead she dead-panned, "I know," and it was my turn to smile.

Later she made a point to tell me she liked my horse. We exchanged phone numbers. I said I would call her.

Once Sapphire was put away I knocked on Anne's office door. I can still count on one hand the number of times I went to her office with a specific question. Once I heard a cowboy say: "There is a fine line between respect and fear; you want to get pretty close to that line." I felt like a horse that Anne had trained well with this rule in mind.

I opened the door and took one step inside. Anne sat at her desk, waiting.

"Anne, do you think I should use a running martingale on Sapphire?" I began.

"What for?" She looked up at me from where she was sitting.

Around her were mementos from the Olympic Games and major Grands Prix she had won. She was filling in the next day's ride sheet, which she would then push-pin to the bulletin board in the aisle on her way out of the barn for the night.

I walked in farther, halving the distance to her desk, but remained standing. "To deal with the way Sapphire tosses her head between jumps."

Anne thought, then leaned back in her chair.

"Tik, you just need to ride better."

"Okay," I stood awkwardly. "Thanks." I backed up to the door and slipped out.

What she said was true. It was the answer to many problems I had. But it was not an easy road to this answer.

What Sapphire needed was to have less tension. Tension could come from different things. Mostly though, I guessed, it came from confusion. Understanding was confusion's opposite—and a much better friend. Another common cause of tension was asking a horse to do something that was really out of his comfort zone. So I struggled to be more clear with Sapphire...and to not ask more of her than I thought she was capable of. And she improved.

Anne's response to my martingale query, however—"You just need to ride better!"—became a slogan that I carried around with me. Eventually, I smiled when I thought of it.

TJ was different.

TJ stopped at fences. He stopped about as much as a cab driver in New York City and just as fast. Then he would lift his head like a giraffe and gaze off into the distance as if the cavalry had just come over the rise.

Anne believed I should be riding good horses, and she told me so. Her theory was riding good horses made a rider good at riding good horses. And that was the role I was hired for.

We decided TJ would return to Vancouver. He was unsuitable, and my goal of preparing him for resale had hit a wall. I had failed in his training. He was loaded on a trailer to go home, by himself.

He didn't call to Sapphire as he was loaded. He did not know he would never see her again.

Asa Bird walked back to the barn with me after the truck pulled out with TJ in back. He fell into step beside me.

"You look funny."

"Yeah?" I mumbled.

"You going to start mixing feeds?"

"I need a few minutes."

He looked at me, squinting. "Whatever, man. That's fine."

I went to the feed room and shut the door. I sat on the cement floor and stared at the wall. I felt fragile and weak, a levee buffeted by endless waves, and each new day saw the water swelling hard. A horse leaving was not something I would normally grieve over—after all, he was going to my parents, a good home. And it would mean shorter days for me, with one less horse to ride. But today, it was the wave that crested the wall. I brought my knees up to my chest. Then I put my arms around them and felt sad.

But soon I was angry. Angry at myself. Was I suffering for TJ or was this all about me?

I stood up and began, slowly, to lay out all the horses' dinner buckets to be filled. They covered almost half the floor. Then I began adding grain to each one…minus one.

CHAPTER 37

Sapphire Is Hurt
and I Call a Psychic

First you have to understand how this works. I will communicate with her through thoughts and scenes. I don't see what she is thinking in terms of words, but in terms of pictures and emotions. After all, that is how horses think and communicate. I will relay what I see. You will have to help interpret it. For example, I once told a gentleman that his dog loved eating from the big brown bowl. "That's ridiculous," the man said. "My dog has a small blue feed bowl." But later he realized it was the garbage bin the dog was referring to. So, I will help, but since you called, it is up to you to make the final analysis. After all, it's you who knows her. Have you ever called an animal communicator before? Of course, no, that's fine. Just sit down and relax. Take a deep breath, close your eyes, and picture her in your head. Breathe deeply once more and say her name three times in your head.

I shifted into park and turned the truck off. Despite it all, we were early. A wrong turn had taken us to the gates of the Aero Club and back. I had peeked through the gates. Picture this: A gated community with a green velvet runway down the middle, and a Piper or Cessna in every garage. I thought of the famous writer, Richard Bach, and the way he described the blood-racing rolling and tumbling of flight. I so easily imagined the steep dive down, and down, and down, till the earth and the devil were shaking hands and grinning up at you, sweat dripping from the pilot's brow, his eyes tearing up, his hand steady on the yoke. Then the thrill of pulling the nose up, almost catching grass in the propeller, laughing as the plane steadied herself and headed into open sky once more. Oh, that great blue sky! It was about living for just one thing. For him it was the freedom above and below you. For me, there I was, on the ground, about as ready to fly as a penguin, and I felt just fine about it. But still, I understood.

I jumped out and went back to check on Sapphire. The trailer had a side and a rear set of Dutch doors. I opened the side top door so my mare could look out. Her long eyelashes blinked as she studied me. Then she furled her nose and sniffed. Freshly cut grass. I looked back at her eyes. I couldn't get enough of them: The oily and mysterious iris, the lighter pupil that twinkled ever so slightly when she saw me. She took a long look around, then drew her head back in and set about her lunch. She took her time with the hay, biting small pieces with the incisors and transferring it slowly back to the molars where she chewed easily and steadily.

Well, now. Let me see if she'll accept me in.

Her head hurts. She banged her head. The right side of her muzzle hurts. She has pain on the right side of the right front leg. Her left rear end slammed hard and her pelvic girdle twisted. Her right eye really hurts. So, what happened? An accident, I see. But let me look deeper.

Normally Sapphire had the whole trailer as a sort of box stall, but this time I had the divider in place, separating the area into two narrow enclosures. The day before I'd had two horses in the trailer. We had gone out for a trail ride along the canals. Today, since the divider was already in, I left it—what could be easier? And since my mare was held at the front of the trailer I was able to lower the back ramp, which allowed me to access her easily without her being able to turn around. So with the back ramp down, and the divider up, and Sapphire eating lunch, I went to sign in at the show office.

Let's see. What is that? I see something. A mouse? Yes, I see a mouse. She hates mice! I see a field mouse. A young field mouse. A young dumb field mouse. Not to make light, of course, but there it is. The mouse got in somehow. How did it get in? I can't see that. Was there a way for a mouse to get in? The mouse went near her left hind leg. She doesn't like mice. Oh, wow, I think she really doesn't like mice!

"Can I sign up for the first jumper class, please?" I asked. Without looking up from her computer the secretary handed me some papers. I leaned over the table to fill them in. No pen. "Can I borrow a pen, please?"

The secretary kept one hand on her keyboard and searched for a pen with the other. She held it out, still without looking at me.

Name: Sapphire. Sex: Mare. Breed: KWPN. Born: 1999.

Then I marked the classes we'd enter, and I paid my thirty dollars. I took my number and asked for a couple of safety pins—I preferred to pin the number to my saddle pad than have it strung around my back.

"Thank you," I remarked. "This is a great show grounds. Not a cloud in the sky. Nowhere I'd rather be today!"

The secretary looked up. She raised an eyebrow.

"Good luck."

She tilted to the right when she went to kick at it. The mouse ran around between her legs. Scurried here and there. She tried to kill it! She wasn't too upset at first. But the mouse ran and ran. She kept trying to kick it. The mouse finally got away, but it did jump on her leg at one point. She rammed her lower leg into the trailer as the mouse scampered underneath her.

I whistled and sang to myself as I walked back to the trailer. *Tweet the magic tweet-tweet* went the tune. I stopped to watch a horse in the ring. *Tweet by the sea.* I had the morning off work…for this! My first show of the year and our first jumper class together in quite a while. *And frolics in the tweet-tweet-tweet…in a land called Honalee.* I didn't know why the children's song came to mind, other than the magic of the day. I smiled to myself and skipped around the corner of the arena as I put the pins on the number for safekeeping.

Her head was the first thing I saw when I reached the trailer. I knew immediately. Something was wrong.

Yes. Her intention was to kill the mouse. She wanted to smoosh the mouse. At first she was startled by the mouse, but then she was angry. When it kept moving around her feet she became determined to get it. But she missed and was frustrated. She became very frustrated. She wanted to kill it. Then the mouse got out and she went for it. She really went for it! She wanted to stomp on it.

Sapphire's head was out the side door, and she was looking right and left, like she was searching for something. The bottom metal Dutch door came up to her chest. It was not a door that any thinking horse would jump over from a standstill. But a scared horse, one that's just reacting, might. The drive to run first, ask questions later, keeps horses alive in so many situations. We try to train that out of them.

Sapphire had been to fifty or more horse shows—she was *trained*. I hadn't imagined anything could faze her.

But I should have.

She still didn't seem panicky. On the other hand, she sure wasn't calm. I wasn't scared—but I wasn't whistling anymore. I started to jog toward her. What was wrong? Flies? Other horses? Maybe there was a draft? I scanned for a problem but saw none. Closer now, I could see her eyes roll upward. I leaned forward into a run.

When the mouse got out she went for it. She was as angry as a bear caught in a leg trap.

The width of a dressage ring, that's how far away I was when she saw me. I was almost at her side in a quick sprint…her ears went forward. I slowed down so as not to scare her more. Then I watched as her energy shifted from a side-to-side motion, to a complete forwardness.

"Whoa girl… Eeeeeasyyyyyy," I called out. *Easy*, I prayed. But her muscles tensed up, and she became one giant spring.

The funny thing was, her eyes didn't leave mine as she jumped. Her front legs came up and somehow made it over the side door. But her hind legs had no chance. She seesawed in the air before sliding forward, the door caught just in front of her hind legs. She was stuck with all four feet off the ground. I saw the whites of her eyes as they rolled back and left me for the first time since she'd seen me.

She jumped out after the mouse. She was trying to kill the mouse; that's why she jumped out. Sometimes horses like rodents, but usually they see them as scavengers. They see them as enemies. They are competing for the same grain. This was not a good situation. Now she is annoyed. She is still annoyed. She still hasn't let it go. She wants me to karmically kill the mouse.

I don't do that!

Hold on while I explain that to her. She still wants me to kill the mouse. She is very stubborn. Very determined. Let me think of what else I can do.

Sapphire's front legs were a good foot from the ground. They hit and scratched the trailer door, her steel shoes ripping sharp edges open in the soft metal, the back of her legs catching on the sharp edges.

There was blood.

Her body rested on the door, which acted as a fulcrum around which she convulsed, obsessed only with getting away. She wanted to run. All her instincts said move. Get away. *Gallop!* But she couldn't get any leverage to get over the door. She couldn't go back and she couldn't go forward. Her legs scrambled for footing, and each time they did, she ripped more skin away.

More blood.

Will she forgive the mouse? No. She is not ready to forgive the mouse. Well, let me see what I can do. I'll put out energy to keep rodents away. It will have to be an energy that surrounds the trailer. If she won't forgive the mouse, we will have to make sure it doesn't happen again.

A man ran over. Then a woman with a white hat arrived. A young girl in riding pants gripped her hand and stood, wide-eyed. A crowd was gathering; unsure of what to do, they stood and watched.

"Call a vet!" I yelled to someone. Stay calm, I told myself. "A vet!" I shouted again.

I put my hands on Sapphire's halter, but she flipped me away. I stumbled forward again and grabbed her halter, cradling her muzzle next to my chest with my arms. She bit into my bicep. She didn't let go and I didn't shake her off. It would only hurt later.

"It's okay. It's going to be okay," I told her again and again. "Easy, girl."

With my arms around her head she struggled less but she didn't relax. Her legs longed to feel the ground beneath them again. Each hoof reached for the ground, a primal urge, like a fish struggling on the deck of a ship in order to get back to water.

A man came up to her other side, avoiding her front legs, which hit the door again and again. I saw more blood appear on her left pastern. Would we have to tranquilize her?

"Did someone call the vet?" I heard someone in the crowd ask.

"I've got an idea," the man on the other side of her called to me. He had to shout even though he was a few feet away at most—the sounds of her struggle were so overwhelming.

"What?"

"I'm going to unlatch the lower door."

"Are you sure? All her weight is on it." I was breathing hard now as I held her head. I struggled to talk normally.

"I don't think we have a choice. Hopefully it will fall open and she will be free."

"What if she gets caught up in it when it falls forward?" I argued.

But the man had already undone one side and was coming around to where I stood.

As he passed me he said again, "I don't think we have a choice."

And then he was there at the door on my side, and it was unlocked.

What I'm doing is I'm putting a white light around the trailer. A light that the rodents cannot penetrate. Hold on. It will surround the trailer and will repel mice. Hold on while I tell her that the trailer is safe now.

The door fell open, extending out like a ship's gangplank. It carried Sapphire forward and down and caught her foot in the moment before it hit the ground. She stumbled, pulling her foot out, and then she was free. I grabbed at the lead rope that trailed her, staying by her side, watching her flank go in and out like a bellows. She marched away from the trailer as if off to battle instead of back from it.

Now, let me see if I can help her. We want her to heal. Physically as well as mentally. I'm going to do some therapeutic breathing. Let's see if we can help her heal.

Sapphire was on a mission, her head low; she didn't glance right or left. Her jaw was set. I was watching her, running my eyes over her wounds, and ignoring the crowd, willing them away. None of the injuries looked life-threatening, but we were both breathing like we had just run ten miles. My skin was cool, and my heart rate was high.

I was still walking her when the veterinarian on the grounds, Dr. Mullin, showed up.

"So what happened?" she asked, approaching us.

"She tried to jump the trailer door. Got hung up."

"Where is she cut?"

"Here," I said, motioning toward her legs, then wiping my face as my voice broke. "And here. And here. And the stifles are both pretty messed up."

"It's okay, you don't have to talk if you don't want to," Dr. Mullin said. "Let's sedate her and fix her up."

I nodded.

"She's going to be fine. She is walking sound. The wounds look pretty superficial."

"Yeah?"

"I mean, I can't promise anything," the vet said, "but I'm sure it looks worse than it is."

I wiped my face again. What the hell was wrong with me? She was going to be fine.

As the vet cleaned and dressed my mare's wounds, she acknowledged we needed to go to a clinic for stitches at the very least. And also to see if one of the cuts went deeper into the tendon sheath than she could tell, which would be a much more serious injury.

"I doubt it," Dr. Mullin said, "but we better be sure."

"I'm going to put her back on the trailer?"

"She's sedated. I'll help you."

I thought about how I sure wouldn't want to get back on that trailer if I was her. But Sapphire trusted me. She walked right on.

"One foot. Now the other," I told her as she went up the back ramp.

She is doing better now. She wants to participate in her own healing. That is a great thing. Her head and neck are stiff. Her right eye is sore. She is sore but she wants to get better. The white light will keep the rodents away. She is healing faster now. Is there anything else I can help you with? Thank you so much. Good luck with her...call again anytime.

The next day at work, I worried about my mare. We had been at the clinic for three hours. Stitching and MRIs.

"Your horse takes three times the tranq as a normal horse and twice that of a difficult horse," the clinic doctor told me. I tried to keep Sapphire calm while he stitched up her leg and cleaned the raw, rubbed skin around her stifles. "You will need to change these dressings every day. Stall rest for a week. Light hand-walking is okay, but really, the less she moves the better. We don't want those stitches to rip out."

I couldn't explain what happened. My mare had never tried to jump out of the trailer before. She crossed the country in that trailer with hardly a fidget or a whinny. As my father is my witness.

I looked at my bicep and saw her teeth marks. Most of my upper arm was the color of an over-ripe banana. I wished there was some way to know what she had been thinking. I suppose we never truly know what others are thinking. All we have is their actions. With experience and learning we might learn the causes and effects of those actions. But it must be either ignorant or bold to say we know what they are thinking.

Fear memories for horses, like for people, are impossible to erase. It is possible to "cover them up" with happier memories, but the fears are never entirely forgotten. They will always be there, just beneath the surface.

I changed Sapphire's dressings that night. Bright red blood trickled out as I tugged at the day-old bandages. She ate her hay and swatted flies with her tail as I knelt next to her in her stall. Her skin trembled a little as I cleaned the wound, but her feet stayed planted on the ground. Her hooves were made for the earth. She could run like the wind and jump like a deer, but she wasn't made to fly.

We would leave that to others.

CHAPTER 38

Quitter

A nne rode over to me. Our horses put their heads together, and I pulled mine away before the mare I was on squealed.

"I want you to ride that horse *round*," Anne commanded. "That horse will go like any other horse! *Get her round!*"

The horse I sat on was nervous and often made her rider—Anne's client—nervous. The mare was in training for a few months; it was my job to calm her.

"Okay," I said.

But since being honored with the title of "Assistant to Anne," I was riding differently. Maybe I wanted to do a better job. Maybe I was in one of those phases where I learned something new, while at the same time realizing how *little* I knew. I was riding the same horses as when I was a working student, but something was off.

I picked up the trot again and Anne called out, "I did not hire you to ride like this. It's almost like you rode better last year."

Anne was honest. I was careful to listen to her. After all, I was not there for the salary, although I appreciated it. I was there for the education. Around Anne I had learned I needed to keep my cool. I told myself to not take her jibes personally. Looking around Wellington, I could see that self-confidence often made up for a lack of knowledge.

On more than one occasion I just made up my mind and blustered through. It was better than being afraid.

"I didn't get where I am today by people telling me how great I was," one rider said to me. The best, I often saw, had their own confidence, which allowed their coaching to be mostly analytical.

In Wellington for the second winter in a row, I was continuing to learn about keeping my mouth shut, watching, and listening. I spent a lot of time at the show grounds—the Wellington Equestrian Festival—but my mare never got to compete. Sapphire was stabled with Grand Prix dressage rider Betsy Steiner, twenty minutes away, in Loxahatchee.

Once or twice a week I ran on the clean sidewalks in the paved subdivisions of Wellington, named after what had been destroyed in the name of progress: Emerald Forest, Meadow Wood, Pinewood Grove, Tree Tops, Brier Patch. I continued to write, but it was lately a struggle.

Anyone who writes knows that it is hard to write honestly. I did not want to look like an idiot in the stories I shared. And neither did any of the other people I wrote about. But want to know the rub? The rub was I did a lot of stupid things. Thoughtless things. I let horses escape. I spooked horses. I missed seeing cuts on legs. I lost my temper. I broke tack. I rode badly. I attempted to teach people stuff I hardly knew myself.

It was hard to admit these failings. Especially in writing. Were these things I wanted everyone to know?

Of course, you might say, we all make mistakes. And that is true. But if an antelope trips he is eaten. If a fox misses he goes hungry. That ability to make mistakes and recover is the great and horrible thing for our species. My snafus could be painted as learning opportunities the way angst in the hands of Holden Caulfield was suddenly cool. But knowing everybody makes mistakes didn't make it any easier to admit them.

The lessons that improved my riding the most, even changed my life, were the ones that went beyond teaching. They were the ones that inspired me.

Ingrid Klimke letting me warm up her Olympic-gold-winning horse.

Karen O'Connor telling me at the Kentucky Three-Day, "You'll be riding here in three years."

Jonathan Field showing me how to get a loose horse to gallop right up to me in an open field. Right up *to me*, then stop, and relax.

In Texas, sitting on a colt that had never had a rider on his back before. I was his first.

I remember where I was both times that Anne told me I was talented. The first time was the night she offered me the job as Assistant Trainer.

The second time was eleven months after the first, the time it takes an unguarded whim to transform into a shaky-legged foal.

Our work days were getting longer and longer as the number of horses showing in Wellington increased. There were many times I was at Market Street until dark, and I didn't get time for Sapphire. Anne wanted to help me, but her horses were the priority. I wanted to help her, but I wanted to ride Sapphire, as well. In many working student jobs I could have brought a horse, but for this job, I shouldn't have.

I was sweeping the aisle and waiting for my boss. I saw her walk in from the jump field and go to her bit box in the tack room. She crouched down and rummaged through it, coming up with a bit in each hand. One was a thin copper bit, the other looked like leather— unusual. She looked at them both, put them aside, peered into the box again. I knocked on the glass door.

"Come in."

"Anne. Sorry to bother you."

She stood up and studied the bits in her hands.

"I want to try a new bit for the next lesson I'm teaching."

I took a deep breath. "I know your horses are your priority. I understand that. But I need to make some time for my horse." I paused. Then, "I really wish we could make it work, but I don't think it's going to."

Anne held the bits at her sides and gave me her full attention. She didn't try to talk me out of leaving. It probably was not that much of a surprise to her. I had mentioned twice before that I wanted more time to ride Sapphire. She had explained that the job was what it was. And she repeated that again now.

"You have to do what's right for you. We will miss you. I wish I could have gotten more horses for you to ride and compete here. You're talented."

I looked at the bits in her hands, then at the floor, then I looked her in the eye.

"Well, thanks for everything."

She nodded.

I got my sweater and helmet and went to my truck. I got in, turned the key, started driving to Sapphire. I had told Anne I didn't have enough time to ride Sapphire, but that wasn't the whole truth. While I loved show jumping, I was feeling increasingly boxed in. I missed eventing. And I wanted to learn more horsemanship. I was like a swimmer dying to get out of the pool, with all the lines on the floor, and out into open water. Or a runner who craved mountain trails instead of pavement.

At the forefront of my mind was the idea that this decision was a turning point in my life. I had worked years for this job, and if I just fell in line in there was a good chance I would make it. I would pick up more rides, get to enter more competitions. Anne would help me. I would be to her like she was to George. I would meet the rich and famous who came to Wellington to play.

On the other hand, if I never jumped a Grand Prix, if I never became a great rider, today would be why.

At Betsy Steiner's barn I went in to see Sapphire, but she was turned out in her field, so I went to my horse trailer. *Two-horse, rear- and side-load, aluminum, small tack room with fold-down bench and water tank. Possibility to sleep on bench,* the ad had said. I sat on that hard, wooden bench. I considered the bridles hanging above me. To my right two saddles rested peacefully, unaware. This is my home now, I thought. What next? When I took the job with Anne, I thought I would be there for years, not months.

I didn't call my parents. I wasn't ready to talk about the last couple of weeks. About this day. Everything had happened pretty quickly at the end. Maybe in a few months I would see the bigger picture—the purpose in coming when I did and leaving when I did. I reached over for the road atlas, stuffed in the corner, and pulled it open on my knees. I looked down at the map of North America. What should I do? I looked far to the left: Just above Seattle a tiny dot represented Vancouver. Home. Was it time to go back?

I took a deep breath, shut my eyes, and thought about where I'd been up to now.

CHAPTER 39

Back Against the Ropes

I ran my hand quickly over her knee and down the back of her tendons. Then I checked the other leg. I felt the old wounds; they were two months old now and healing well. The scar on the inside of the cannon bone was salmon pink with hair growing through. Another scar, on the pastern, was darker and blistered. I felt where the stitches had left bumps. I stood and ran my palm over her withers and down her back. I knew every inch of her body well now.

I bent over to look at her left stifle. On both sides the wound was still open and snaked upward from the corner where the hind leg meets the belly. I opened the lid on the antibiotic cream. The ointment was soft from the heat.

"Easy, girl," I soothed, but she winced and swung her rear end away from me.

"Sapphire, you're braver than that." But I knew she was sore. I rubbed a circle around the wound for a minute before trying again. Her skin puckered, but she didn't move away. She turned her head and looked back at me. "Don't give me that doe-eyed glare," I said. "I'm trying to help you."

Sapphire was strong. She was a Dutch Warmblood and built like one. In nature she was feminine. One summer I was lucky enough to ride for a few days with American Olympian Amy Tryon. She told me: "If you treat her like a bitch, she will act like a bitch. Treat her like a lady, and she will act like a lady." I touched Sapphire's heavy neck and rubbed her stern withers. She sniffed me, then took a mint from my hand.

We were still at Betsy Steiner's barn. She was helping me with dressage. I heard Sarah, her working student, on the other side of the barn, chatting with a client as she tacked up a horse. When the client was mounted and away, I heard her boots on the circular stone driveway, approaching.

"Healing up pretty well?" Sarah slipped her dark curls behind her ears as she crouched down to take a look. Her hair fell forward again.

"Not bad. Thanks to you."

Sarah had been looking after Sapphire for me since January, when I had been still working for Anne. Before I left my job.

When asked, I was saying, "I left my job." I could have said, "I quit," but I hated the sound of it. I did not want to be a *quitter*. It wasn't a sin...but it didn't make me feel super, either.

Since I'd left Anne's I was spending more time with Sapphire. If I hadn't had my own horse, maybe I would have stayed a lot longer with Anne, but there were just not enough hours in the day. The time I spent with my mare was always rushed, and I had discovered that rushing leads to mistakes. I didn't know if she jumped out of the trailer because of a mouse, or something I could have done differently, but I wanted to slow things down.

There are so many nuances with horses that I was learning seconds too late. The past few years had felt like I was in a war against mistakes, and I was determined not to lose the same battle twice.

"What are you going to do now?" Sarah asked me.

I didn't know and I didn't feel like answering. So I replied with my own question: "Do you think she'll be ready to compete this year?"

"You mean here? In Wellington?"

I gave her another question: "You think she could be ready in a month for the event at The Fork?"

"You still want to event her? She was bred for show jumping."

I gave up. I leaned against the stall doorway. "The truth is I want to event her."

Sarah looked closer at the marks on her stifles, and very gently traced her fingers along the edges. They looked like bolts of lightning. "I hope you don't go back to Canada."

"I'm not sure if my visa is valid now that I left Anne's. I better ask a lawyer."

"You want to stay in the United States?"

Did I want to stay here? Of course I wanted to stay! I wanted to go home, too. But yes, I wanted to stay! I had once been criticized for judging the United States too harshly. But in truth I was a fan of the country and the people, of the horsemen and the horses. I loved the writers, the thinkers, the teachers, and the friends I had made.

There were also aspects of America that made me sad. I'd lived a quarter of a century in Canada without ever hearing the "N-word." Then one day, in the United States, on a day like any other, I heard it, sudden and unexpected, like bird shit landing on your head. The young guy said to me, "Let's nigger-rig this motor while we wait for the parts to arrive." I'd frowned. Really? I thought we had given that up decades ago. Then a month later, from someone else, a woman this time: "You're gonna be the head nigger while we're gone." And then, on another day: "Nigger rich! You gonna spend all your cash the day you get paid?" the man asked.

These were phrases that I understood without ever hearing them before. Evil, like love, is mostly simple. But I am embarrassed that I was left speechless each time. It was later that I knew what I should have said: "Every time you use that word I lose respect for you. You will have to work pretty hard to earn that respect back." And while I didn't say anything at the time, it has stayed with me.

The United States is a country that loves a work ethic. It is believed that someone smart and talented and driven will get ahead. The equestrian world is a place where the ones who *have* gotten ahead are easily seen, especially in Wellington. The ones behind have a long, hard climb ahead of them.

"It's great to have you here," I overheard one boss say.

"I am happy to be here. This is a great job," the young man, a new hire, replied.

"You will start at six. There is no lunch break. You are done at five. Every other night you have night check."

The young man bowed his head. "Thank you for this opportunity."

"What part of Mexico are you from?"

"I am from El Salvador."

"Ah. Well."

"We work hard in El Salvador."

"Of course you do. Hey, Jose!" The boss waved another young man over. "Can you show this guy the ropes?"

"Of course," Jose said, probably thinking, *He will have his back against them in no time.*

Most of the workers I'd met in the horse industry, both American-born, and not, were transient. They rarely lasted six months. They complained that the work was too hard and the pay too little. Those in charge said the work was tough, but fair. "I used to work *harder* than that," they said. "They are *lucky* to have any job."

And there is always somebody ready to replace them, they probably thought.

At Market Street I played the role of both rider and groom.

Whatever needed to be done, I did it. I thought of one young woman I met at the show grounds—she was memorable for her royal posture and pearl earrings. She explained that she was allowed to miss high school for two weeks every year to show in Florida. The first three times we ran into each other I was on a horse, we chatted, and we found we knew people in common.

The fourth time I saw her I was leading a horse; I had my head down and was schlepping along. I wore jeans, instead of riding pants. I had a towel and hoof pick in my back pocket. I looked up at her as I passed the De Némethy Ring.

"Hey there! Hot, isn't it?" I called up to the girl on her horse.

I was sure she heard me, but she didn't answer. Maybe she didn't recognize me. But, on the other hand, she didn't look down either. She was on a gray horse with legs so long they could have been stilts. I shrugged and just kept on going; left foot, right foot, left foot. The difference between me and so many others leading horses around the grounds was that sometimes I was in the saddle; I had the possibility of a future that some of them did not have—no matter how hard they worked. And that difference was purely chance: who my parents were and what country I was born in.

I was proud of my family and my country. But really, that pride was not based on anything *I did* to achieve what I had. I had what I had because of dumb luck. It was nothing to be ashamed of, but the ones who sweated and dared for their dreams or their family or their citizenship had fought a more valiant battle.

I had seen many types of America, and many types of Americans. I would be honored if I could stay in America, I told hard-working Sarah, because I knew there were so many people just like her. And there were also opportunities that did not exist at home. This country, like a truly Great Horse, was worth the time to figure out.

Sarah looked at me. "You really should jump her, you know. She's talented."

"I'm just happy to have some time to spend with her. She'll heal and I'll make a plan. Maybe we can event *and* show jump. Does anybody do that? Do both?"

"Hmmmm," Sarah said, now squatting and looking at the mare's fetlocks and pasterns. "I'm not sure."

"See something?" I asked.

She had a hand on the leg, and she looked closer. Sapphire swished her tail.

"No, no. Looks like it's getting better."

"I feel so bad about it," I admitted and paused. "You know, I've written all these articles about horsemanship and what I've learned the last few years, and then I go and let my own horse get scared and hurt."

Sarah stood up. "It's not your fault."

"Whose fault is it?"

"She just jumped out. Not everything has to be somebody's fault." The sun came out from behind a cloud and highlighted her; she was caught in the shine like an actress on stage. I didn't think Sarah would tell me it was my fault—even if she thought it was.

"Sometimes somebody has to take the blame. This time it's me." Sapphire was standing quietly again, and I untied her. I was going to turn her out in the paddock again.

"You did everything you could."

"Maybe." I started to lead my mare, and Sarah fell into step beside me.

"Well, she's looking a lot better. You must be happy about that."

Now the sun was fully out, and the clouds were disappearing.

"Yes, I am," I said quietly. Then, "I spent the first week after I left Market Street sleeping in, riding, reading, but now I really need a job."

"Yeah. You're living in your horse trailer," Sarah said with a laugh. She took her sweater off as she walked, and tied it around her waist.

I had left the camper in New Jersey. I hadn't thought I would need it in Wellington. And the pickup seemed much more maneuverable without it. Now, sleeping on the floor in the tack room (the bench didn't work out so well), I regretted that decision. There wasn't enough room to straighten my legs when I lay down.

I stopped at the gate and waited till she looked at me before I said, "No, I *really* need a job." The chain and snap on the gate gave me some trouble so I handed Sapphire to Sarah.

The young woman put her hand on my mare's head, between her eyes, and rubbed a small circle. She watched me struggle with the double-ended snap.

"You look a little desperate."

I assumed she wasn't just talking about my issues with the gate.

"I feel like I'm on stall rest. I need to get out and run around. I need to *do* something." Finally I got the snap open. I opened the gate, took Sapphire from Sarah, led her into the grassy enclosure. I took the halter off.

Sapphire just stood there. She eyed me warily, not leaving.

"We all need a job, don't we, sweetie?" Sarah said to her. Sapphire widened her eyes and blinked as if to agree, or at least to accept that she didn't, and that was okay, too. Her body was healing well, and so was her mind. She had learned a lot—and also been tested. What were the limits to what she could learn? She kept surprising me. And how much could she endure? That I didn't want to find out.

Sarah and I left Sapphire alone in her field. I went toward my trailer, and Sarah went back to the barn.

"See ya later," Sarah tossed over her shoulder as she headed back to work.

The accident was a tough wakeup call for me: I was going to put

Sapphire first for a while. There, on the floor of the trailer, so close to where it had occurred, the whole thing ran through my mind again, as it often did. I tried to shake it off but couldn't. Normally I was tired and slept deeply, but that night I woke many times.

CHAPTER 40

Still Hungry

"Don't be an idiot!"

"But sweetheart..."

"Just because you're confused about what you're going to do now doesn't mean you have to be confused about us!"

"I'm not confused. And I don't want to talk about this on the phone." I lay on my back in the trailer, the phone to my ear. I looked at the ceiling.

"Trust me," Sinead sighed across five states. "You're confused. I know you. Come here and we'll talk about it in person."

Sinead was still in New Jersey, and her new business was growing. She was busy, and had big goals. Normally I liked that about her, but right now it made me feel more lost.

"I don't know."

"Why are you so moody? Stop acting like a child! Everything should be great. You ended your job with Anne on good terms. You're getting lessons from Betsy Steiner—who loves you, by the way. Your horse is healing well, and you've just spent the last fucking month at the beach!"

"I'm not sure."

"Look..." she started, but I kept talking, pulling myself up, slipping into my flip-flops, opening the door to look out. The sky was hidden by the leaves of three palm trees, but light squeaked through and the ground was dappled with sunshine. "I've only been to the beach twice. It was too cold to swim once. The second time there was a shark warning."

"Meet me in North Carolina, and I'll help you figure out what you're going to do," was her reply. Sinead was a problem-solver, I would give her that. It would make sense to meet at The Fork, a stable in Norwood, North Carolina, where we could both rent stalls and make plans. But I wasn't ready to let go of my bad mood that easily.

"You don't have to call me an idiot," I said.

"I didn't call you an idiot. That's a sure sign you're confused. Besides, I'm going to help you!"

"Help me with what?" I stepped out of the trailer and walked over to where I could see Sapphire. She was about 200 yards away. Her head was down. She was eating.

"There aren't many things I know a lot about, but I know a lot about horses. If you want to do this I can help you." A pause. Then, "And when has the water *ever* been too cold for you?"

Well, she had me there. And by knowing me, she helped my mood. I stood under those palm trees and smiled. "I went in, but it wasn't swimming weather."

"That's more like it, my brave soul, now get going! You head north, I'll head south," she instructed from all those miles away. "I'll meet you in the middle."

My suitcase had one rigid side so its wheels were sturdy. I needed to move everything from the trailer to the back seat of the truck. Then there would be room in the trailer for Sapphire's tack trunk, saddle, bridle, blankets, boots, and her ointments and wraps. I was using the suitcase, but I really wanted to be able to fit everything I owned in a backpack. I rolled socks and folded shirts. As I organized I thought,

I don't *have* to go to North Carolina. I could drive west. I could look for a job on a ranch. There might not be a frontier to conquer, but there are still sprawling ranches. Maybe Montana? Or Colorado? I'll work the range. It will be a job where I hardly meet anybody. Ever. Just me and my mare, checking fences. Foaling. Calving. Wrangling. Roping. We will join the cattle drives. Of course there are people there, but no crowds. And in every group of cowboys there is one man who is silent. That will be me. I'll sit by the fires in the evening watching the flames, my gun on my knees. I'll poke the embers with a long stick and then lean back and pull my hat over my eyes. From under the brim, I'll watch the others sleep. The stars will be light enough to cast shadows on the ground. As the sun rises I'll rouse the still-warm ashes into a searing flame and boil water for coffee. With the orange orb behind me, to the east, I'll swing my leg over the cantle. "Gonna get a head start on the day," I'll announce. Then I'll whisper, "Let's go, girl," and my horse and I will disappear into the woods.

Or maybe I'll find a lonely flat spot where I can park the camper by a brook. A place with fresh water will take us a long way. If I get there quickly there will be time to plant tomatoes, lettuce, maybe carrots and corn. Potatoes grow anywhere, don't they? White-tailed deer will be aplenty and if I'm slow on the draw, or sloppy with the bow, I'll deserve to be hungry. My horse will learn to stay near for that is where she will be fed and looked after. I'll shoe her myself. We will drink from the pools that gather at the base of the hills. We will sweat together in the summer, and in the winters I will let her coat grow long.

But…if I kept quitting these adventures as soon as it got tough, it would be like having a bunch of jokes with no punch lines. I needed to see something through.

Why did these thoughts come to me? Maybe I'd been in Wellington too long? Been to too many competitions? Maybe I'd been around too many people? Or too much affluence? I needed to find a better balance. I'd seen what other people did with horses; now I needed to find something that was right for me.

Now when I imagined a dream stable, it was not one with a dozen Olympic horses, it was one where everybody liked each other. It was a place where every day we worked toward a common goal. It was a place with more work than gossip. It was a place where I would continue to learn about horse behavior. A place where I could practice with rope halters, teach horses to jump on-line, and have them work around me at liberty. But did that mean I couldn't compete at a high level? Were the two ideas mutually exclusive?

It was evening when I had finished packing my bag and moved to the barn to prepare Sapphire's trunk. I suddenly heard a quiet voice: "Tik? Is that you in there? The barn is so dark."

"Yeah, it's me. I'm packing."

A silhouette entered the barn. The dark form slowly advanced and then revealed Betsy Steiner's contagious smile.

"What are you doing packing? It's pretty late."

"I'm going to leave a couple days early. I'm going to head to North Carolina for a bit while I figure out a plan."

"You're leaving us?" she asked me quietly.

I nodded. "It seems like every time I turn around lately I'm leaving."

But I was glad to see Betsy. She and Sarah had been my saving grace the past few weeks. Betsy gave a good lesson. She taught beginners as well as Grand Prix riders. Some people taught with rough honesty. "Tough love," they said. But Betsy taught everybody like they rode better than they did, and because of this, often, we became better than we were.

"Your long-lining is improving," she told me. And so it did.

"Your position is way better," she said. And I straightened my back, and my heart pushed my chest out, and the way I sat a horse developed.

Long-lining strengthened Sapphire's back muscles and hind-quarters without having the weight of a rider on her back. Ingrid Klimke told me: "No matter how good a rider you are, no matter how exceptional your seat, the horse will always move easier and more elegantly without you. It is up to us as riders to be invisible so that we may show these creatures off."

It was the same reason George Morris liked his riders and horses clothed in neutral colors: we were there to show off our equine partners, not ourselves. When we did our job well, we became invisible and the eye of the spectator was drawn to the horse.

Betsy treated her horses the same way she treated her students. She expected greatness. Then she received it into quiet hands and with calm eyes.

In the very small world where riders were dependent on patrons, why should someone like me expect someone to buy him a horse when there were better qualified, more experienced, and more deserving people, all doing the same thing? Anne was the best show jumper I'd seen and she had not had an Olympic horse for years. Eiren was the most deserving dressage rider I'd ever met, and she did not have a Great Horse. Betsy, too, needed an owner to step up and say, "Here's a Grand Prix horse, you've earned it."

Wouldn't that be nice?

How could *I* ever ask for that? I had such a long way to go. But I was also seeing how many ways there were to get where you're going.

A few months before I had urged a young horse to canter, and her trot quickened briefly before she picked up the canter.

"Use your *outside* leg!" Anne reprimanded when I didn't get the transition cleanly.

But the week before, Betsy explained: "It's the *inside* leg that asks for the canter."

The trot-canter transition is a common act. But there are different ways to do it and definitely different ways to describe it. Three-time winner of Badminton, British eventer Sheila Wilcox, wrote:

> *The aids to canter are preceded, as always, by the warning half-halt. The horse becomes attentive. Raise the inside hand slightly, sit on the inside seat bone, and apply the inside leg just behind the girth. The very application of these aids means that the rider's weight is greater on the inside and eventually this weight balance, coupled with the vibration of the raised inside rein will be enough to make the horse strike off correctly.*

The Principles of Riding, the classic text from the German National Equestrian Federation, also suggests it is the rider's *inside* leg that tells the horse's inside leg to step forward with these instructions:

> *To strike off in right canter the following aids should be applied.*
> 1. *The rider's right leg applied close behind the girth causes the horse's right hind leg to reach further forward.*
> 2. *The right rein, taking and giving a little, produces flexion at the poll to the right.*
> 3. *The rider's left leg, lying further behind the girth, controls the quarters and prevents the horse's left hind leg from stepping sideways.*
> 4. *The rider's weight should be predominantly on the right seat bone. (The rider must learn to put more weight on the right stirrup, which will prevent him from collapsing the right hip while trying to put more weight on the right seat bone.)*
> 5. *At the moment of strike-off the rider should ease the right rein to let the horse's stride flow.*

Colonel Bengt Ljungquist, coach of the US Dressage Team in the seventies, wrote that it should be both legs:

At the departure the horse must think forward. Call him to attention by a half-halt. Sit inward, lower your inside knee. Squeeze the inside rein a little more that the outside. Do not bend the horse outward. Keep your inside leg at the girth and the outside leg behind the girth and urge him into canter by squeezing with both legs. Do not forget to squeeze with your outside leg. If he gets used to the signal with the outside leg, it will be easy later on to teach him flying changes.

Back home in Vancouver, the German way was gospel. But *The Pony Club Manual of Horsemanship*, a continuous bestseller since it was first published in 1950, gives a solid, basic how-to version. An amalgam of knowledge from past and present professionals, it seems to suggest the use of the *outside* leg more:

The horse must be going forward in balance and with impulsion and accepting the bit. You should indicate with your inside hand the direction of the canter (with a quick 'take and give'), sit for a few strides, bring the outside leg back behind the girth, and give a definite nudge to the horse's side, while at the same time maintaining the impulsion with the inside leg. As the horse strikes off into canter you will feel the alteration of pace, and you must be particularly careful to remain supple, relaxed, and in balance.

Of course, if the horse understands what is being asked, who cares how it is done? It might as well be with a cluck or a whistle or a "heigh-ho." The answer is two-fold. One: Some cues inherently make more sense to a horse when they are first learning. The cues are almost like onomatopoeia to a horse. *WHAM! BIF! POW! Batman fought. Tattarrattat! was a knock at the door. Tick-tock went the clock.* Aids that are simple and obvious in a young horse can slowly give way to a more subtle aid as the horse matures. And two: Cues are meant to be universal. A horse trained in Poland should be able to step off a plane in California and be ridden by a new rider immediately and effortlessly.

With more complicated movements, it is important that the aids do not overlap. For example, does the rider's outside leg *back* mean haunches-in or a canter transition? Of course, it is the degree and the *feeling* that may mean the difference.

How to ask for the canter depart also depends on the maturity and training of the horse. *Teaching* a horse to pick up the correct lead is different than *asking* a trained schoolmaster to do it. (This is one reason why Grand Prix riders are not always good with young horses, and vice versa. It is a different skill set.) Another Pony Club book, *The United States Pony Club Manual of Horsemanship: Advanced Horsemanship* by Susan E. Harris, explains this progression:

> *There are three types of canter departs, which require progressively higher levels of riding and training. All three must be executed with clear, coordinated aids, and at the right level of training. The horse should always be prepared for a canter depart with one or more half-halts.*
>
> *Canter departs are developed progressively. A very green horse usually canters from the trot, using an angled canter depart and outside lateral aids. As he becomes better balanced and responsive to the aids he can canter from a working trot, with diagonal aids and a straighter canter depart. A trained, supple, well-balanced horse can canter from the walk, using inside lateral aids,*

which result in a more precise depart, and a straighter, more collected canter.

Harris then goes on to explain each of the three methods in detail. But basically the outside leg is recommended for a young horse that is learning, the inside leg for a mature partner.

What this all means is that Anne and Betsy were both right. While there may be some wrong ways to train a horse, there are also many right ways. All horses are different, and I have seen many great trainers break the rules or create their own. When I asked, they told me this: "You must know the rules before you can break them."

Before I left Florida, I stopped at the Agricultural Inspection Station. I presented my papers. Florida demanded health certificates for horses when they crossed the border. I parked and went into the building. I knew the guard would photocopy the papers and my driver's license. Then he would follow me out to the trailer where he would match the photo of the horse on the paper against the real horse standing in my trailer. For others this was a simple formality, like showing ID when buying beer, but my pulse quickened. I watched each page being photocopied. I winced inwardly when he said, "You're a long way from home," and I was aware of the gun on his hip as he followed me to the trailer.

In the end my papers were in order. I could move on. Soon after, I stopped for gas and called Sinead. It had been a three days since I last talked to her, and I knew she was already in North Carolina waiting for me. She was at The Fork, her stepfather's farm, with him, her mother, and her brother. All through the winter I had talked to Sinead on the phone two or three times a week, sometimes for an hour or more. We talked about horses, but we also talked about the future. Now I was going to stay with her. And her family.

Was she my girlfriend?

"Hey," she said. She sounded distracted. She was probably feeding the horses breakfast.

"Hey, I just crossed the border. You sure you want me to come?"

"Tiiiikkkkk. You're killing me."

"I should just go home." I finished pumping the gas and switched the phone to speaker. I put the truck in drive—the I-95 was to be my fate for most of the day. I turned the volume up on the phone, and I could hear water splashing into buckets in the background as Sinead continued her morning chores.

"So you can be a big fish in a small pond? If that's what you want, I'm not going to stand in your way. And you wanted to be a working student for *a year*—it's been *three*! I think you need to give it a shot on your own."

The traffic was light as I pulled onto the highway, and the lanes were wide.

"I dunno."

"Come here and we'll talk about it."

"You *think* it's a small pond. Just 'cause everybody from Canada goes south, and everybody from the West goes east. And then everybody from the East goes to Europe. And everybody from Europe goes to England, or wherever they go. But aren't there people who will succeed no matter where they are?"

"Look." I could hear irritation in her voice. I imagined her doing that *tap-tap-tap* with her hand that she only did when she was impatient or anxious. "If you want to raise your game you have to go where the better courses are, where the better coaches are, and where the better competitors are. This is the right place for you now."

"I should have just stayed at Anne's." I got into the slow lane, and settled in behind an RV doing sixty. Why hurry?

"What?"

"Maybe I can go back. She said I could come back."

"Don't be stupid."

"I hate it when you call me stupid," I said. But I didn't mind, really. It was how she said it. Like she liked me.

"That job was great while it lasted, but I really think you're over it now."

"You know, there is some really basic stuff that I'm still trying to figure out. I don't know if I'm ready to run my own place."

"What are you confused about?"

"What do you mean?"

"I mean, what are you confused about?"

"You want an example?"

"Give me an example."

"Well. Let me think." I drove in silence for a few seconds. I passed the billboard that asked about John Galt. It felt good to recognize something.

"Should the outside leg or the inside leg ask for the canter?"

"Anything else?"

"Can a program have longeing and round-penning that co-exist beneficially?"

"What else?"

"I dunno. Isn't that enough?"

"You know what?"

"No."

"You're not confused about how to ride. Those are just excuses. You're confused about how to live." I could tell by her tone, Sinead was just getting started. "Know why? Because you know how to do a transition! It's about feel more that anything. You *have* all this knowledge. This *amazing* knowledge. And it's great that you are still asking questions. And it's great that you are still figuring this out. But now you need to start to make all this your own. You're not the type to work for somebody forever. I wouldn't tell this to someone sixteen, or twenty, or even twenty-five. And some people not at all. But you're almost thirty. You're smart and talented and it's time you grew up. I don't mean stop learning. I mean start living. Keep taking lessons, but take a chance on your own. You need to have your own place and make your own mistakes."

"That's not even what I was asking."

"It seems like you are taking all these chances and putting yourself out there. But it's time to take the next step."

"I don't want to end up just another small-time trainer." I studied the national park stickers on the back of the RV. Yosemite. Carlsbad. Acadia. "I'd rather work for somebody. At least at home I have friends and family. My dad wants me to take over the business. It's a 'made' business. I'm guaranteed more success if I go home."

"Wasn't it Asa who told you to *man the fuck up*? Sometimes that can mean staying, but sometimes that means going. You need to learn the difference. You think it's a sign of loyalty or perseverance to stay in a relationship that isn't working? It's a sign of immaturity. Right now you need to put yourself out there as your own self. Forget all these guys who teach other people's methods. What you should do, what you are capable of doing, is taking everything you have learned and making it your own. Didn't you call it 'Cafeteria Riding'? Did you forget about that?"

"You read that?"

"Yeah. I read that."

"I love you sometimes."

"Thanks a lot."

I drove another three hours. At the next station I filled up with diesel and went to the trailer to check on Sapphire. I saw the scratches on the side door where her front feet had fought for footing that day, which now felt long ago. I checked her hay and water. She had always traveled well.

"How you doin'?" I asked her, and she sniffed at me and then went back to her hay. She was relaxed, and I wondered how she became so trusting, so forgiving.

In the previous three years the days were sometimes fast and sometimes slow. Sometimes *really* slow. Monotonous chores made time slow down. I watched the clock, *tick, tick, tick, tick, tick, tick.* But while the clock may have struck slowly, the pages of the calendar always fluttered, turning more and more quickly, as if caught in a wind. As each page turned, I learned something. Sometimes I learned what to do; often it was what *not* to do.

I remembered my mother humbly explaining the half-halt to me.

"I've trained three green horses up to Grand Prix and I still don't know a *great* half-halt," she said. "The half-halt is an idea, such a simple concept really, but it can separate good riders from great riders."

I was proud of what my mother did with horses, and while I did not listen to her as much as I should, I always heard her in the end.

"In a sport that is all about balance and timing, the half-halt separates the men from the boys. Or more commonly these days, the women from the boys," she proclaimed. "It is the foundation of all the other work. Some might say that the half-halt allows you to do all the other movements, from extended trot to piaffe to passage. But, no, the half-halt is an end in itself! The half-halt is the moment of creation. And creation *is* an end in itself! It is art. And like in any artistic endeavor, each artist will create something different—there are only a few great ones who can take a horse and create something beautiful and memorable and eternal.

"Remember, you will always keep learning. You will always look back after a year or two and think: *I knew so little then.* That is the nature and the genius of this sport."

I was behind a Mini now, and it slowed suddenly. I hit the brakes, apologizing silently to Sapphire. The other cars ahead slowed, as well. Once past a car looking to pull over, its engine smoking, we all surged forward again. I saw another sign: WELCOME TO NORTH CAROLINA. My mind started to wander. I thought about home as we approached, and passed, Albemarle.

I liked to drive with the windows open, and I noticed the temperature change as I entered Norwood. It was colder than Florida, but this was good weather—it reminded me of home. The sun was still up but I saw, too, the moon already high in the sky.

That evening Sinead's family was around so all my questions were put on hold. I drank beer while the others drank wine. They talked about the farm, and the hay, and the town, and the price of gas, but mainly they talked about horses. For the most part I just listened.

"I don't know how this sport is going to survive."

"What do you mean?"

"Land is getting more expensive and more places are being developed. It costs more and more to own horses and compete."

We sat at the wooden bar shaped like a "C" that faced the kitchen. Sinead's stepdad was cooking pasta, and there was steam, and tomatoes being diced, and pots being moved, and probably more action than was needed. We didn't need the TV on.

"Something will have to change. We need to bring in some new money."

"We need some big sponsors."

"But it will never be like in Europe where it's part of the culture. Where they have people lining the courses four deep. Where there are beer gardens by each fence, and trade fairs at every entrance."

"Do we really want eventing to be a big sport here?" I queried. I took a sip of my beer. "I wonder if that would change it?"

"Of course it would change it," somebody said.

"Imagine if eventers made as much money as show jumpers!" someone else offered.

"Imagine if show jumpers made as much as hockey players!" I challenged. "Imagine if hockey players made as much as baseball players!"

"What's your point?"

"Where's the finish line?"

Although I realized the necessity and inevitability of change, it scared me. Much of what I liked about eventing would disappear if serious cash was involved, as was evident in the show jumping world. Yes, I needed to make a living, but I sure did not do this for the money.

Every sport and every hobby had its own sphere, where people gravitated toward certain people and certain places. I knew there must be famous ping-pong players and handball heroes, with groupies who knew their names. But if they took a small step outside that small world, they were no one, and that kept all of them humble. I didn't think these worlds should be big enough that one didn't have to—sometimes—leave.

After dinner I left the beer behind, and switched to a rum and coke, with lime. A Cuba Libre. Then I slipped out to the patio, tilting my head at Sinead as I left. A few minutes later she joined me. She touched my arm.

"You've got goosebumps."

"The air is real tonight." I breathed in, felt my lungs swell. "I think I can smell the river. I love being near the water. You know in Vancouver I lived near where the Fraser meets the Pacific?"

"You miss home."

"Take a deep breath."

She did. I sat down and looked at her. She wore tight jeans, faded, with small rips in the thigh and knee, and a clean white shirt. She took another breath.

"Can you smell that?" I asked her.

"I'm not sure."

I took another deep breath of my own. I grinned as I said, "Now I don't think I can smell it either."

Sinead pulled a chair closer to me. To one side of us was the house, with the windows lit. To the other side were dark woods. We faced slightly away from the light.

"Do you know what you want to do now?"

"Well, I guess the two big questions are: Do I go back to Canada or stay here? And do I get another job or start my own program?"

"Do you want to know what I think?"

I drank. What a delicious evening. "Hmmm?"

"This is what I think: You should come back to New Jersey with me after the competitions here are done, and you should find a barn to run your own business out of. You will pick up clients really fast. I know you. And you can compete your own mare how you see fit."

"We could have a great business in BC."

Sinead paused, then looked at me. "Would you be happy in Vancouver?"

I wanted to say yes, but I told her the truth.

"You don't really want to go home. You need to make it on your own first."

"But I don't know if I'm happy here either."

"Look. I want you to stay, but you are totally free to go home. You are free to be miserable. Sometimes I think you like it. Or you can try to make it happen for you here."

We sat in silence then. I put my hand on her leg, and she put her hand on mine. After I while I said: "I do miss home. I miss winter even. I haven't had a real winter in three years. I miss snow. I even miss rain. Nothing has felt real lately. Here, though, something feels real. I don't know if it's you or the weather or being on my own."

"Thanks a lot." It was her turn to grin.

"I think I have a real problem with change."

"No you don't. You might have a problem but not a *real* problem. If you did you wouldn't be here."

"Do you think change is a good thing?"

"Yes. And you need to change what you're drinking. What is that?"

"Try it."

She took it from me, and sipped. "Oh my god. That is strong. Wait here, I'll grab you a beer." Sinead returned with a Malbec for herself and a Corona for me.

We drank and talked and laughed...and then I took her to bed.

The next morning came early. I went up to the barn while it was still dark. I rode in the arena first. The trot-canter transitions were easy if I didn't think about them. Soon Sapphire and I decided to head outside. I looked around and liked what I saw: no fences. Now this felt real and good. What *was* real? Hunger, loneliness, failure, fighting, fighting back, pride, swallowing my pride.

It was uncomfortable being hungry. But I wrote better when I was hungry. I was a better competitor and better student when I was hungry.

Sapphire and I began a slow canter along the tree line, away from the barn. Soon we entered the woods, and I slowed to a trot. I hadn't been this way before. I came out of the woods and found myself on a ridge. I looked around. There were pine and red cedar all around me. This was a place to think.

Time fell away both behind me and in front of me. Two abysses. I was on a precipice that was about to break, and grace was allowing me to choose which way to fall: forward or backward.

I chose to start something new. This would be the end of my working student positions. Forward, I thought, and I asked Sapphire to walk. In her first step there was a burst from the underbrush. Quail. My mare spun and started to canter again, but instead of pulling her up I decided to let this one take its course, maybe something to distract me. We ran along the trail, and then out into the field again. Her tension left her quickly, but she didn't slow down.

We flashed past a stand of trees, and I ducked to miss the branches. I looked down and the ground was a blur. We headed into the fields. They were freshly hayed and the short grass made perfect footing. Her feet moved confidently as we raced along. My eyes watered as the wind whipped my face. Something different was coming. "What's going to happen?" I asked Sapphire. She did not answer but kept on galloping. I let the reins out and we ran on. We started up a hill and reached the crest, and then I saw forest and more forest. The world seemed ready and we were a part of it. The wind was in her mane, and the dawn sun was on my back. I had made up my mind, and there was plenty of time to work, for the day was still ahead of us.

PART II

PROFESSIONAL

CHAPTER 41

Troncones

Cameras flashed like a swarm of fireflies, lighting her smile. The seven-piece mariachi band drowned out the waves; talking was impossible. The dance floor was full, but I only saw one woman. I spun her, and dipped her; we danced apart—me, all arms, her, all hips—and we danced as close as two people can dance. The floor became slick with sweat, and I wanted to sit down. Eamon took my arm and led me to the bar, where he poured.

"Tequila will revive us," he declared.

I don't know how much later I stumbled out the door. I held my shoes in one hand and looked down the beach at the walk ahead. Eamon appeared in front of me, made me promise I would meet him in three days' time, at dawn, on the beach, at the north end of Troncones.

"Don't forget," he said, as Sinead joined us.

I reached for his hand, missed, grinned goofily, and hugged him. "The earlier the better," I lied.

"Three days" was important because that was when I would marry his daughter. I had my doubts Eamon would remember our rendezvous. It was likely he felt the same way about me. Neither of us mentioned it the next day, or the next, but he was already standing barefoot in the sand when I arrived at our assigned time. His linen shirt looked light and thin in the golden morning light.

"This is the first sunrise I've been up for."

"Me too."

"Shame, isn't it?"

As we walked sandpipers skirted ahead of us. Eamon talked; for the most part I was content to listen, but I did want to find a minute to apologize for not asking his permission before I proposed to Sinead two years before. It had been a mistake to not ask him, but at the time, he seemed out of the picture.

"Tik, I'm not a good role model. I've made a lot of mistakes. Yes, I've paid dearly for them, but I've made a lot."

"Eamon…"

He slowed his speech, looked out over the water. "I just want to share some things with you. You are going to marry my only daughter today. Maybe you can learn from some of my mistakes."

I nodded. The sky was turning tangerine in streaks, and I felt the salty air on my face.

"I grew up on the streets of Dublin. Fighting. Bernadette, Sinead's mother, came from class. Her dad knew it wouldn't last; we were too different. But we made it work for twenty-three years."

I did not believe that Eamon and Bernadette were a mistake, not with Sinead in my life. I asked about his marriage, then about my fiancée's childhood. We chatted about what it had been like living in Irmo, South Carolina.

"Remember this, there is no book on parenting. There is no book on relationships. You have to figure it out. If you have any questions, I want you to know you can ask me."

I smiled. I was sure there *were* books on parenting…and on relationships. But I also knew Eamon had figured his own life out—one handshake, one knockdown, one get-back-up, at a time. The lessons he learned himself were the most real. I remembered asking him if he had read *Angela's Ashes* the first time I met him.

"No way," he'd replied, laughing. "I *lived* that. We all lived that. I don't need to read about it."

We walked until the smooth beach gave way to rocks, and then we stood looking out onto the Pacific Ocean. There was a movie I saw as a kid where two brothers swam out into the ocean at dusk. The first one to turn back for shore lost a bet. The challenge was repeated, time and again, and one brother always turned for home first, until one day, his mind made up, he went farther and farther into the dark, until he was swimming by himself. Years later, when the boy was asked how he won that day he said simply, "I never saved anything for the swim back."

Troncones lay to our right—small buildings and villas along a shallow bay. Eamon began the walk back and I ran a step to catch up. The wet sand felt firm and strong beneath my feet.

"Character. Class. There is no substitute for class," he proclaimed. "There are people who have PhDs, gold medals, great jobs, who have no character. Most of the people at your wedding have success. They understand ambition, perseverance, hard work. Most of them don't have life experience, though. Experience is part of class, having it, for sure, but also appreciating it in others."

I was coming to understand Eamon and his standards. He had expectations from his family, his career, and his friends, but he also looked deeply into himself...and out into the world. One minute he could be completely present and the next he would be looking right through me. He saw things I did not.

Eamon was an Irish Catholic by birth, but in Paso Robles he stood a large stone Buddha in his front garden. He was a gift-giver: At a funeral in Maryland I had admired his hip leather jacket, and in a moment he had it off and held it out to me. I tried it on.

"Keep it," he said with a smile.

"I can't accept this," I replied, taking it off, pushing it back toward him.

Sinead, watching, whispered to me, "Just take it. You know him. He gets more pleasure out of giving it to you than he would wearing it."

I felt Eamon was placing a lot of hope in my marriage to his daughter. I watched seagulls squabble on the sand, and then take off as we approached, as I thought about that.

Neither Sinead, nor Eamon, had made a big deal out of me not asking Eamon for Sinead's hand, but over the last two years I had grown to understand that I had underestimated their love for each other.

The smell of brine and kelp came on the breeze. I tapped a shell with my foot. I decided that I would apologize another time. There was plenty of time. I wanted to just listen today. Eamon kept talking, sometimes looking out to sea, sometimes looking at me, and I tried to hear, and internalize, everything he said. Then, as we stood on the path directly in front of our rented villa, he gave me his last advice.

"The biggest challenge I see for you is your jobs, your ambition, your separate careers. I don't want either of you to stop that, but you have to acknowledge something else equally as important: each other. And you have to work at it."

He was not expecting an answer, so I stayed quiet, but for the third time I made a silent pledge: *I will.* I will work at it. Sinead is as important to me now, Eamon, as she is to you.

Eamon made his way back along the water after that. I could see him looking out to sea. I walked up the short path away from the beach, entered our bungalow, and started coffee. The kitchen had no walls, so as I stood waiting, I watched the gulls circle, and behind them, the shimmer of the distant blue horizon. I took two coffees up to Sinead, still sprawled in the bed we shared.

"Wake up, love bug," I whispered. "Today is the first day of the rest of our lives."

CHAPTER 42

On Enthusiasm

Our place, we were practically stealing it. We paid probably half of what our landlords could have gotten if they had fixed it up even a little bit, but they didn't want to bother, and besides, we all got along and had dinner together once a week. It was in Hunterdon County, an hour from New York City, but still a place with farms. Our apartment was in their former carriage house, on the second floor. From there we could look out the window and see their typical, old, New-Jersey-style house: white, grand, with grass spreading out from its base like a skirt.

Two things I liked about our apartment: First, it was *ours*. Second, it had a red door at the foot of the stairs. That is an inviting door, I thought, the first time I saw it.

One Thursday evening I sat down on our couch. I patted the cushion and Zeppo, our black-and-white mutt, jumped up. He circled twice, and then sank into place next to me. I loved that word, "sank." Anne and George always would say: "*Sink* into the saddle. Don't sit. *Sink!*"

To my right was a bookshelf. To my left, a television. In front of me was a low brown table, and on it, a box the right size for a small saddle. In the box were videos from Road to the Horse; Pat and Linda Parelli; Jonathan Field and George Morris; Ray Hunt; Tom Dorrance;

Guy McLean; Dr. Robert Miller; The Jeffery Method; dressage and show jumping World Championships; Burghley. Many of them were competition videos, but my interest in horses was evolving, and more and more of the DVDs were about different kinds of horsemanship (whatever that was). Riding was still fun, but it was not enough.

In my pursuit of this Next Real Thing, I also watched YouTube videos: Tommy Turvey, Clinton Anderson, Dan James and Dan Steers, Tristan Tucker.

I read too: Monty Roberts articles during a lunch break; a Mark Rashid paperback on the plane; *The Revolution in Horsemanship* by Dr. Robert Miller and Rick Lamb. I struggled through more technical books like *Evidence-Based Horsemanship* by Martin Black and Dr. Stephen Peters. By the time I found Dr. Andrew McLean I was hitting my stride, and I could understand more technical concepts.

Few people, even those with degrees, could give clear definitions of concepts of behavior training like punishment and reinforcement. Did it matter? I wondered. Their skills might be far ahead of their ability to explain what they were doing and why.

Each of the trainers I was watching and reading about approached horses from a unique place. Some had a scientific background; some used horses for ranch work; some were in the business of entertaining; many of them taught for a living; a few of them competed. Besides having various backgrounds, everybody was at their own point in his or her journey with horses. I tried to respect that. It was too easy to get all caught up in what was at odds. Of course, there *were* differences. But hey, I thought, people sail all kinds of boats.

When I studied these horsemen, I found three levels on which to compare them:

First, the *techniques and tools* they used varied widely. One trainer used a Western saddle, another used English. One trainer used yachting line, another used nylon, while a third didn't use ropes at all. One trainer shook a lead to ask his horse to back up; another trainer used a stick and a tap on the horse's chest; another said, "He will back up when he is ready."

There are easier ways, harder ways, quicker ways, and slower ways, to work with a horse, but mostly, if something looked like it was not quite right, the problem was with the person shaking the rope, not the rope. Yes, using the most effective tool for the job is important. But having the right kind of flag or stick does not a horseman make.

When I began my adventure I wanted to learn from people who went by the book, but I had a growing appreciation for the innovators. There was room to do things differently, to explain concepts more clearly, to try new techniques, to do things better.

After *what* they did, comes *why* they did it. These were the theories that the trainer understood and used as the basis for his or her training decisions. Although not all the individuals I studied could clearly verbalize these theories, they all applied them. I also saw that there was plenty in common here when it came to the good trainers: The discipline or style of training did not matter as much as effective teaching methodology. Horses learned in a few distinct ways and being able to pinpoint and understand these was vital.

On a deeper level resided the philosophy of the trainer. I never saw two trainers with exactly the same doctrine. The philosophy of my parents differed. It differed between Karen and David O'Connor. It differed between Johann Hinnemann and Ingrid Klimke. It differed between Jonathan Field and Bruce Logan. It differed between George Morris and Anne Kursinski. A differing philosophy in training horses might be similar to differing parenting ethos. Do we let the kids stay out late and they can learn for themselves going to school tired is no fun, or do we set a curfew? Do we want to be their friend or their leader? It had taken me years to begin to see philosophy in training and riding horses; seeing techniques was much easier.

To a certain extent, I did not care what Monty Roberts' background was or what kind of halter Mark Rashid used. What I wanted to know was, could I learn something from them? If I could, I would go after it. I would not be a learning victim. I would not wait for the knowledge to find me. I would not only feed off the knowledge that hung at head height. I would look deeper or ask questions. If I found I could not learn something from a trainer, I was going to go somewhere else to learn. We could still be friends. Or perhaps not. No hard feelings.

Watching trainers with different techniques *was* frustrating at first, especially when I was trying to find my way through something new. But after a while I appreciated it more, for it gave me more viewpoints from which to create my own. It was the same in other disciplines I studied: When I saw Olympic show jumper Rich Fellers in such a forward seat, and the other riders not, I thought, Interesting! What do all these riders have in common? The better horses all traveled in an uphill balance; they were looking forward, drawn to the next jump, like an arrow fired out of a bow. These traits seemed consistent, despite different rider positions. It seemed what horses disliked was not a certain rider position, but an *unpredictable* rider position. They wanted to know where their rider was. It was the same with handling the reins: Horses would rather have more tension in the reins than lighter but inconsistent tension. The consistency helped them understand. *Understanding* helped them *relax*.

The scale of tension I had pondered years earlier in my mind was filling out as I came to know more and more horses. Although I loved watching competitions, competing seemed to be the easy part. But preparing a horse to be in the right mindset to learn. Wow! *That* took some thinking.

So, I watched what others were doing, but I did not feel obligated to copy them, only to comprehend their views and techniques.

Natural horsemanship did not seem to have established rules the way show jumping or dressage did, and yet it had evolved into a unique discipline. It had gone from being a means to an end, to an end in itself. For some, the goal was to entertain crowds or to have fun, which was a different mindset than if the goal was to compete or to create a working horse. This evolution is not unusual—consider the path other sports have taken. Running to hunt or to avoid being hunted is now an end in itself. Watch Britain's Mo Farah run; you will see poetry.

For a few, natural horsemanship—both on the ground and in the saddle—has become an art. Something as simple as bridling a horse can be done so smoothly, with such politeness, that it is as sweet as an apple.

Buck Brannaman, who gained mainstream fame when the documentary *Buck* won the Sundance Film Festival Audience Award, took difficult-to-load horses and showed them they had nothing to fear from the trailer. I thought if I were a horse, I would like to be *his* horse.

Cowboy Chris Cox started young horses, a discipline that is inherently difficult and dangerous, and he did it without making mistakes. How could he make it look so easy?

I watched my friend Jonathan Field play with horses at liberty as if he and his horses were a school of fish, dancing and weaving together through a reef.

There were so many different approaches to natural horsemanship that for some it became all about the name. There were so many kinds of "horsemanship" available, it was hard to know where to begin. At the heart, though, it was simply training horses "the way it should be." After all, what was "natural" about taking a horse's instincts and changing them or molding them to our purposes? Did "natural" necessarily mean "good"? Murder, cancer, rape, and incest all occur in nature. Does nature have morality, a sense of right and wrong? Nature can be as harsh as she can be beautiful.

I was watching a video when I heard the red door to our apartment open. Footsteps. "Hello," I said. No answer. "Hello?" I called.

Zeppo got off the couch and tilted his head, waiting to see Sinead come up the stairs. His eyes—one brown, the other mostly blue—were totally still and focused. He was a rescue, most likely a blend of Collie, Husky, and Shepherd.

"What are you watching?" Sinead asked as she appeared. Zeppo ran to her and "frapped" around her feet. "FRAP" to dog trainers stands for Frantic Random Activity Period, also known as "the zoomies." The vocabulary dog ownership had introduced!

Sinead sat down on the couch next to me and Zeppo immediately rolled onto his back, pushing his chest toward her. She rubbed him.

"Last year's Road to the Horse. Listen to this quote," I looked down and read from the notes I was keeping. "'A trainer works on getting the horse better for himself; a horseman works on getting himself better for the horse.'"

"I like it. What are you drinking?"

"Cuba Libre. Can I get you something?"

"It's been a long day."

"Wine? Did you like the quote?"

"Yes, please. Who said it?"

I went and got her a glass of Malbec. "I did. Just now." She looked at me with those raised eyebrows that meant she was just about half-way between amusement and annoyance, so I said, "Chris Cox, I think. You want me to put something else on?"

"This any good?"

"It's a little like watching the Tour de France. It goes on for a long time, and if you can appreciate the subtleties, and you are patient for the exciting moments, you can watch it for hours. There are some crazy moments."

"Okay," she said, looking at Zeppo on his back. He was still push-ing his chest toward her as if he was a gymnast.

I kept watching the cowboys. One was on his horse already, bare-back, as I replied, "Okay what?"

Sinead still watched Zeppo, whose hind legs moved as if riding a bicycle upside down.

"Let's leave it on for a bit."

"If you don't like it we can change to something else", I conceded. "And rub that poor dog. He missed you."

We studied the horsemen on the television. Road to the Horse was a competition where horsemen "started"—they used to say "broke"—colts in a head-to-head format. Three (some years four) horse-and-rider pairs were assigned their own round pens, side by side in the center of the main arena at the Kentucky Horse Park in Lexington. I'd never seen anything like it: sold-out crowds, announcers, television cameras, judges. The trainers tried to go as fast, and as far, as they could with their colts in three days. There was a ridden obstacle course to prove yourself on the third day. There were also rules about how long a trainer could work a colt, what tools and equipment the trainer could use, and how many breaks he or she had to take. Still, it was a lot to get done in a few hours. If a trainer crossed a line, the horses felt it, the crowd—a discerning bunch— saw it, the judges judged it, and I'm sure the trainer knew it. The format of the competition brought out a battle in the trainers' souls: a battle between patience and urgency.

We watched them move on the TV screen, so smooth and confident and experienced that the word *natural* did spring to mind. We observed their attitudes. Which attitudes did I want to exude when I was around horses? Thoughtfulness and empathy? Definitely. Patience? Yep! Joy? Yes! Enthusiasm? For sure!

I wanted to be thoughtful about how and when I used a whip. When we approached a jump and the horse seemed unsure, I arranged my position and supported it with the whip to help me emphasize, "We have prepared long hours for this moment, I believe in you!" The better I got, the less I used the whip to tell a horse, "No." An educated viewer saw that difference. Horses, for sure, knew the difference.

I wanted to be patient with a horse that was not ready to jump. Every time I put my leg on I expected the horse to go forward (over, under, or through). But I tried to never put my leg on *unless* he was prepared and *could* go forward. If we did not make it over a jump, that reflected on our partnership, not on the horse.

Empathy. There was a difference, I thought, between the kind of empathy that understood a horse's motivations and fears, and the kind of empathy that treated a horse like a dog or a child—even with the best intentions. I was aware that empathy had, in the past, rendered me paralyzed. Perspective, I was learning, was important.

Perhaps most of all I wanted to remain enthusiastic. I wanted to smile when I was with horses. During my years on the road, and now as a head instructor, I was working the hours of a legal student. Every once in a while I thought I needed more balance or I was going to burn out. I thought about writing again, or more often, but it was not a priority. The horses were too interesting, and besides, they were paying the bills. One day, I promised myself.

I glanced at my wife. Her riding clothes were tightly fitted to the lines of her body. Her blond hair was down. I picked a piece of hay off her shirt. I took her hand in mine. "Sinead?"

"Yep."

"This is cool, isn't it?"

She squeezed my hand. "Shhhh, I'm watching."

I grinned. It was addictive. One of the horses was being saddled for the first time. I might have seen hundreds of horses saddled for the first time. But *that* horse would be saddled for the first time only *once*. It was an initiation.

"When I was in Texas with Bruce I thought I would learn

something about riding. I don't think I learned *anything* about riding. But I learned more about horses than I had in all my previous life."

Sinead finally leaned over and rubbed Zeppo. He gazed at me, making eye contact, until he could stand it no longer, then he flopped his head back, and his eyes shut. Sinead rubbed his belly. "I remember you saying that."

I put my drink on the table and rubbed Zeppo as well. If he could have purred, he would have. "Riding and understanding horses are two different things."

"But I think the more you understand horses, the better the rider you are."

"Of course. But it is so easy to get caught up in learning just what we *think* will help us reach the end result faster. Sometimes if we learn how to go a step backward or a step sideways, we can actually go farther forward. And we can get there faster."

Sinead stopped rubbing Zeppo and leaned back on the couch. "What are you saying?"

I sat up and turned to her. "I think some people like to compete, some people like to just have horses as pets or to dot the landscape, some people like to start horses. I'm saying people are interested in different things."

"Wow, Tik. That's really incredible," she said, deadpan.

I raised my eyebrows. Zeppo growled, and still looking at Sinead, I went back to rubbing him.

"You know," she remarked, "all these horses—they all like *grass*."

I laughed. "I guess I'm saying when people want to jump, it can be hard to see how this is relevant. It's like, you want to drive a car, but you don't see the need to know how to make one."

"*Is* it relevant?"

"When I understand what these guys are doing it makes me more versatile. But you're right: Most horses are so forgiving it probably doesn't matter. And if you have a trained horse, it matters even less."

I stopped rubbing Zeppo for the second time, and he growled softly for the second time, eyes looking straight into mine. I went back to rubbing him. Sinead rolled her eyes.

"At least one of you is getting trained." Suddenly Sinead's attention was on the TV. "*That* horse isn't very forgiving."

"Jesus. I haven't seen a horse bronc like that in a long time."

I'd heard criticism of Road to the Horse—that starting horses should not be a competition. But competition is fun. It drives us to improve. This particular model brought attention to methods that may not have been in the spotlight before, so people like myself could learn. Yes, sometimes trainers advanced more quickly than the horses were ready for, but honestly, that is the trouble with young horse classes in *any* discipline. Hell, that can be the trouble with *all* horse classes, for *any* age. We all have to take responsibility and prepare ourselves so we are in the position to make the right decision for a horse. Some horses progress more quickly than others. Just because a competition exists does not mean we *have* to enter it. And just because we *do* enter it does not mean we *have* to finish it. There is no shame in losing a competition and winning a friend.

"You want to keep watching this?" I asked. We had both been riding horses all day, and now maybe we'd benefit from different subject matter.

"Just a little more."

Sinead leaned back, one hand in mine, eyes on the horses. We couldn't get enough horses. Even while we watched I finished our earlier conversation in my mind: Horses are forgiving, and we can get away with a lot with them, but that doesn't mean we should. Zeppo, finally, gave up his soft growling and slept at our feet.

CHAPTER 43

"Can He Ride?"

In 2014 the off-the-track Thoroughbred Icabad Crane and Olympic eventer Phillip Dutton stole the show at the inaugural Retired Racehorse Project's Thoroughbred Makeover. The point of the now annual contest was to garner more interest in re-homing ex-racehorses—those that were no longer wanted on the track.

I could see the video of Phillip and his Thoroughbred play in my mind's eye as I ran my hand over the horse in front of me. Icabad earned the nickname "Mr. Adjustability" for putting four, five, six, seven, and eight strides between two jumps in a line. Not a bad feat for a horse that had raced the year before. Was there a way to top it?

Horses are mainly motivated by people through the contrast between discomfort and comfort—commonly called *pressure* and *release* (for example: pulling on the reins, squeezing your legs, using the whip...and then *not*)—but riding can become art when that motivation is based more on curiosity, play, and even a sort of contagious enthusiasm for work. Watch the soft hands of eventer Lauren Kieffer as she rides, or the confidence her fellow competitor Buck Davidson gives his horses as he jumps, and you start to see how some of their mindset rubs off on the horse.

I remember watching a video of Olympic dressage rider Steffen

Peters in a training session. Something out of view of the camera got the horses in the ring riled up. The camera's focus was on Steffen, but in the background you could see the other riders, trying to bring their horses back to the work at hand. Steffen felt his horse get excited and what did he do? He changed his plan, instantly. Instead of the working trot, he smoothly shifted his weight, looked up, smiled, and asked for passage. And then both the rider and the horse got what they wanted: harmony.

I have replayed that scene so many times in my mind that it has become personal myth, something seen, then exaggerated; a beautiful thing that has meaning, so that even if it had never really happened, it would not matter.

The search for that kind of connection and willingness is the main reason I sought out another horse of my own. And when I learned of the Thoroughbred Makeover, with the chance to perform, compete against others, and perhaps win prize money—I admit, I was all in. I approach a contest like a duck to a pond.

Others must have been thinking the same as the Makeover organizers had to incorporate a cutoff for entries at 350 and start a waitlist. The rules stated each participant could start working with an off-the-track Thoroughbred as early as January of the year of intended competition (the Makeover was held in October in Kentucky). That gave us nine months of potential training and preparation.

But it wasn't until June that Sinead heard about Mr. Pleasantree from Liz Millikin in Virginia. Liz was an Advanced Level eventer known for a great eye when it comes to finding horses. After seeing a short video of him, Sinead called me immediately.

"Tik, I found a horse for you. You need to go see him."

"I'm on a horse, can I call you back?" I always felt obligated to answer the phone when I was riding, but I didn't like the interruption and distraction. I often thought, I will know I've made it when

I can just have a landline. I'll return my calls at the end of the day.

"The horse is in Middleburg. Can you get there tomorrow?"

"Tomorrow?"

"A horse like this does not come along very often."

"I can't do tomorrow."

"*Tik.*"

I knew that tone. I winced. "I bet I can get somebody to go look at him for me."

"Try Lynn."

I asked our friend and four-star eventer Lynn Symansky, who lived in Virginia, if she could check out this horse that Sinead was so excited about. Lynn came back with a positive report: "Classy, good conformation, great canter, solid feet, nice walk." Her only criticism? The horse was green to the jump. But that might be expected in a horse that had only been ridden off the track a handful of times.

I took the next step and called Dr. Christiana Ober, the Canadian Equestrian Team Vet, who was based out of Middleburg, asking her to look at the horse's X-rays and do a pre-purchase exam if they looked good. Dr. Ober gave the thumbs up, adding, "This is one of the nicest Thoroughbreds that I have ever seen."

Now it was my turn to get excited. But because I had lessons to teach, and horses to look after, I couldn't get away. All this had happened within four days and more and more people were getting involved. I was reminded what a team sport horses are.

Finally, my father, who had just arrived for a week to visit, and whose trip coincided nicely with this whirlwind of activity, volunteered to take a look at this supposedly very nice Thoroughbred— Mr. Pleasantree. Betsy, a student and friend of mine, said she would go as well. They drove from New Jersey to Middleburg while I taught and rode. Liz Milliken was skeptical when I phoned to say my dad was coming to try him for me.

"This is a young horse, he can spook a little," she said. "Can your father ride?"

I grinned. You bet your ass he can ride, I thought. But, "Better than me," was all I said.

Betsy and my dad liked Mr. Pleasantree right away. And wouldn't you know, they had brought a trailer with them—so they loaded him up and brought him back.

Now I had four months to get him ready for the Makeover.

In 1939 there still wasn't a road across Canada to connect the Atlantic to the Pacific. When my grandparents drove west from Ontario, it took a bit of planning and a lot of bravery. In order to go west, they first had to go south; the majority of their drive was through the United States. They drove a flatbed truck that my grandfather had used to deliver bags of coal in Toronto until their wanderlust overtook them. They meandered like pilgrims through various provinces and states until they found themselves in the Okanagan Valley, in British Columbia. After a summer of leasing a hotel on the Okanagan Lake, trying to make a go of it, they gave up and wondered, Which way now? And that old answer was apparent: West again!

Heading west from Okanagan there were no paved roads, but rather than head south to go west again, they sold the truck and bought two horses. They completed the trip to Vancouver, sometimes on deer paths, sometimes on goat paths, on two stocky part-Clydesdales named Patches and Lady.

In 1957 my father decided to recreate the last leg of his parents' journey. He and his friend Brian took a bus from Vancouver to Penticton, a city on the Okanagan Lake, where they bought two horses. They rode on logging roads from there to Summerland, on the west side of the lake, then on to Princeton where the Tulameen and Similkameen Rivers converge east of the Cascade Mountains.

The thing was, Brian had lost his finger in a sawing accident only a day before they left Vancouver. His finger was throbbing. Each hour they rode the hand was getting bigger and darker, and the pain was worsening. He was worried about the risk of infection. Halfway home to Vancouver, Brian threw in the towel. When he broke the news to my father that he would have to cut the trip short it was not a surprise.

The horses arrived in Vancouver, by trailer, a couple of days after the boys made it back by bus. Brian's horse, Acadena, stepped out first. The second horse, Remarkable, jumped out and skipped up to my dad.

"Remarkable!" My father took the rope and gave the horse a rub between the eyes.

A few years later my dad sold Remarkable and eventually lost touch with the horse's new owners. Even though my father went on to own many horses and to be short-listed twice for the Canadian Eventing Team, he told me he often thought about that horse and that trip. Brian, his childhood friend and fellow adventurer, was his best man when he married my mom. Brian died the year before we bought Mr. Pleasantree.

In honor of that trip, that friend, and that horse, we renamed Mr. Pleasantree.

He was now Remarkable.

CHAPTER 44

On Remarkable

I turned into our driveway and almost hit a white-tailed doe. I dimmed my lights and she ran across the road. Then another. And another. Then a buck. Seven deer altogether. Maybe deer are like horses; they have better night vision than us, but it takes them longer to adapt to sudden changes in light. I would have to look that up.

"Hello?" I called up the stairs.

I took my shoes off at the front door, and was halfway up when I heard, "Hello!" I smiled. I liked this ritual. And again, "Hello!"

"Sinead, I want to write another article about Remarkable."

"Hello," she said coyly from where she sat on our couch with Zeppo, legs curled under her, looking completely relaxed and beautiful.

"Sinead, be serious for one second. I want to use a quote about Kate Albey for an article."

I was still catching up on American authors since moving to New Jersey, plus I was always looking for new ideas for my next piece. Sinead knew the drill.

"Who is Kate Albey?"

"Probably the worst mother ever."

"What's the quote?"

I picked through my backpack and found the old copy of *East of Eden,* now coffee-stained, and read aloud to my wife:

In human affairs of danger and delicacy successful conclusion is sharply limited by hurry. So often men trip by being in a rush. If one were properly to perform a difficult and subtle act, he should first inspect the end to be achieved and then, once he had accepted the end as desirable, he should forget it completely and concentrate solely on the means. By this method he would not be moved to false action by anxiety or hurry or fear. Very few people learn this.

"What is the end she is trying to achieve?"

I smiled. "Murder."

"Do you really think that relates to riding?" Sinead asked doubt-fully, eyebrows raised.

"Yep."

"Why?"

I paused. I moved around the room, but I didn't sit down. "I guess it's because being in the moment, and having patience, are two of the most difficult and most important skills for working with horses."

"Is that part of natural horsemanship?"

"I don't think love or hate is any more natural than the other. I think it is up to us to choose which one we prefer."

"I think I need to read the book."

I passed it to her.

"Actually, I think wanting to win is more natural than the incli-nation to go slow and do better by the horse," I admitted, kneeling down to scratch Zeppo behind the ears. He immediately rolled on his back. I rubbed his stomach.

"You think that's good?"

"No, but I think it is *natural*. Much more Darwinian. But I will *choose* not to go that path."

I was entered with Remarkable in the Thoroughbred Makeover—only two months away now. I was entered to win, but I needed to seek that balance—to be ready to change plans, or back up, or abort if need be. The hardest part of horse training might be, knowing *when to quit*. If I drive three hours to school my horse cross-country, and my horse is too anxious when I get there for it to be a positive experience, I want to have the discipline to not jump a single jump. And the same should apply in its own way to starting a horse or deciding when to begin competing a dressage horse at Grand Prix.

The Horse Park of New Jersey Horse Trials was marked to be my first competition with Remarkable. I felt underprepared; I was ready to withdraw if necessary. I approached the weekend like a training session, but I was still nervous. We used the dressage as a flat school. I was happy to keep him fairly calm and forward. Then I gave Remarkable the chance to take a good look at fences before jumping them on the cross-country and in stadium. In both phases he broke to the trot a few times, which I didn't mind at all. I would rather have him slow down, look, and then go, than run anxiously. Thoughtfulness and relaxation travel well together, so we hit that road and just took it slow.

Millbrook Horse Trials was our second competition two weeks later. We improved our dressage score. We had three rails down in show jumping, which was an improvement from the four we hit at HPNJ. Remarkable still didn't really understand the game, but the light bulb was glowing!

Bucks County Horse Park Horse Trials was our third Beginner Novice event, and our first clear round in show jumping. It was starting to feel like Remarkable and I wanted the same thing, at the same time, more often. It wasn't fun for me to ride a horse that wanted to go fast when I wanted to go slow. Or vice versa.

This is what I told him, my big sweet gelding:

There is a solution to every problem. Believe in me.
I will never ask you to do something you can't handle.
Do not panic! Think.
Trust me.
Try!

A working cowboy, one making the clinic circuit with his wife, once told me: "A horse should try to go up a telephone pole or into a rabbit's burrow for you, if you ask. You should never ask." And when I thought back to my working student days I realized that that *try* was so important to Ingrid, David, Karen, Bruce, Anne, everybody. It had begun to come clear at the end of my time at Market Street, it was not just about teaching horses; the bigger picture was about getting them in a frame of mind to learn.

There would be $100,000 in prize money at the Thoroughbred Makeover, split between ten categories: Barrel Racing, Competitive Trail, Dressage, Eventing, Field Hunter, Freestyle, Polo, Show Hunter, Show Jumping, and Working Ranch. Each horse could be entered in two categories. Remarkable and I were signed up for Eventing and Freestyle. On the last day of the contest, all the finalists would then compete against each other for the title of "America's Most Wanted Thoroughbred."

And *that* was our goal.

The Eventing test would be the United States Eventing

Association's Young Event Horse Test for four-year-olds (regardless of the entry's actual age). For the Freestyle category, contestants would have the ring all to themselves, with whatever props they wanted, to demonstrate "the trainability and talent" of their Thoroughbreds.

Sinead, who had been skimming through Steinbeck, finally looked up.

"So what are you going to do for the Freestyle?"

"I have six minutes. So I think three minutes on the ground without a halter or lead. Playing with Remarkable at liberty. Then three minutes riding him without a bridle."

"So you'll be doing horsemanship?"

I answered with another question, a game I like to play sometimes: "What is horsemanship?" It was even odds that I would annoy her if I pushed this game too far, though.

"What you do."

"No. I'm asking *you*. What is 'horsemanship'?"

"Do you mean 'horsemanship' or 'natural horsemanship'?"

"Either."

Sinead's eyes narrowed with suspicion.

"I feel like you are leading me down a path when you already know the answer."

"There is no real answer as far as I can tell. Ask a dozen people, get twelve different answers."

"So, what are you doing with Remarkable?"

"It would be interesting to start a collection of people's answers to the question, 'What is horsemanship?'" I mused.

"So, what are you doing with Remarkable?" she repeated.

"You know what, I'll show you. Grab a sweater." It would be dark soon, but there were lights in the indoor arena at the property where I rented stalls. It was about fifteen minutes away. "Zeppo can come." I filled a water bottle in the kitchen as I kept talking: "When you think of horsemanship do you think of somebody working on the ground? Or do you think of Bernie Traurig letting a young horse investigate an obstacle up close before coming around to jump it?"

Sinead went slowly down the stairs. Zeppo ran down ahead, missed the bottom step, and tumbled. He looked back at us, paused, then ran off again. Frapping again.

"I think of the first, but I see what you are getting at."

When we drove together we inevitably took Sinead's truck, and I was content to let her drive. When I drove I was usually too slow, and occasionally too fast, for her taste. Driving might be like bringing a horse along: The speed I go is the best speed. Everybody going faster is crazy, everybody going slower must not have a job. I talked as she started the truck up.

"A halter should not define a horseman. It's more about how a person understands a horse."

Sinead navigated the long driveway as she said, "But what about somebody who understands a horse and just takes advantage of him? Like a con man. Just because we can read a horse's thoughts and feelings doesn't mean we always use that knowledge for good."

I liked her answer, so I decided to push it a little further. I asked her: "Well, what's *good* to a horse?"

Sinead turned left. She was thinking. Then left, then right, to go through Oldwick. We passed the la-di-da Tewksbury Inn, then the old blue General Store, which had a bit of everything and a classic grilled cheese, and finally the stand-alone yellow Magic Shop. We were through in thirty seconds. Sinead accelerated and finally spoke.

"I guess it depends on the horse and the situation."

"Exactly. Causing a horse stress when you set boundaries does not always appear nice. But anytime something really new is learned the horse is out of his comfort zone and may experience some stress. That's what I was thinking. It's like a bell curve. A little stress is beneficial to performance, but pretty quickly it can become anxiety."

I had thought about this a bit, was all ready with my follow-up question—but I also had no agenda. I really did not know what I was trying to know.

"So it's not clear exactly what *good* is. But do you think a horse can get used to being out of his comfort zone?" I asked my wife.

We passed men making hay, then drove by sheep, then horses. Then we approached a long hill. On either side were trees, enough to call it a wood, if not a forest. Occasionally we passed a dirt road. I'd heard it was more expensive to live on a dirt road than a paved one in this part of the county. Quiet and good for riding horses, but it meant affluence for dirt to transform from impractical to quaint.

Sinead spoke clearly. There was very little left anymore of either her Irish accent or her southern one.

"I think once a horse is used to it, what once was out is now *in* his comfort zone. If something is really *out* of his comfort zone, then he is uncomfortable."

"Hmmm," I responded, staring straight ahead. That got me thinking, but it wasn't until we arrived at the barn that I pulled out a notebook and a pen and drew two lines that connected in the bottom left of the page. "Take a look at this XY graph. One side is the level of the rider; the other is the level of the competition. You would imagine that a person would sign up for a competition that matches her level, right?"

"I guess so."

I drew a line that went at forty-five degrees up to the top right corner, so that there were now three lines. Along this last line I wrote: *The Zone.*

"Well, if she does, that's great. This line I just drew is where one is most likely to be 'in the zone.' You know, that 'unthinking' place. That place where time seems to slow down. Have you ever seen the movie *The Greatest Game Ever Played*? That golf movie with Shia LaBeouf?" Sinead shook her head; I could see it didn't ring a bell. "Well, everything except the golfer and the ball fades into the background. Noises disappear. Distractions are gone. That's being 'in the zone.'"

"I love that spot," Sinead admitted, remembering now. "That's what my first Kentucky Three-Day was like for me. I felt like an underdog there, but I'd put in the hours. I was ready. Any pressure on me was pressure I was putting on myself."

I drew a long thin bubble just above the line. In it I wrote: *Improvement.*

"Well, if you compete above that spot, that's where you are most likely to be *out* of your comfort zone. You're not likely to win there… but that's where the most improvement is made."

"If you go much above that line though, time seems to speed up."

"Yep," I agreed, and above the *Improvement* bubble I wrote *Danger.* "And things can get out of control."

Sinead was nodding. Now I drew another bubble just below the forty-five-degree line. In this bubble I wrote *Confidence* and pointed to it, saying, "Look at this other side. Competing just *below* that middle line is where you gain confidence."

Sinead nodded again. She could see where I was going with this.

"But you can also go too far, and then things just get easy," she said.

"Yep, you're wasting time, money, effort." And below the *Confidence* bubble I wrote: *Boring.*

"Makes sense," Sinead agreed.

Now that we were at the barn Zeppo was eager to get out, and he moved around restlessly in the back seat as he looked out first one window, then another.

"Hold on one second," I said to both of them. I quickly flipped the page of the notebook, and drew a second XY graph. I filled it in just the same way: *The Zone* along forty-five degrees, *Improvement* above the line, *Confidence* below, *Danger* well above, and *Boring* well below. "The interesting thing for us is that we have two of these graphs: one for the rider and one for the horse. So which one do we follow?"

"The one for the rider," Sinead said immediately.

I waited. I could see different scenarios playing out in her mind; her fingers tapped her knee as she tried to make sense of it.

And then: "The one for the horse."

I looked at her. Waited again.

"Oh, I see!" she exclaimed as it came to her. "You follow the graph for whichever one is at the lowest level."

I grinned. "Yep."

I opened the door of the truck and stepped down on the gravel; heard it crunch and skitter with each step. I opened the back door for Zeppo who flung himself out the door and into a new adventure. Then I waited for Sinead. As she walked beside me to find Remarkable, I explained further: "Just picture those graphs. They are why if you want to compete at the international level, it makes sense to have a horse that is always better than you, so that you are always competing at the place that is right for you. Above the line if you want to improve. Below the line if you need to get some confidence. And right near the line for the big classes."

"But what about somebody like Christilot Boylen? She took her first horse to the Olympics as a teenager!"

I laughed. "Good point. That was in 1964 for one thing. But, you're right—there are always exceptions that prove the rule."

"How does that prove the rule?"

"I have no idea. That's just what they say."

At Remarkable's stall I held out a horse cookie, which I often had with me (many clothes came out of the wash with pockets full of grainy mush), and waited for him to come to me, which he did. I let him stretch his neck the last few inches. His whiskers touched my hand. His ears went forward like antennae. He took the treat politely. Giving treats involves skill and timing; it was not something to be done thoughtlessly.

"Sinead, the other caveat is that not everybody wants to go to the Olympics. If you want to get good at starting horses, you need to start *a lot* of horses. If you want to be great at dressage, you need to ride *a lot* of dressage horses."

"And I guess you can have 'horsemen' with different skill sets."

"Yep." We were on the same page now. "I think you can. Look at people like George Morris and Ingrid Klimke. They may never have picked up a rope halter in their lives, I don't know, but they are both great horsemen. And Bruce Logan maybe couldn't compete at the Olympics, but he's a true horseman, too."

I put a saddle on Remarkable, took him to the arena, and set him loose. But he didn't leave. He stood with me. I asked Sinead to stand beside a jump so she would be out of the way.

I asked Remarkable to canter, and he did—boy, he left with a buck! He did what I asked, but he did it *his* way. I was fine with that. I loved watching him! I asked him to circle, then to come to me. I gave him a rub, then asked him to follow me as I zigged and zagged and sprinted and stopped around the arena. After a few minutes of this I let him stop next to me.

He took a deep breath, and I waited for him to lick and chew before I got on. Then I rode him bridleless. My arms were relaxed; I had no reins. I could steer with the neck strap, but when he wanted to speed up, or cut left, I often just went with it. Better to be on the same page than to grind away at something I wasn't going to get anyways. I picked my battles; I compromised a lot.

After trotting, and cantering, I came to a stop and lay along his back. My feet were by his tail, and my head just to the side of his withers. He hardly twitched. I put my arms around his neck.

"That was a little over six minutes, but essentially that's what I'm going to do."

Sinead is not one to pass out compliments easily, but I could tell from the way she took me seriously that she liked it. I asked her what music I should use, and she knew right away:

"'Pompeii' by Bastille. 'Firestone' by Kygo. They will be perfect."

I nodded in agreement. Perfect. "I knew marrying you would be useful someday."

Sinead withheld a smile from her lips, but I saw tiny wrinkles at the corners of her eyes. She knew her smiles were like candy to me, and she liked to ration them.

"Now don't get too big a head or you'll have to get a new helmet."

I laughed and hugged her. Zeppo ran over and jumped against our legs.

I led Remarkable back to his stall. I rubbed him in front of the saddle. He was learning to respect me, trust me, as I was learning to respect and trust him. We were finding our own brand of horsemanship, just the two of us.

CHAPTER 45

Horses, Too, Are More Forgiving Than We Deserve

"I will never forget seeing this gelding walk out of the stall for the first time. He was *huge*. Legs that went on forever." Reed, known to folks at Turf Paradise Race Course in Phoenix, Arizona, as Dr. Zimmer, was a vet. He felt the legs of hundreds of horses each month. He watched thousands of horses jog up for him every year. "But this one was special."

It was during lunch, January 12, 2015, six months before I bought Mr. Pleasantree, when Reed heard that he might be for sale. He had been watching him for a while. He didn't rush over, but he also did not leave it until the next day. And as the horse came out of his stall, a smile spread across his face.

"I'll take him."

"You want to see him move?" the trainer asked.

"Nah."

"You don't even know how much I'm asking."

"Doesn't matter. I'll take him."

The trainer shook his head. "Well then, I guess you will."

Reed called his girlfriend, Kara, as he led the horse away, through the track stables.

"You have never seen a Thoroughbred like this."

Kara, of course, took that with a grain of salt. She knew Reed was a cowboy. From Texas. His first true love was Quarter Horses, then racehorses. She wasn't so sure he knew what made a good jumping horse. So she kept asking him questions.

Exasperated, he finally said: "Just come and see him."

It was Kara's first experience having a vet jog a horse for her, instead of the other way around. As Reed and Mr. Pleasantree stopped, the horse looked off into the distance. His eyes were bright and bold. Kara took the lead rope right out of Reed's hands.

"I love him."

The gelding fell in line politely next to her as she headed straight for her father's barn at the track. Her parents were both racehorse trainers. People stopped and stared at the pair. The horse was tall and bright as the evening sun. In a zoo full of zebras, he would have been a red giraffe.

Mr. Pleasantree ran twenty races and won four. His sire certainly ran his share of races: Pleasantly Perfect was an American racing legend. Born in 1998, he won the Breeders' Cup Classic in 2003, and the world's richest horse race, the Dubai World Cup, in 2004. In 2005 he retired as the fourth richest American horse in career earnings.

Pleasantly Perfect was born in Kentucky, raced many times in Kentucky, and then stood at stud in Kentucky until eventually he was sold to Turkish interests. As of 2015, he was standing at the Turkish National Stud.

Mr. Pleasantree's mother? Spare That Tree.

I never found out much about her, but at least I could tell people where his name came from. Spare That Tree's father was Woodman, an American bred horse that was famous for siring many winners. And I can only assume her name came from that famous poem-turned-song penned by American George Pope Morris:

Woodman, spare that tree!
Touch not a single bough!
In youth it sheltered me,
And I'll protect it now.
T'was my forefather's hand
That placed it near his cot;
There, woodman, let it stand
Thy axe shall harm it not.

Although the tree is spared, the relationship between the boy and a tree reminds me of Shel Silverstein's *The Giving Tree*. In that tale the tree gave herself to the boy, piece by piece, until finally she was cut down. But even as a stump, good only for sitting on, she remained forgiving...and happy.

Horses, too, are more forgiving than we deserve.

Kara was the one who started transitioning the big chestnut from his racing life. He was her only project at the time and she kept him close; he became more than a project, he became a friend. She would ride him around the backside after training hours. The two of them would sneak out to school in an adjoining round pen and arena that were once home to the Phoenix mounted police. They also hauled out for lessons, ponied a three-year-old filly around, and trail rode in the desert. He would bathe and clip and stand tied to the trailer.

"He never faltered once," claimed Kara, "except when it came to cows..."

In the end she and her family were devastated to have to sell him because he was such a lovable horse.

"He's never met a stranger," Reed said when I spoke to him.

I like horses like that, I thought.

Reed also told me: "I am so proud of what he has become. It is cool to see how many lives he has touched in less than a year.

Thoroughbreds are very versatile animals as we all know, but most are judged by their performance on the track. It's my opinion that he was a jumper from birth; he just needed someone to realize it. After getting his chance to do what he was truly born to do, he has become royalty in his own right."

"So you don't think he was meant to be a racehorse?" I asked.

He chuckled. "He would rather eat the turf than run on it."

I could picture the other horses galloping, dirt flying, and Remarkable standing there, wondering what all the fuss was about as he lowered his head and took a bite.

Remarkable has been called by many names…but never Forgettable.

CHAPTER 46

Letter to Myself

Tik, this is a letter to yourself. Read it in ten years. I'm curious. Have you had kids? Do you still have Remarkable?

Do you look back and think, "God, what have I done with my life?" Yes, I am naive compared to you. I don't own property or an Audi, but I married a woman who gets me. And there are horses that nicker and poke their noses out to greet me each morning. So it's pretty good.

I have goals in my life that are important. The Olympics, still. Constantly bringing in two- and three-year-old horses to start. Also finding the next Great Horse, finding a way to pay for him, growing my business, and finally, my most short term goal: the Thoroughbred Makeover with Remarkable in a few days. How many of those things do you remember at age forty-three? Do they still seem as important to you as they do to me?

Have you found balance between the thrill of competing at the upper levels and the joy of creating relationships with younger horses?

Please tell me you are still competing! Remember, there are two kinds of athletes: Some say, "What a relief! Thank goodness that is over." Others shout, "Yes! YIPPEE! I am in my element. Now. Here. If only this moment could slow down, so I could be here longer."

The type of athlete is unrelated to the chances of winning. I have seen both types win…and lose. But the second one—wow! That is a feeling that cannot be bought.

Tik, do you remember your modern pentathalon days? The 2007 Pan American Games in Brazil? You stood on the edge of that swaying bridge leading to achievement. You boldly stepped out...

But it was not to be. You finished thirteenth and you felt a deep emptiness. But there was also relief. An end to the bubbling pressure that was pushing against your chest.

The next spring, in 2008, you tried to make the Olympic team. You were at the World Cup in Mexico City when you broke your clavicle. You were riding a horse that jumped the way Lance Armstrong shows remorse. The horse hit the jump with his front legs, and you both met the ground like lead tumbleweed.

So you retired. You gave up. You quit. But isn't there a time when it is better to cut and run?

You decided to travel and work for a year. You chose horses over everything else.

In Germany you rode big Warmbloods during the day and studied Bonhoeffer at night:

In normal life we hardly realize how much more we receive than we give, and life cannot be rich without such gratitude. It is so easy to overestimate the importance of our own achievements compared with what we owe to the help of others.

You were lonely but alive. You went for walks in the dark. You were fired from that first job for not being a good enough rider. But you got a second job nearby and learned that bad things may not happen for a reason, but if you persevere at least your odds of improvement are better.

Later, in the States, you worked hard and were told: "This might be your calling." You found in horses that second feeling: The feeling that seeps through your muscles into your soul, so you feel whole in yourself, but at the same time know your place as part of something greater.

It is the way Jonathan Livingston Seagull felt after he climbed high above the earth and then hurtled down through the sky, moving a single feather at the edge of each wingtip to navigate. Learning: We did it in school for grades, now we *crave it* and do it while eating breakfast, and in bed at night!

Remember Loving, Texas? Remember Bruce, who somehow tried to treat horses and people the same way? I hope you haven't forgotten about that and what you learned from it.

Do you still live on the East Coast and love it, but think of Vancouver as home? I hope so. (Or do I?)

If you won the Thoroughbred Makeover with Remarkable, I hope you gave him a vacation. I hope you took one, too. I hope you kept him, even if you didn't win. He is one of those horses where time disappears when you are with him. Simply vanishes.

So I hope you thanked him, thanked everybody who helped you.

One more thing: If you are reading this aloud to Sinead in 2025, look back together for a minute and consider a few of the horses and people who, over the years., made you who you are.

And maybe remind Sinead that you used to have a lot more hair under that helmet—does she remember?

CHAPTER 47

Winning Is the Easy Part

Iplanned my performance to be simple. There were to be as few props as possible. I wanted it to be about Remarkable and our partnership. When the rider before me finished, I took off Remarkable's halter and prepared to enter the ring. I waited for the music to start, and I hoped he would follow me in.

The day before the Freestyle we'd been allowed to enter the arena and walk around. Remarkable shied away from every banner on the rail. I asked my father, and Emily, my assistant, to walk around the outside of the ring and stop at every banner with a carrot.

So during the performance, when the music started and the judges picked up their pens, I knew that he wasn't scared of the banners anymore. Of course, that didn't mean he wasn't going to be afraid of something else. I had only our training to keep him with me as we played in the ring together.

We entered the main arena shoulder to shoulder. We looked around—the crowd was a lot to take in. We started to trot. We turned. We stopped. The people started to disappear and blur until it was just the two of us in the building. I was about as close to being in The

Zone, that place near the forty-five-degree line, as I had ever been.

The first three minutes, I was on the ground and he was at liberty. He ran and he bucked, but he kept an eye on me and he kept coming back. The second three minutes I rode with no bridle. We galloped around the ring, but we walked as well. We jumped and we halted.

We stood together and alone as the music stopped. Six minutes had passed in an instant. I looked around. People were clapping. I looked at Remarkable and he looked back at me. I stood up on his back and waved. Then he got a carrot, and we walked out of the arena together.

Remarkable and I won the Freestyle competition at the Thoroughbred Makeover.

We then made the long drive back from Kentucky to New Jersey with Emily, the working student I had first met in New Jersey at Bow Brickhill Stables five years before. I was teaching a jumping lesson, and I noticed she had come out on her horse, Bella, twenty minutes early for her own lesson, which was to follow. Emily decided to follow another kid and pony out of the ring, down a drop, and out onto the grass field. The drop was about two feet high, and Bella said, "No way."

Emily tried to get her pony to go. She kicked and she clucked and Bella backed up. Nothing worked. Emily used the whip and Bella spun and galloped halfway back to the barn. By the time my jumping lesson was finished in the ring, and I went over to help her, Bella wouldn't go anywhere near that drop—she would pin her ears and back up.

Every horse is born with innate motivations. They are drawn to open spaces, other horses, water, food and play. They are curious. They don't like predatory acts. They tend not to like things that move quickly, erratically, or toward them. They are often scared of sudden loud noises, especially new ones. Wind in the branches?

Probably danger. A change in footing, a drop, or a ditch? These are also scary things for an animal that relies on his ability to cover ground fast to survive.

Once the horse enters the human's world, we start to influence those likes and dislikes. Whereas a feral horse is scared of humans and barns, he can quickly associate them with food and comfort. I wanted Emily to look at the situation from Bella's point of view. This problem was a common problem, for inevitably some things pushed a horse away, some drew him closer, and some were neutral.

"How's it going, Emily?" I stopped about ten feet from her. She wiped the back of her glove across her cheek and just looked at me. "Remember when Bella was scared of a water crossing, we made it neutral by offering her food when she walked up to it? Remember when we had trouble catching Sapphire? She would rather be in the grassy paddock than with us, so we made it neutral by doing some of the harder work in the paddock and then bringing her to us for a rest?"

Emily nodded, but still said nothing. Her breathing was returning to normal.

"Why don't we try that today?" I suggested. "Try to make her world neutral. If we get there we should be able to shift her interest by adding the tiniest amount of leg or by giving her the smallest treat. Let's try to get it to be like having an hourglass that is balanced equally, and then all we have to do is shift one grain of sand to adjust her interest and movement."

Bella started to back up again. Emily closed her legs, and went to use her whip.

"Easy. Just hold on," I said as I walked closer. "Right now you're trying to move so much sand it's like you're at the beach with a shovel and wheelbarrow." I mimed the work it would take. Emily wiped her cheek again, but this time her eyes were brighter.

"Why don't you hop off and go grab a rope halter and a longer rope from the barn? We can start this process from the ground."

I walked right up to her now and held Bella's reins while the girl dismounted. As she ran off I thought about trying to make the horse's world neutral, and how it was not something we were going to get done today. But maybe we would get a little closer. One of the first things my mother ever explained to me was, with horses, we needed to think in months and years, not days and weeks. Improvement is a lifelong pursuit.

I worked with Emily's horse for about forty minutes. I showed Bella the bank, but didn't force her. I took her away from it, where we worked on backing, and turning, and then drawing her back to me. Then we took a break—and we took it by the bank. A horse can stop a dozen times and still be improving. Was the mare looking ahead more each time? Was she studying her options more clearly? Was she looking down off the bank as if somebody had spilled a bag of grain, and she wanted to stretch down and get it?

The mare's confidence slowly grew, and eventually she took the leap. Once she could jump down easily, I had Emily get back on. For ten minutes Emily and Bella went up and down the bank at the walk, then the trot, and then the canter. All on a loose rein. We talked about the importance of building a relationship with your horse. By the end, I thought it was one of the better lessons I had taught.

But later someone asked: "Emily only rode for ten minutes. How is that a full lesson?"

The next time I taught Emily I started to explain how important trust was to a horse and why I had helped her the way I had during her last lesson. I was a little awkward and struggled to find the right words, and Emily stopped me.

"Tik," she said, meeting my eyes, "I get it."

"How old are you, Emily?"

"Thirteen."

"Some people are thirty and still don't get it."

I was still studying horses, and I was becoming more experienced with young horses and "difficult" ones. I might have still preferred to have a barn full of athletic, fully trained horses, but I was paying the bills and learning a lot.

It was in another lesson that I explained to Emily that people have a lot of ways they try and communicate with horses, but horses have two main ways they let us know what is going on: They show more tension, or they show more relaxation. So I asked my student not just, "Is Bella relaxed or not?" but also, "How relaxed is she?" or "How tense?" It was the idea of the tension scale that I had started to play with at Anne's; it was becoming clearer in my mind all the time.

When Emily graduated from high school, she came to work for me. That felt funny...because suddenly *I* had a working student! Soon she graduated from apprentice to manager, and we brought on a new working student. By seventeen years old, Emily ran the whole barn, managing the care of ten to twenty horses year round. She was in the barn mucking stalls, in the office recordkeeping, at the shows grooming and riding, and on the phone liaising with clients, owners, veterinarians, and farriers.

One afternoon the wind picked up and the horses started cantering—then spinning! Stopping! Bucking! Cantering!—in their paddocks, anxiety written all over their high heads and quick legs. One horse in particular was not settling. Sinead was about to ask for the horse to be brought back into the barn when she saw Emily catch him and start some basic groundwork exercises in the paddock: She circled the horse left, then right. Then she backed him up. She paused, and then he was licking and chewing as she took him to his pile of hay where he started to eat. After another minute Emily left him. He continued to stand quietly and eat.

"It was fantastic," Sinead told me later.

Emily's abilities with horses surpassed her confidence in her abilities. This was not ideal, but more pleasing than the opposite.

I knew that at some point Emily would move on, just like I had. And, "that is okay," I told her. "It is good to learn from different people. I spent a lot of time with different trainers."

"I get confused when I take lessons from too many people."

"Well, I always had a solid foundation of knowledge to fall back on," I said. "I rode with my parents until I was twenty-six. If I had not had that foundation, and I had gone to be a working student when I was eighteen, I think it would have been different. You're right, at the start it is smarter to stay with one trainer for a number of years. If you find a good fit, even decades. Look how long Anne stayed with George! Look how long Leonie rode with Hinnemann! Jonathan studied with Pat for ages!"

"How did you know it was time for you to start your own business?"

"After a while, no matter what barn I went to, I caught myself thinking, 'Hmmm…I would do that a little differently if I was running things.'"

Emily laughed. "I don't think that yet."

"One day you might."

When I watched clinics, if an idea did not make sense, or seemed to contradict another idea I thought to be true, I asked one of my parents, or Sinead, to help me figure it out. I also often called Jonathan Field with horse-related questions.

"Somebody wants to send me a donkey. Do I know how to train a donkey?"

"They are similar to horses," he responded, without laughing, bless him, "but you will get away with less. They are less forgiving, and they have less of a flight response, so your timing has to be better."

Another time: "I am working with a young mare that pins her

ears and seems to hold her breath when she is away from me on the circle. She only licks and chews when she is back with me. What is that all about?"

"Sounds like what I call 'connection tension,'" Jonathan said. "Why don't you send me a video? I'll give you some tips on how to work through it with her."

When I started teaching horsemanship clinics, I caught myself stealing all his lines.

When I asked Jonathan about it, he said that was normal.

"I used to feel that way too," he admitted. "Remember, there is not much new with horses. Just put your own take on it, and as you start to gain experience, you will feel more comfortable saying what you need to say, because it will not only come from somebody else's experience, but also from your own."

On the drive home from Kentucky, I thought about the Makeover, and what I was going to write about it. I didn't want to write about winning. I had heard George Morris say, "Winning is the easy part," many times, and the older I got, the truer that seemed. I wanted to write about something I'd learned.

I could write about all the details that went into the preparation, for there was an Olympics for dressage, eventing, and show jumping. But what would Olympic-level saddling look like? What would be the four-star of trailer-loading? I imagined a World Cup for ground-tying: Not only would each horse stand untied where he was placed, but he would do it with relaxation and understanding, his head low and mouth salivating. And he would do it with horses galloping around and crowds screaming.

What about the Burghley of leading? Each horse staying with his partner without lead rope or halter, stopping when his partner stops, going when his partner goes. Turning in unison, just as a mare and foal might.

Before Remarkable and I left for the twelve-hour trailer ride to the Kentucky Horse Park where the Makeover was held, we could walk, trot, canter, and halt, without a halter. He would ground-tie and wait for me patiently. Trailer-loading? Not a problem.

Trying to be the best at such basic skills gave me and Remarkable a concrete foundation that I knew would serve us well. At a major competition, there will always be the unexpected, and the stronger a horse's basics skills the easier it is to deal with new experiences.

Or maybe I would write about the cowboy, I thought. Yes, that's a better idea.

I started to make notes. A cowboy was much more interesting.

CHAPTER 48

"If There Was a Bunch of Indians Headed My Way…"

For the second time during the Trainers' Forum I heard Dale say, "Well, I dunno. This is all getting more complicated than I'm used to."

Dale Simanton, a trainer from South Dakota, was one of the presenters, along with Lainey Ashker, Louise Robson, Eric Dierks, and myself. Lainey, Eric, and I were there as experienced eventers. Louise was there for her perspective on dressage. Dale, wearing cowboy boots and a button-down shirt, was the voice of simplicity in our evermore technical discussion on everything to do with Thoroughbreds.

Dale went on: "I just ride 'em." To be more clear: "Sometimes I'll ride for a while." To be even more precise: "I ride 'em till they figure it out."

I believe Dale gave this answer not because he couldn't have explained something more clearly, but because it was the opposite to what the rest of us were doing, which was giving a complicated answer to a simple question.

I appreciate complicated answers sometimes—when I can understand them. But most of the time I don't. I guess it depends who your audience is. What Dale brought to the table, besides a lifetime of successful horse training, was much-needed balance. It was like what I was trying to find in my work with horses: my own balance when I was on them, of course, but also being vigorously aware that I was helping the horses find their mental, emotional, and physical balance, too.

Usually a simple answer is the best one.

A lady near the front of the auditorium stood and asked: "How do I get better bend in my Thoroughbred? She is only off the track a few months and always seems so stiff."

I was happy to let Eric field this one. And then Louise took a shot at it. This forum was valuable for having different points of view, rather than unanimous ones. It gave me the chance to make up my own mind.

When members of the audience asked questions, sometimes we gave specific, technical answers. Most of the time though, I noticed, we gave broader, theoretical ones.

"Next question?" our moderator asked.

One woman stood up and looked right at me, saying, "Tik, I have a horse that won't go near liverpools. Sometimes I can get him over one, but the issue returns in new situations. Often it gets worse the harder I try, and soon he thinks the whole ring is one big liverpool."

"Well," I said, pausing to put my words together, "that is a tough question."

Giving the woman a specific task to try in response to a question like this, without seeing the problem firsthand, would be, at best, a guess. And at worst, dangerous. Some horses with a specific fear can overcome it, with patience and good timing, in one session. Other horses may struggle with an issue for years. Often, in the case of the person doing the training, it is possible to replace skill and experience with patience and empathy. But not always.

"Let me tell you about something Buck Brannaman has done. And just bear with me, because I'll get to your question at the end." We had about a hundred people listening, and I looked out at them all, but then focused on the lady who asked the question. She was nodding.

"With two horses that are really attached, that call for each other and can't concentrate when separated, Buck has them go through something he calls 'The Divorce.' He has the slightly better behaved horse stand in the middle of the arena while the other is ridden around. The rider keeps the horse working when he is near his friend, and he gets a walk break when he's away from his friend. The walk breaks start to happen farther and farther away from his friend. He starts to associate being near his buddy with work, and being farther away with rest."

The woman in the audience smiled. She looked like a librarian and was taking notes. She could see where this was going.

"What I'm saying is, you can apply this same principle: Work your horse around the outside of the ring. Every time you go near the liverpool, take a break. You could even give him a treat when you are next to the liverpool. This process might take a while. Progress might be like growing pumpkins. But I think after a while you will look at your horse and see a difference."

In school I had always been self-conscious in front of a class. When speaking to a group I would lose my place and pause, searching in my head for where I was. The longer I was silent the harder it was to find my spot. They say that animals facing a threat will decide between two choices: fight or flight. But there is a third option: Imagine a walking deer that hears a twig snap. "A cougar?" she thinks. She freezes.

But now, like Jonathan Field had predicted, knowing something from experience gave me the confidence that knowing something from a book never had.

And I also felt comfortable explaining that most behavioral questions have only one real answer: "It depends!" There are so many variables with horses that what might help one particular kind of horse might actually make another one worse. Still, I tried to improve my ability to explain things, and to give answers that would help a variety of situations.

Usually, though, "It depends."

The last question at the forum was from a lady in the back: "When you are looking at a Thoroughbred, how do you decide if you like him?"

Lainey took that one first. She explained how she relied a lot on her mother's opinion—that her mom had a unique way of seeing the potential in an off-the-track prospect. She didn't ask for the horse to be jogged, or free-jumped, or ridden. Instead she asked, "Can you please let him go in the round pen?" She then watched how the horse reacted. Did he take off bucking? Or was he dull? How was the quality of his gaits? Was he curious about his surroundings? Was he scared and nervous?

Most riding and training can be reduced to science, but there will always be an art to it as well. Some may even call that art *magic*, and I wouldn't be the one to disagree. I also suspect the best riders do not necessarily have the best eye for picking horses. They tend to be two different skill sets. I have seen Olympic riders who tend to pick horses that are going nowhere, and I have seen men and women who don't even ride, but can, and sometimes do, make a living from being able to pick a horse with potential. Like Lainey, I recognized my weakness in picking horses, and I asked others for help.

I passed on the question, as I didn't feel I had a good "system" for picking Thoroughbreds, and I didn't want to make something up. Lainey handed Dale the microphone. He took it and leaned back, not quite ready to answer.

On the man's head was a cream-white cowboy hat, which he now took off. He wiped his brow, and then replaced the hat.

"Well," he said after a minute, and shrugged. "I just think, if there was a bunch of Indians headed my way, and I had that horse tied up nearby, would I like to get on him to get away, or would I have a better chance on foot?"

Grinning, I wrote that down.

CHAPTER 49

On Pain

The Thoroughbred Makeover was supposed to be a turning point. It had been a good year. With the help of some friends we had bought and imported a young mare from Germany. What an athlete she was! What a beauty! Dapple gray like a stormy morning; supple and sweet; the swaying trot of a tigress! There's an old expression that every time a horse rolls back and forth their value is greater. Well, when I first saw this girl in the quarantine facility she rolled over fourteen or fifteen times. And, what a puppy; it was so easy for her.

Her name was Karma.

In August of that year I was away for a week teaching clinics in England and Scotland, when I received an email that began: *Karma jumped out of a paddock at some point this evening and has injured her right hind stifle. Emily called the vet out and she came and took radiographs but has not been able to get a clear read...*

The break ended up being so severe the vets suggested euthanasia. But they did say there was a slim chance she would recover with months of stall rest. The owners and I could not reach a unanimous decision on what to do.

With my vote being the swing vote we started nursing her back to health. She would look at me with large liquid eyes when I brought her dinner. She stood docilely while her stall was cleaned. Her breath was slow and shallow as if she was conserving energy. She put her whiskers on my hand and smelled me. I wondered what my scent meant to her. She watched me leave the barn and walk, looking back over my shoulder at her, to my car. She was tied in her stall, not even allowed to turn around, lest movement made the injury worse.

Sometimes it is not clear what is in the best interests of a horse.

Then that year there was Dutch Times and of course Sapphire, two horses that I had the ride on. They were giving me a chance to qualify for the 2015 Toronto Pan American Games. But Sapphire was injured in the spring in Ocala, and Dutch Times was hurt later that summer at the Bromont Horse Trials. Although both horses recovered, I felt the question, like a sharp knife jabbing me in the gut, *What should I have done differently?*

Then there was the mistake I made one Saturday morning at Bucks County Horse Park, just across the river in Pennsylvania. I was there to help a client with her cross-country school. We had a good session and were heading back to the trailer when her horse stopped. Stopped as if he was a boulder that had rolled to the lowest point.

"Try taking only the left rein," I advised. "Now only the right rein. So you are tacking back and forth, like a sailboat. That way maybe you can get him moving without adding more leg. More leg might make him rear up."

And just as I said that, he went up on his hind legs.

"Why don't I get on," I said. By this time, I was dealing with lots of difficult horses, and I felt casually convinced I would be able to get him going. I put a foot in the stirrup and mounted from the ground. "This should just take a minute."

There is a now-common phrase that often comes to mind in situations like this: *Make the right thing easy, and the wrong thing difficult.* More leg, or the stick, when he was standing; a rub, or a rest, when he walked. But it was not working. The rears were getting bigger. And he was starting to feel pretty committed to them, like a surfer after a fall, fighting through the water for the surface and his first breath.

And then he went over backward. I was underneath him when his back came down. He rolled over my torso and head as he scrambled to find his feet. As he righted himself I jumped up, reins in hand. Before he had a chance to look around, I had one foot in the stirrup. A second later I was back on.

That same scene played itself out three more times. Each time we flipped over I would stand up with him and be back in the saddle before he had taken a single step.

I probably got the concussion the first time we went down, which is why I do not know the details of each consecutive fall. All I remember is walking toward my car and having the strangest feeling, like I was waking up: *My feet are moving, but where am I going? Oh, there is my car. I'll go there. I recognize this place. What am I doing here? I should see what time it is. Noon. Weird! What have I been doing all morning?*

For the next few weeks I felt vulnerable, weak, and useless. I had a lot of time to think about what I had done wrong. The most obvious: I had not been wearing a helmet. Stupid. It was one of the few times in my life I have not worn a helmet while riding and the most mortifying. I was almost disowned by my parents and divorced by my wife for doing such a dangerous thing. But the concussion and two perforated eardrums were the real reminder.

Every year there are riders who are not as lucky as I was; riders who are not able to stand back up. They have life-altering injuries... or worse. I remembered the letter writer from my Hinnemann days. The one who would have said it was not confidence, but hubris, that got me up on that horse.

I would not argue with her.

I also did not *think* enough. Like the old carpenter's saying, "Measure twice, cut once," I should have spent more time figuring out *why* the horse did not want to go forward, and less time trying to fix it.

I also might now say, if there is an easier way to get things done, why not take it? I could have just led my client's horse back to the trailer.

A few days before leaving for the Thoroughbred Makeover I got an unusual call to come check on Karma.

As soon as I saw her I knew we were in trouble. Her hind end collapsed with each movement. We called the vet immediately. He gave her something for her pain as soon as he arrived. He took X-rays, but there was little hope. Sinead arrived and the vet talked to her. They didn't really need to say anything to me. I knew.

Karma was euthanized that cloudless morning. In her last minutes she felt no pain. She stood in the sun. She ate green grass. She didn't look up once.

That year I often wanted to lean on, and sometimes celebrate with, my wife, but she had nine horses in training, and four competing at the FEI levels: Top Gun, High Altitude, Gray Area, and Forrest Nymph. Her top horse Manoir De Carneville ("Tate") who had competed at the World Equestrian Games the previous year, was out for a while with an injury. Our schedules, as for a lot of partnered athletes, were different, and I think we spent about six months apart that year. So it was a treat and a relief for us to visit my family in Vancouver that fall—together.

As can happen, we found ourselves looking at photo albums. My family had an album for every year. Each photo within was labeled with a date on the back. Many noted location, names, and included a short description.

"Here, Sinead, this is from my parents' wedding."

"God, they look young."

On August 29, 1968, Jennifer Wright, twenty-one years old, became Jennifer Maynard at the Unitarian Church of Vancouver. I went to the same church growing up, a big beautiful box of a church that, no matter the time of day, always seemed to have sunlight pouring in. Her new husband, Rick, was twenty-five. Ten years later they would have their first child, Telf, named after Rick's father. Then, just over three years later, a second son was born.

Telf, with a limited vocabulary (typical I could say, for a baby), started calling the newborn "Tik." Unusual for sure, but it caught on. Jennifer and Rick made it into initials. A new birth certificate was issued. *Thomas*, it read, and there were two middle names: *Ian Kevin*.

That was me.

Six years later a third son was born, Jordan. The three of us, like many brothers, grew up to be similar, but different. In height we were all tall, but tallest was Jordan. (Six feet two-and-a-half inches.) He started chubby, but ended up a runner, loping through his first marathon in 2:36. He was always a minimalist, once spending several years living in a tool shed.

In ambition, we all had plans, but Telf had the most. Since registering his first company (Canadian Computer Consulting) at age thirteen, he had: worked as a pizza delivery driver, barista, security guard, database architect, web programmer, and General Manager of Southlands Riding Club; moonlighted as a PADI Master Scuba Diver Trainer and Pony Club Examiner; and become certified as a ham radio operator and a pilot with night and float ratings. Telf could fix anything; do anything.

We all liked horses, but I liked them the most.

We were a close family, and without anybody ever saying it, traditions were important. So I thought I would be going to that church as long as there were birds in the sky, and water in the rivers. Then as I grew older I realized my favorite place to worship was outside.

I closed the cover on the fourth album. "Want to go over to the riding club?"

"It's cold."

"I'll find you a jacket."

Sinead swung from boiling to freezing to steamed with the regularity and fickleness of West Coast precipitation. I took her hand in mine and led her away from the albums.

"Besides," I said with a grin, "if we wait for it to stop raining, we might be waiting months."

We pedaled two bicycles the half-mile over to the riding club to meet my dad. Many men his age were retiring, but he still rode and taught every day.

We leaned the bikes against the fence and then leaned ourselves against the fence. Sinead stood close to me, for warmth. I put my arm around her; I was proud to bring her to my home.

"I think he has to be the most underrated instructor in Canada. I don't know why people aren't lining up to take lessons from him."

"I don't think he cares about that." Sinead had a way of cutting to the chase. We watched as my dad walked behind a diminutive girl on her tall horse and corrected the angle of her leg yield. *Too much angle. Not enough angle. Just right—there you go.*

"Do you think we will ever move back here?"

"We can't be here with our jobs," Sinead said matter-of-factly. My brain knew her to be honest, but something creeped through my chest, like a coyote in the dark. Was it *my* decision to not return home? Or was my marriage keeping me away?

When my father finished teaching his lesson, we pedaled home with him. We passed a blue heron standing as still as a statue. Now that is patience, I thought. No matter how much somebody has, nature has more. A small chickadee landed at our feet and just as quickly flitted away.

Over dinner, all of us spread around the kitchen and living room, we talked about horses. There was a question I had been thinking about, and I put it to the group: "Why do you think horses stop?"

Seeing a horse stop at a jump was all too common and this was a good crowd to discuss it. Between my parents, Sinead, Telf and his wife, and Jordan and his girlfriend, we came up with six reasons. One: Pain. Two: The anticipation of pain. Three: The rider inadvertently made stopping easier than jumping. Four: The horse is overfaced. Five: Stopping had become a habit. Six: The horse was distracted.

The only one of these categories where we agreed we would use the whip is when stopping had become habit. The whip, we concurred, should be used to give confidence, to say, "Yes! We can do this! We should be doing this." It should not say, "You are wrong!" Or worse, "I hate you."

The most difficult part was being able to read which cause was at play. Or even more confusing, it might be a combination of more than one. I wrote notes. Maybe all we'd debated could be an article one day.

Finally we settled around the fireplace. Sinead was still cold so Jordan made hot chocolate for everybody. It was fortified with Irish Cream, of course. And I decided to tell a story. I held Sinead's hand as I spoke.

"Before the World Equestrian Games in France the United States Equestrian Federation held a big party in Virginia. In Middleburg. White tents, white wine, black tie. While Sinead chatted with Lynn Symansky, I escaped to the fire pit and joined a few other husbands and boyfriends. It came up that I was newly married, and so I asked what the secret to a long marriage was. There were a few answers not worth repeating, but then one man, gray-haired, put both hands around his whiskey, leaned forward, and said, 'Let me tell you a story...

"'When I married my wife we made an agreement. Myself, being the man, of course, would make all the *big* decisions.' All us husbands and boyfriends stood around the fire pit there, just like we are sitting around here, and we nodded at each other. 'My wife,' the man went on, 'being the woman, of course, would make all the *little* decisions in our life going forward.' More nodding all around. That seemed fair. 'Well...' the man said as he took a sip of his drink—I remember it was straight up, no ice. 'We have been married forty-seven years, and we have never, not once, had to make a *big* decision.'"

I waited for the smiles, and I got them. Then Telf laughed, and my mother cheered. The dogs picked up on the excitement and barked. I glanced at Sinead and the soft firelight danced on her face. She squeezed my hand. It started to rain outside. Being inside felt even more pleasing.

The next morning, we woke with the light and flew to Salt Spring, part of the Gulf Islands chain that rested between the coast of British Columbia and Vancouver Island. Our float plane landed gently and pulled up to the dock in the tiny town of Ganges. Eamon flew to Vancouver and took the ferry to meet us. We stayed at the Quarrystone House Bed and Breakfast, with the best muffins in the mornings, and in the evenings, the best views. I was proud to show my father-in-law around.

"Perfect," he said, looking at us, then looking at the sunset.

Later the same year I was in Vancouver again to teach a clinic. It was my last morning. The phone rang early. It woke me, but I didn't answer it in time.

I heard the horses banging in their stalls, waiting for breakfast.

Probably TJ, I thought. I'll go visit him later. I rolled over, away from the light. Just a little longer…this is so nice.

The phone rang again. I looked at the screen. *My Beautiful Wife*, it said. I answered.

"Tik?"

I knew instantly something was wrong. I sat up in bed. I held the phone to my ear as she spoke. On the walls were shelves and shelves of books. I stared at them. The spines were in many colors, and many sizes, like stones in a river. I looked out the window and saw my dad throw hay over a stall door. TJ quickly brought his head back in to eat.

I could almost see Sinead as she spoke. Her crystal blue eyes open but seeing nothing. Her world blurry, confused. I imagined her fingers anxiously tapping on her leg. She would be curled up, making herself small, as if chilled. I wanted to hold her.

I have never felt so powerless as when my wife told me her father was no longer part of this world.

He had taken his own life.

CHAPTER 50

It Is Unbelievable That Magic Like That Can Vanish

The lectern didn't hide his size at all. He was an oak of a man. Rough looking. Skin like bark. Tattoos peeked out from above his collar, and on his wrists. His voice carried through the still air down the nave: "I am speaking because my wife is unable. Sometimes there are just too many tears."

That day there were enough tears that I worried about drowning. I noticed Sinead's finger tic had returned so I placed my hand on hers. The twitch continued in my palm, as if I held a tiny bird. I let her hand go. I knew when held she could feel as claustrophobic as a wild Mustang. The only thing I knew to do was to just be there.

This large man was the last of a dozen or so to speak. The way he had held his wife's hand, and then half stood, and then looked back at her, made it seem likely that his speech was a last-minute decision.

"My wife worked for Eamon," he said. "She knew him well." A few people glanced at the woman in the front pew where the man had been sitting. Her head was down. Her hair shielded her face. "The first time I met Eamon he looked at my sleeves of tattoos and asked, 'Are you in *Sons of Anarchy*?'"

Laughter behind us. Thank God. There were eighty-odd people that had assembled, and our somber mood was lightened briefly. Only Eamon, we said to ourselves. Only Eamon could get away with something like that. Eamon was magic. Our laughs floated above the tears, like oil on water, for a short time.

The eulogies all had a common theme: Eamon was worldly, but could be so present; he was loved, he was passionate, he was funny. It was easy to imagine him ribbing this Grizzly in front of us. The vision gave us something to grasp at as we tried to make the world make sense.

Then, just as quickly, the laughter ended and I heard quiet weeping behind me. I did not turn around.

In a sea of adjectives during the past three days, *magic* was the word I'd heard most. Eamon had outrageous Gift-Giving-Fun-Magic, like Aladdin's Genie. He had also the more mysterious Wise-and-Full-of-Surprises-Magic, like Roald Dahl's Willy Wonka. It was unbelievable that magic like that could vanish. We were in disbelief.

The big man looked down at us and paused. He looked at Sinead, then his wife. Then went on.

"What I will remember most about Eamon is his hugs. He would give me a hug, and I was the most important person in the world."

The long, old church was silent.

"Bear hugs," he whispered. His arms came up, grasping, in vain. My wife shook beside me. I squeezed her hand, but I sensed she did not feel it. "Hugs that carried the understanding of a man who knew a hug could touch the soul. I hardly knew him compared to most of you, but I'll never forget him."

Sinead took a sharp breath in, and I knew what she was thinking. *My dad never met a stranger.*

The man with the tattoos stood for a minute, and then walked back to his wife.

I had gotten my crying out two days earlier. I was jogging down the hill behind his house to downtown Paso Robles. I ran by the café where Eamon and I would never have coffee again. There was Bistro Laurent's, where the sommelier would never pair a wine for us again. I kept running. I looked away from the event center on my right, where we had attended a horse demonstration together. It had been the first time I had hung out with him without Sinead, and although not a horse person, he had been captivated by the cowboys and how they began building a relationship with a horse.

Eamon and I would never smoke a cigar, drink tequila, go to the gym, or practice yoga together again. We would never laugh together again. Man, could he laugh! Eamon would never meet his grandchildren. He would never make me another kale smoothie. I ran across the street. He would never play golf with Sinead's brother Greg again. (Who had won that last game? Was it Eamon? Or maybe it was Greg.) *Goddamn it!* I was so mad at him. Greg loved golfing with his dad. I ran harder.

Eamon would never call Sinead "My Baby" again.

I would never be able to apologize for not asking for his daughter's hand in marriage.

When I couldn't run anymore, I walked. I took the long way back.

Sometimes horses aren't the only ones that need to run. I wish more people understood that.

After my exercise, I was saner, and I could be there more for Sinead. I heard once that a child's birth is called the "Common Miracle," and a parent's death is called the "Common Tragedy," but an emotion's rarity does not relate to its intensity. We still *feel* it. I believe that not only do animals grieve, but in grieving we become more like animals.

It is a wonder nature allows us to feel so much love. And, truth be told, what I was saddest about was not my pain; it was the hurt in my wife. She was like a foal weaned before her time. Her crying ripped at my heart until I turned inward and was silent. I was so angry at him.

Even when he was alive, and he could be *so* alive—*so goddamn alive!*—people either wanted to slug him or hug him.

At the memorial, I overheard someone say, "No one will ever know Eamon as an old man." I imagined that being a small consolation for some, just as our image of James Dean is forever as he supposedly wanted it, strong and cool, at twenty-four. But my new family had so many dreams still ahead of us, dreams that would now be shy one.

I went outside for some fresh air. I called my own father, and I told him I loved him. I don't think I had ever done that before.

The next two days passed in a blur, and before we knew it, we were leaving California. Greg drove the rental car back to Los Angeles with Sinead next to him. We were headed back to our lives. There was no choice. We had horses to care for, train, and ride. We had clients to teach. We had bills to pay. I was in the back seat. I reached forward and put my hand on Sinead's shoulder. I felt her touch me; take my hand in hers.

We drove in silence for the most part. Then Sinead turned the radio up, and Adele called out from the other side.

Sinead began to sob quietly again, and I knew there was nothing I could do, again, so I did nothing.

Sinead took her hand back after a few minutes.

I sat against the rear seat, taking my hand with me. I wanted to leave it there. I longed to comfort her. But it would have been like squeezing a pilot's shoulder as his plane silently dove, the blades not turning.

CHAPTER 51

On Horsemanship

George Morris wore an orange shirt and tall boots the color of mahogany. He had on dark sunglasses with apple red rims and a black helmet.

"The basic principles all go back to the same thing," he was explaining, when suddenly he shouted, "Shut up!"

"Shut up," he barked again as he slid off the dark bay horse, and handed it off to the rider who was waiting nearby. "I have no respect for you." He walked over toward those of us in the audience. "Him I do." George pointed at Peter Gray, our host and a two-time Olympian. "You?" He looked at the rest of us. "You, I don't. You've done nothing in the horse world. Nothing!"

I was sitting in a group of about twenty Canadian, mostly young, event riders, at a clinic in Ocala with George and dressage rider Christilot Boylen. Two auditors had whispered and looked at a phone while George was demonstrating the importance of leg and the benefits of a light seat.

"Christilot and I are dictators here today," George went on, his voice getting raspy. "Maybe benevolent dictators. But dictators. PAY ATTENTION!" He then signaled for some water. A bottle was handed to him. "I'm getting soft," he admitted quietly as he took it.

I liked him for that.

At the end of that day I brought a Thoroughbred over for George and Christilot to look at. Johnny Football was a six-year-old gelding that I had competed at the 2016 Thoroughbred Makeover. I knew George and Christilot were both fans of the breed. I wanted to know why. I wanted to know how they trained them. Did they handle them differently than for other breeds? And I wanted to know what they thought of Johnny.

George's favorite Thoroughbred from when he competed was Sinjon. Sinjon, now in the Show Jumping Hall of Fame, started his career on the track, then was transformed into a great jumper by Harry De Leyer (of Snowman—*The Eighty-Dollar Champion*—fame).

"He was weedy," George said, "but he could jump the top of the standards. He could do tricks in the air. The first time I saw him I wanted him."

When George speaks, he often repeats himself. It's like he is taking a highlighter to his words—he is letting us know what the important parts are. And when he spoke about Sinjon, he might have been describing all thoroughbreds: "Hot, but honest…brave, but careful." Then again, "Honest," and again, "Brave."

Christilot, a six-time Olympian, got Bonheur, a five-year-old gelding, off the track when she was only thirteen years old. Four years later they competed at the Olympics in Tokyo.

"Bonheur was never a top horse, but he did his job," she said. "He taught me a lot. Thoroughbreds will do that. I learned about temperament. I learned not to override."

Christilot and George were both horsemen who respected other horsemen without prejudice for what kind of saddle they rode in. During George's group lessons on the grass, Christilot stayed in the shade by the dressage arena. She referred repeatedly to the Classical Training Scale: Rhythm, Suppleness, Contact, Impulsion,

Straightness, Collection. George agreed, but constantly stressed impulsion. "It's like turning the key on a car. It's the first step." The horse having the desire to go forward is nonnegotiable.

"Be perfect in the little things, and the big things happen by themselves," Christilot told us.

"You will never be a top trainer if you don't know history. You can be a rider, but not a trainer. Not a *top* trainer!" George said.

And then: "The basic principles all go back to the same thing. First: Calm, forward, straight. Second: Leg, leg, leg! Third: Hold, don't pull." George took the hand of one of the riders nearby and held it. "Hold," he said. Then he pulled on the girl and shook his head. "*Don't* pull!"

"What about Thoroughbreds?" I asked. "Do you train them differently?"

George looked at me as if I was asking him to repeat himself.

"There is no difference. No difference! The principles are all the same. You want the same things. But with a Thoroughbred, you are already ahead. They already have impulsion. And they are more sensitive."

Christilot nodded in agreement. "Sensitivity," she said. "And feel. *Not* overriding. We are all improved by riding a Thoroughbred. And that can make you a better horseman."

I agreed with them both: Thoroughbreds were often more sensitive. But George's claim that this put you ahead was not totally correct. Horses can be *too* sensitive. When I asked Johnny to trot, I didn't want him to underreact and just walk faster, but I also didn't want him to overreact and canter. I wanted him to react appropriately. With some Thoroughbreds, we don't start ahead of the game because they are sensitive, we start *behind* because they are *too* sensitive.

But then again, maybe it wasn't about the horse. Probably I just needed to ride better.

I thought about that as I proceeded to school Johnny over some jumps. He jumped with quick feet and a light heart that day. The sun cast shadows at the fences, but Johnny didn't care. He reminded me of a young Billy Elliot. George watched and said nothing. At the end, he suggested I take him in the hunter ring at some shows.

"You'll get people interested," he said.

I nodded and gave Johnny a rub. I dismounted and led the horse over to where George and Christilot were sitting in a golf cart. I had one more question for both of them.

"What does being a horseman mean to you?"

George looked at Christilot. "Want to go first?" he asked.

She nodded, then leaned back to gather her thoughts.

"Horsemen are people who spend their whole lives around horses. They understand the twitch of an ear or the nod of a head. They have empathy and they understand immediately how to react. They are always aware, and they react to the first signal. They know when to hold on, and when to let go. They put the horse in a position to win, not lose."

Christilot is a quieter teacher than George, but no less aware. Now she paused to find more words...the right words.

"It's subtle...with horsemen, you don't see the problems because they don't go there. With others, they see it a second too late. Then you have issues."

George was watching Christilot as she spoke. Then he looked at me. His sunglasses reflected my face.

"First, everybody who is successful for a long time has an innate love for the horse. A horseman has a deep empathy for horses," he began. "Second, they are interested in all phases and aspects of horses. *All* aspects."

"And what about people like Buck?" I asked. I knew he had done a clinic with Buck Brannaman years before. I knew he'd made a DVD series with my friend Jonathan Field.

"There is definitely a place for people like Buck and Jonathan. Not as an alternative to what we do," and he brought his hand up as if to include Christilot, "but as a supplement."

Christilot nodded.

"Remember, Thoroughbred or not, the basic principles all go back to the same thing."

If the American jumping scene were the Mafia, George might be the Don. "I'm not teaching this clinic to be with all of you, but to be with her," George had told us earlier in the day, as he pointed at Christilot. "Why? Because I will learn. I have always been a student. I didn't have talent, but I had ambition. I wanted to learn. I still do."

These two riders, so full of passion, started their careers on Thoroughbreds, and had gone to the Olympics. Thoroughbreds are often credited with having more "try" than other breeds. They say you can even see it in their eyes—that "look of eagles." When I looked at George and Christilot, when I looked at a lot of top horsemen, when I looked at my wife, I saw that same glimmer there.

I went forward and shook both their hands, thanking them for their time.

"The basic principles all go back to the same thing," George said for the third (or fourth) time, as he made more room for Christilot on the golf cart. Then they drove off past the dressage ring together, chatting.

There was another fine horseman who knew Thoroughbreds: I had the chance to meet Michael Matz while interviewing him for an article for *Off-Track Thoroughbred Magazine*. Michael was a show jumper who went to three Olympic Games but more recently he had success as a racehorse trainer. He might be best known for being the trainer of Barbaro, who decisively won the 2006 Kentucky Derby, but tragically shattered his leg two weeks later in the Preakness Stakes.

I met up with Jennie Brannigan, professional event rider, in the lobby of The Diplomat in Fort Lauderdale at five-thirty one morning. The night crew was polishing the floor. The lights were dimmed. Elsewhere, we knew, jockeys and exercise riders were up, maybe even in the barn already, preparing for the first set of horses to go out. Some of the riders and staff lived onsite, but we had an hour drive ahead of us. We would meet Michael Matz and his crew for their second set.

There was security at the Palm Meadows Training Center gate, but once inside, the place was like a small city. There were rows and rows of barns. I got lost briefly. There were hundreds of horses, maybe thousands, many of them being led or ridden. All the riders moved with purpose, searching for that mystical balance between patience and urgency. Veterinarians did their rounds. Grooms carried saddles. Trainers watched, like owls, or generals.

I felt out of place. Too big and too tall. But those on Michael's staff were easy and welcoming. Jennie galloped horses with them regularly, and she greeted them with hugs and a box of donuts that we had picked up on our way.

This was the second time I had gotten to gallop as part of an interview for *OTTB Magazine*. The first time was at Oliver Sherwood's stable in England the previous year. Oliver was famous for having trained Many Clouds, a Grand National winner. Upon arrival I had been legged up on a small horse and we had walked through the old streets of Lambourn, and out to the gallops, which were set on a grassy hill behind the stone town.

This morning, however, Jennie and I rode three sets on the wet oval track. The first horse was assigned a long trot and a slow steady canter. The second was a short gallop. The third we took into the starting gate. I could feel my horse's heart beating through the saddle. *DE-DUH-DE-DUH-DE-DUH.* Double time. I could see the muscles taut like guitar strings. But we didn't break out. We just backed out and went for a gallop.

The theory behind backing out of the starting gate is that if the horses break forward every time, they get anxious and anticipate the break. But if you back out sometimes, they become quieter, because the gate isn't always associated with racing.

In England, however, trainers never back their horses out. Their theory? The gates have one way in, and one way out. Why confuse the racehorses?

Thoroughbreds are bred to gallop—a relatively easy job compared to some, and yet one of the most competitive sports in existence. You don't find "amateur" or "recreational" racehorses, like you find with human runners (we call them "joggers"). The slow are quickly cut.

As we galloped around the track, it was as if gravity was turned on its side, and we were being drawn forward instead of down. Faster and faster we went, until I had to say "sorry" to my mount. I pulled on the reins, and held him from going faster. Not today.

Truth be told, I wanted to go faster, too. It was like driving a Porsche and having to stay in third gear. Oh, to open her up! To say, *Let's go!*

Jennie laughed later when I told her how I'd felt out there. "You have to be an exercise rider a little longer than one day to breeze them!"

When I finally had time with Michael, I of course asked him about Thoroughbreds. But what I wanted to hear about were his thoughts on training and horsemanship. So I popped the same question I'd asked George Morris and Christilot Boylen.

"What does horsemanship mean to you?"

Michael sat down on a tack trunk and so I did the same. It did not take him much thought before he said, "Common sense."

Jesus, Michael, I wanted to say. Common sense? You have got to be kidding me! Horsemanship is about as common as a horse that produces a profit.

But I didn't say anything. I just wrote it down.

Michael's answer was so simple and so profound, because to him, that *was* what horsemanship was: something easy and obvious. And yet, if it wasn't so rare and special, *everybody* would be going to the Olympics and winning the Kentucky Derby. And I wouldn't be traveling all over asking the same questions all the time.

No, horsemanship is more like a riddle: obvious once you know the answer, nothing to brag about, but wizardry to everyone else.

From a horse's point of view, it must be similar: Figuring *us* out must be a riddle to *them*.

The difference is, we work with horses because we are driven to figure out that riddle. Imagine if we took a general sample of the human population and randomly assigned some people to be horse owners. Lacking the ambition to figure horses out (maybe they would rather be golfing, or fishing, or reading *Longmire*), there would be more frustration and anger than there is in politics. *That* is what it is like for horses; we don't ask them, "Which of you want to be ridden by people?"

And then add, "Oh, and by the way, you do not get to choose who your person will be."

Maybe if we did, we would not like what we would hear.

CHAPTER 52

No Sulking

I am sitting in the kitchen of the small yellow house that Sinead and I are renting. It is down the road from where our horses live—there isn't a house for us there yet, but one day there will be. We have called our property Copperline Farm, in honor of Eamon's favorite song by North Carolinian, James Taylor.

Out the window I see Bahiagrass that grows in a "'Y'" and is ready to seed, and I think, Our grass needs to be cut. I see horses in the paddocks. I know my wife is still at the barn riding her horses, but it has begun to storm so I hope she is almost done.

Sinead and I have our own working students now, and most of them, most of the time, do a much better job than I did at their age. Sometimes though, I send them back to the barn if they have the wrong saddle pad, or their horse is not clean enough. Sometimes I send them to the round pen if their horse is overly anxious. When I do, I try to remember that it is not always *what* I say, but *how* I say it. I remind myself: How I treat the greenest student, or the poorest, is as important as how I treat the most talented, or the richest. How I treat the least impressive horse is as important as how I treat the most.

Sinead and I have merged our businesses, and we are growing more and more optimistic about it.

For a while, after Eamon's death, it was as if every step we took was through deep mud. There were horses to ride, bills to pay, clients to please, fences to fix, grass to grow. There was also a constant voice in my head: *Look after your wife!* Add in our first mortgage in Citra, Florida, and it was more stress than I was used to. Sinead ended up looking after me just as much as I looked after her, which was not fair, so I worried about that, too.

In my family, worry and guilt run like a thin vein through marble. When my dad was fourteen he adopted Bandit, a baby raccoon. He made a neat little collar out of baling twine for him and led him around Southlands. Bandit was curious, but shy. At home Bandit acted the clown: He turned the sink on, played with kitchen utensils, poked around the trash, washed all the fruit. One day, the still young raccoon did not return. Of course, my father hoped Bandit had found a raccoon family to join; that he had not been eaten by a coyote or run over by a truck.

In Vancouver, at that time, the idea that *all* animals should be treated with curiosity and respect was not a trendy one. When he became a vegetarian in the sixties, as a young man, in a farming community, he was a rarity. But he believed, "Do unto animals as we would wish done to us."

With that in mind, his heart beat easier. Freedom was the best thing for Bandit.

Until he woke at three in the morning and realized his mistake: Bandit was small. The collar of baling twine was small. Soon Bandit would be bigger. The collar would not be.

My dad still felt the criminality of this mistake five decades later. He could imagine the worst, just as if it was happening right in front of him.

As the months rolled by, I tried to honor my silent pledge to Eamon. Sinead and I helped each other with the horses, and we had "date nights." Sometimes though, I just held her while she cried. We missed him terribly. On top of her father's death, she was dealing with an emotional roller coaster that was her journey with Tate, her top horse, a Selle Francais that was on the verge of retirement. Sinead coped bravely, and I wanted to tell her I was proud of her, and I wanted to do it publicly, so one day I wrote this for her, and shared it on Facebook:

I want to say something nice about my wife. Sinead has had a tough go recently—as we all do sometimes—and she has bounced back. Again. I get worried that as we age we will lose some of that bounce—that we won't rebound as high. So, I thought maybe something nice, said in public, would help keep that bounce alive.

Here is what I have to say: Sinead is a survivor.

When life is sunny she works hard and improves—that's easy to do. But when life is a hurricane, she puts her head down and keeps going—and that's not easy to do.

Sinead competed in her first FEI event when she was a teenager. Those years (I've heard) were a little out of control. She didn't know what needed to change, but she knew something had to. So she moved to Middleburg, Virginia, and got the best help she could find. She waited tables at night and exercised racehorses in the morning, and in between she took lesson after lesson after lesson from David and Karen O'Connor.

In 2007 Sinead was getting by, but there was something missing again—some small piece. And Sinead is not one for little dreams, so she moved again. She went to work for William Fox-Pitt in England. She came back with the idea that if she didn't do a four-star by the time she was thirty, it just might not be meant to be. It might mean that she just wasn't a player.

In 2011, when she was twenty-nine (and a half) she completed her first four-star in Lexington. She finished third. (After Mary King, who finished one, two.)

I visited Sinead in England before the London Olympics. She was getting ready for the Games with the US Team. USET flew over the short list to prepare, and then picked the team at the last minute. She was named the first Olympic alternate. She and her horse, Tate, drove through London and went through security the day before dressage. But after the other horses jogged up sound, Sinead was sent off, her accreditation stripped.

Was Sinead upset? Yes. But she cheered on her teammates, and she went back to work.

She competed at Burghley a month after the Olympics. Burghley is the biggest, hardest track in the world. She and Tate kicked ass. Second place. The top American finish in years.

Two years later, in 2014, Sinead was fourth in Kentucky. After that she was picked to go to the World Equestrian Games in France, where there were six riders: four on a team, and two individuals. Sinead wanted to be on the team, but again she was placed as an individual rider.

In 2016, she was tenth in Kentucky on Tate—her own horse that she has kept sound and happy through twenty-seven FEI competitions over eight years. They are currently one of the most experienced combinations in US eventing. But Sinead and Tate were alternates for the Olympics in Rio—again. So what did they do? They went to Millbrook and kicked ass! They were picked as the favorite and they delivered.

I'll tell you—from a husband's point of view: Sinead is no joke. She just keeps putting one foot in front of the other. Again and again. No sulking. And that's why she wins.

Of course, she hasn't done it by herself. She has done it with great support. She has a once-in-a-life-time horse. She has a talented team. And supportive owners. Sinead knows she needs a great team around her. She loves the camaraderie and the pressure. It motivates her. Sinead's life is full of travel. It is exciting and tough and fully lived. But she has earned it, literally, through blood, sweat, and tears (and twenty-three broken bones).

Kids get told, "No, do not make a profession out of this," "You should go to college, you will never make it in this industry," "You should have a backup plan, this is no way to make a living," "It's dangerous." But Sinead did not listen. She would not listen. She did not want a backup plan. She just ignored everybody. She knows something very few of us do: the difference between a "job" and a "calling."

And that luck is spelled "w-o-r-k."

Sinead is brave, and stubborn, and persistent, and passionate. But more than anything Sinead is a survivor. (Love you, Sweetheart.)

It wasn't good, but it was honest.

Sinead smiled when she read it. I glimpsed her dad when she smiled. I saw him when she worked and when she laughed. I saw him when we argued. I did not know if Eamon believed his work was his calling—maybe it was, maybe it wasn't, although I guessed not. I thought his purpose was two little kids: the first, a boy born in Dublin, Ireland, in 1980; the second, a girl, in Arlington, Texas, in 1981.

In 2016 I got an unexpected call. It was from Trafalgar Square Books, the same book publisher I had written to four-and-a-half years before, but from which I had never heard back. I had started writing for *The Chronicle of the Horse* again, which I enjoyed, but my heart was not in it the same way as the first few years. Those years in Germany, in Florida, in Texas and New Jersey. It felt like I was trying to go back to something, trying to relive something.

This publisher wanted to know if I wanted to write a book.

"Say that again."

"A book."

Yes, I thought, and then a second later, *Holy shit*. And then a second later: It's been years since I wrote to you.

"Are you still there?"

"I'm sorry. I thought you asked if I wanted to write a book."

"I did."

"Well, I'll have to think about it."

I thought about it for about five seconds.

At first we discussed a training how-to book, but I admitted I did not feel I had the experience to *teach* on the level that a book implies.

I did have lots of experience *learning* though; maybe I could write about that. They liked that idea.

"When can you have it done?"

"How long does it take to write a book?"

"Would six months be okay?"

That is soon, I thought, but, "No problem," I said.

There were two questions I had to answer before I began.

First, if I was sharing my journey, and what I learned, how would I address the mistakes I'd made? Mistakes were not only *part* of it, they were *the blood* of it, and yet my first instinct was not to share them.

Second, if I could have a "do-over," would I do any of it differently?

To the second question, there was a quick answer: No. No matter how many mistakes I'd made, no matter how humiliating it is to think of the ignorance with which I approached this adventure, it was *my* adventure. That broken collarbone, that lost girlfriend, they were like the turning of a key in a car. The motor caught and never stalled. I may have been in reverse a few times, been off-road, but the engine was always coughing and growling.

To the first question: It was a problem I'd had all along. I'd faced it writing articles as a working student, and now I faced it again in a bigger, badder beast—a book. It made me feel naked, staring out at a crowd. There was, there is, an overwhelming urge to cover up. To hide. To lie. To think of an excuse to stop.

Some people have been quick to criticize—sometimes to my face, sometimes anonymously. But the confident ones gave me advice, or simply let me make my own mistakes. I have learned a lot from watching other's mistakes. I never tire of watching great horsemen work. It is as fine and sweet as music to me. My hope is that just as I have learned from *their* mistakes (and truly, they all make mistakes), others might learn from mine. So many of our lessons are learned at the expense of our horses, and so, I think, the more we learn from books, the better. Of course, in the end, some things can never be explained properly on a piece of paper. For some lessons we must be outside, with the sun, or rain, or snow above us, and a horse beneath us. And even then, some things cannot be taught. They can only be learned.

No matter what words are spoken, *I* am my toughest critic. The number of times I've shaken my head at myself, and said, "Stupid!" are like cones on a pine. My only response, to myself, is that if I had known more when I began this journey, I might never have started. This adventure is the only thing I truly own. I would not trade it for anybody else's.

Reflecting back once more on my stay at Hinnemann's, I now see new lessons. I was so frustrated then that I was not improving, but maybe I grew in exactly the way I was meant to. Hinnemann showed me professionalism. His staff showed me what a work ethic really looks like. I learned about discipline. Perhaps I could have been more patient.

Recently I heard a good definition for confidence, and it is based entirely around our self-talk. We never know what another says to himself, and so we should consider twice what we think is arrogance, confidence, shyness, meekness. Hinnemann's journey is his own. With humanity. With himself. With horses. So I thank Herr Hinnemann for allowing me to learn what I did.

I wanted to be a Great Rider, now my ambition is greater: to be a Great Horseman.

Anybody can sit on a horse, but that does not make that person a rider. A rider *rides* a horse, getting the best out of him that day. And that is no small thing. A trainer trains a horse, preparing him for tomorrow, teaching him something new. And that is something special. A horseman, however, goes deeper, thinks about the heart and soul of the horse, as well as the body. A horseman not only knows his horse, but his horse knows him—this is a true relationship.

Now a *Horseman* (capitalized!), having graduated the first three, is working on himself for the horse, not the horse for himself. *Great Horsemen*, these are the rare people that achieve about all one can achieve of that journey in this lifetime.

I cannot call myself a Horseman. I am still learning too much about the first three. But I want to be! Oh yes!

Right now my laptop is open, I have coffee brewing. Six months have passed since I got the call from Trafalgar Square Books. Ten years have passed since I lost my job, my dream, my health, my girlfriend. I still have the scar from my broken collarbone, but the other wounds have long since healed. Healed stronger, I suspect, than they were before. I look out the window and see sheets of rain. Dark clouds and showers are common in Florida in the summer afternoons, and the drumming on the roof makes for pleasant background music.

So here I am thinking about horses. And still writing about horses. And about Horsemen. I look at this word again: *Horsemen*. Wow! What a nice word; what a nice goal. And so I continue on: one foot in front of the other. One sentence after another. Writing and riding. A good way to make a living. A good way to *live*!

There are many animals (and a few people), I could dedicate this book to, but I would be remiss if I didn't write it for my parents. It would not, in so many ways, exist without them. So, *Mum and Dad, thank you for inspiring a respect and empathy for animals and a big old-fashioned love of books.*

Now I smell the fresh coffee, I stand up to fetch it, and when I do I see a big black truck pulling up the driveway. Sinead. My wife! In a moment, she will look through her window for me, and I will wave.

I am, as always, excited to see her. When she gets in, we will discuss the new farm and upcoming competitions. We have lots of projects in the works to keep us busy.

The rain is strengthening now, and she does not see me when I wave. I wait, but she is hidden by the shower between us. I look forward to her walking in the front door. With Zeppo.

As I write this last chapter, I remember the first. It was raining then, too.

Finally Sinead is there before me. Her hair is wet, her shirt sticks to her skin, and her eyes are bright. She sees me and smiles.

I have never minded the rain.

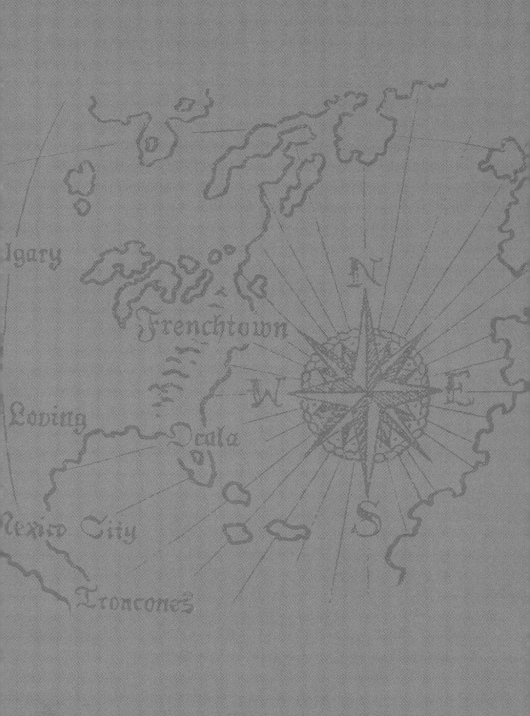

Acknowledgments

First, thank you to my wife. As I write this Sinead is five months pregnant. There are still a lot of question marks in front of us about what direction our life will take. Will we stay in Florida? How will our careers change as we age? Will we agree on a name for our son? But we face these uncertainties together, just as we should.

I already dedicated this book to my parents, but I would also like to thank my father in particular for Sapphire, and my mother in particular for enjoying a good argument.

In September 2008 when I began this adventure Christine Mazur at *Gaitpost* magazine printed the first of these articles. Thank you!

Kenna, thank you for lending me *Letters and Papers from Prison*.

Thank you Kelvin for taking me in during the winter of 2008.

In September 2009 *The Chronicle of the Horse* began publishing my "chapters" online. Thank you Sara Lieser. You were a good editor, and more importantly, a much needed friend as I sorted my way through some tough times.

Parts of this book have also previously appeared in *Practical Horseman* thanks to Sandy Oliynyk and *Off-Track Thoroughbred Magazine* thanks to Steuart Pittman, Stephanie Church, and Alexandra Beckstett. Also thanks to *Eventing USA Magazine* and *Horseman's Journal*.

A big thank you to Kathy Page, a very talented novelist, who took the time to edit so much of my writing. She began helping in January 2009 after I had written four "chapters" and helped me through these and other projects until about 2012.

Thank you to the horses in my life. One of my favorite quotes is from the front of Christopher Bartle's book *Training the Sport Horse*, a book that Ingrid Klimke recommended to me in 2009, and although I have forgotten the exact wording, I have never forgotten the sentiment. I will try to paraphrase it here: To the horses. You didn't choose to be with me, but I owe you so much. You gave me the opportunity to learn, and inevitably I made mistakes. I must say sorry to many of you, and thank you to all of you.

To Greg and Bernadette: Thank you for letting me share some special but also some deeply sad moments in this book. With every single word I have tried to respect and appreciate your generosity in this regard. You are my family now, too. I love you.

To Eamon: We love you and miss you and no words will ever do you justice. We will never forget you.

To my brothers: Thank you for your support. Jordan, I wish we got to run and talk more. Telf, I wish I got to spend more time with your family! And thanks for reading the manuscript—you could be a professional editor!

To every single person mentioned in this book—I appreciate all of you. I have learned something from each of you: Johann Hinnemann, Steffi, Julia, Eiren, Jamie, Ingrid Klimke, David and Karen O'Connor, Lauren, Hannah, Max, Kyle Carter, Ian Millar and family, Bruce Logan, Rhiannon, Anne Kursinski, Asa Bird, Liz, Michael Matz, George Morris, Christilot Boylen, and Emily.

I deeply hope that I have made it clear my respect and appreciation for everybody that appears in this book. No relationships are perfect, and while I shared some fleeting interactions in these pages,

I do not judge a person from a single meeting, and I hope you do not either.

To Jonathan Field for being a mentor throughout everything. I can't imagine a better one.

To Zachary Gray and The Zolas for letting me use some of the lyrics from their hit song "You're Too Cool." I first met Zach when we were six years old. Much later he sang songs by Bryan Adams and Britney Spears at my wedding.

To the people that managed the barn, the business, and the horses while I was writing: Emily, Arielle, Rory, Aurelie, Cian, Kellie, Erin, Mollie, Brynn, Sharon, Gabbie, Stacy, Kate, Dorothy, Brianna, Nell, Lauren Grace, Lauren Taylor, Lynn, Margaret, Madlen, Payne. Thank you all!

To Meg, who helped Sinead with her horses for years, and who also read the manuscript: Thank you.

Also to the others who have read some or part of this along the way and been critical or supportive, or both: Betsy, Barbara, Larry, Sarah and Sarah. Thank you.

To the Books, Jarrells, Hartzbands, Dumonts, and Schaeffers for your invaluable support, and to Christina, owner of Dutch Times: Thank you.

Kathy Russell, thank you for the incredible photos!

Matthew Martinez, I will resist a lawyer joke and just say thanks. You went above and beyond.

Thank you to all the vets at Furlong and Associates. You really are lifesavers!

Thank you Pat and Linda Parelli, for your support and knowledge over the last few years, and also for letting us use your magical Ocala campus for the cover photo.

To Erik Schmidt for the map, and the doodad: Thank you.

And saving the most vital for last: Thank you Trafalgar Square

Books. If you had not given me a deadline this book would still only exist in my mind. From the moment we started working together I have been impressed by your insight and professionalism.

Caroline Robbins, the Publisher, thank you. Martha Cook, the Managing Director, thank you!

And very last: Rebecca Didier, my editor at Trafalgar Square. Although I took the first step by myself and many, many people have been there for me along the way, it is Rebecca that has helped me and empowered me to get this book across the finish line. If this book is any kind of success, or failure, I suspect the person who will feel it the most keenly besides myself will be Rebecca.